A

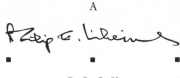

■          ■          ■

B O O K

The Philip E. Lilienthal imprint
honors special books
in commemoration of a man whose work
at University of California Press from 1954 to 1979
was marked by dedication to young authors
and to high standards in the field of Asian Studies.
Friends, family, authors, and foundations have together
endowed the Lilienthal Fund, which enables UC Press
to publish under this imprint selected books
in a way that reflects the taste and judgment
of a great and beloved editor.

*The publisher gratefully acknowledges the
generous contribution to this book provided by the
Chiang Ching-kuo Foundation for Scholarly Exchange.*

*The publisher gratefully acknowledges the generous
support of the Philip E. Lilienthal Asian Studies
Endowment Fund of the University of California
Press Foundation, which was established by a
major gift from Sally Lilienthal.*

Fantasy Islands

# Fantasy Islands

*Chinese Dreams and
Ecological Fears in an Age
of Climate Crisis*

JULIE SZE

UNIVERSITY OF CALIFORNIA PRESS

University of California Press, one of the most distinguished university presses in the United States, enriches lives around the world by advancing scholarship in the humanities, social sciences, and natural sciences. Its activities are supported by the UC Press Foundation and by philanthropic contributions from individuals and institutions. For more information, visit www.ucpress.edu.

University of California Press
Oakland, California

© 2015 by The Regents of the University of California

Library of Congress Cataloging-in-Publication Data

Sze, Julie, author.
Fantasy islands : Chinese dreams and ecological fears in an age of climate crisis / Julie Sze.
    pages cm
Chinese dreams and ecological fears in an age of climate crisis
Includes bibliographical references and index.
ISBN 978-0-520-26248-5 (cloth : alk. paper) —
ISBN 0-520-26248-4 (cloth : alk. paper) —
ISBN 978-0-520-28448-7 (pbk. : alk. paper) —
ISBN 0-520-28448-8 (pbk. : alk. paper) —
ISBN 978-0-520-95982-8 (ebook) —
ISBN 0-520-95982-5 (ebook)
    1. Urban ecology (Sociology)—China—Shanghai.    2. Sustainable development—China—Shanghai.    3. Urban renewal—China—Shanghai.
4. Urban ecology (Sociology)—United States.
5. Chongming (Shanghai, China)    I. Title. II. Title: Chinese dreams and ecological fears in an age of climate crisis.
    HT243.C62S477 2015
    307.760951′132—dc23                    2014017607

Manufactured in the United States of America

24   23   22   21   20   19   18   17   16   15
10   9   8   7   6   5   4   3   2   1

In keeping with a commitment to support environmentally responsible and sustainable printing practices, UC Press has printed this book on Natures Natural, a fiber that contains 30% post-consumer waste and meets the minimum requirements of ANSI/NISO Z39.48-1992 (R 1997) (*Permanence of Paper*).

# CONTENTS

# Introduction

I stood on a wooden deck overlooking the Dongtan wetlands in the blistering August heat and humidity. The wetlands are a stopover on the East Asia–Australia migratory shorebird flyway and located on the eastern edge of Chongming Island. The island is located twenty miles east of Shanghai's glitzy downtown, seven miles across the Yangtze River. It is the world's largest alluvial island, formed by deposits from the river. The island has doubled in size since the 1940s, and it is either the second or third largest island in China.[1] Chongming is on the proverbial rise, fast-tracked for ecological and economic development of all kinds (Chongming was rumored to be the site for the first mainland Chinese Disneyland, a prize lost in 2009 to the Pudong district). According to the county website, Chongming Island is "a tourist attraction for urban people to find a return to nature where they can experience a spiritual integration of humans and nature."

I wasn't here to look for a "return to nature" or to birdwatch. Rather, I was here to see something that was supposed to be here but was never built: the world's first great eco-city. In its glaring absence, I saw something else: what eco-dreams and fantasies are made of, in an age of emergent global climate crisis.

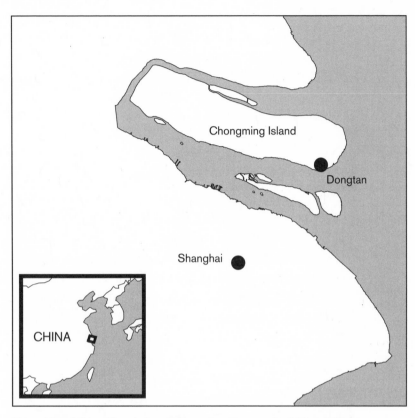

Map 1. Map of China, Shanghai, and Chongming. Cartography: Michele Tobias

## DONGTAN: THE QUEST TO CREATE A NEW WORLD

Dongtan and Chongming were all over the international news in 2006 with the announcement of the world's first major eco-city. Dongtan eco-city was slated to accommodate a population of five hundred thousand people by 2050, and to be a "carbon-neutral" and "zero-waste" city where all inputs for energy come from collected waste, using renewable sources and technologies. Dongtan was to be built by Arup, the UK-based global planning, engineering, and design firm, for the Shanghai Industrial Investment Corporation (SIIC), the investment arm of the Shanghai municipality. Dongtan was supposed to exemplify a "green" approach to urban design, architecture, infrastructure (including sustainable energy and waste management), and economic and business planning.

Arup described Dongtan as "the quest to create a new world." This "quest" included a "different model" for Chinese urbanism, one that explicitly rejected the idea that one must have economic development first and environmental protection second. Rather, this model asserted that economic growth and environmental protection go hand in hand. Arup's original master plan for Dongtan had a planning trajectory of forty-five years and was intended for completion in 2050. As imagined, Dongtan was to be three quarters the size of Manhattan. The plan provided twenty-nine square meters of green space per person, more than four times the amount in Los Angeles, and which also ensured that no place in the city was farther than 540 meters from a bus stop (a density of 160 people per hectare was planned to make public transportation feasible). The Dongtan plan was divided into two sections: an eighty-six-square-kilometer conservation area of farmland and aquaculture; and exterior wetlands on the sea side of the 1998 dyke. Dongtan's ecological footprint was modeled as less than half that of a typical Chinese city. Ninety percent of all waste was to be recycled; and 95 percent of all energy was to come from renewable sources. Biogasification of rice husks was to supplement wind and solar power. Only cars with zero tailpipe emissions were to be allowed inside the city; all others were supposed to be left in a parking lot on the edge of the development. Dongtan city was to be formed through the integration of three towns (Marina Village, Lake Village, and Pond Village). In addition to the town and city plan, the comprehensive master plan included three leisure parks, each focused on a different theme: equine and water sports, science education, and vacation villas.[2] Yet, despite these ambitious plans, no significant construction took place. In the face of this inactivity, SIIC continues to actively bring government officials to tour the wetlands.[3]

Dongtan's vision was big business and politics, involving leaders of nations and heads of international architectural, engineering, and design firms. When I first heard about Dongtan, I almost fell off my chair. I was pleasantly surprised—and thoroughly confused. My father was born and raised on Chongming and we still have extended family there. Growing up, I associated Chongming with being rural. Now it was supposed to be the site of the world's most cutting-edge eco-city, around which China and the United Kingdom were modeling the future of Chinese cities. For me, Chongming was the repository of complex ideas and emotions, a place my family, old relatives, and family friends were "from." When I was growing up, my mother would routinely make fun of my father's occasional slipping into the Chongming dialect (distinct from the Shanghai dialect that they shared).[4] Their teasing was an en famille reprise of the divide between city sophisticate and country bumpkin. How did Chongming become the staging ground for the bold new eco-future for Shanghai? What did it all mean?

In 2006, Chongming Island instantly became the locus where politicians, technocrats, and planners in Shanghai and in the West made fantastic claims about sustainability, the green future of Chinese cities, and global environmental nirvana. Chongming and Dongtan became the focal point of fanciful dreams and ambitions of Chinese politicians and developers, and transnational politicians, planners, and architects. Collectively, they painted a lovely picture of a green future where one could bike, boat, and eat locally grown Italian cheese (and apparently become white, at least according to the pictures in the Dongtan promotional materials).[5] And these eco-romantic notions were not just *imposed* by off-island outsiders. Chongming Island is defined by its own local government as having "back-county ways" and being characterized by its unique "folkways, the place without hullaba-loo."[6] It's also long been a place the rural populace left to seek economic opportunity, especially in the past three decades of China's breathtaking urban and industrial development (virtually all of Shanghai's taxi drivers, for example, are from Chongming).

A decade earlier, when I traveled to Chongming with my dad, he offered to lend his cousin's son money so that he could move to Shanghai to be a taxi driver. "Who stays in Chongming?" my dad asked. (The answer: little kids and old people.) To be young and ambitious meant moving to Shanghai. To stay in Chongming meant immobility and economic stagnation. Thirteen years later, this same relative greeted me proudly, when I stepped off the ferry boat, in a shiny black car—having "made good" while remaining on the island. When I told my dad about this car, my dad raised an eyebrow. To be sure, some of this disbelief reflected my dad's dislike of being proven wrong. His beliefs were shaped by his own migration history, sprinkled with an American Horatio Alger worldview. His skepticism also reflected a well-worn narrative and experience. This storyline is of opportunity that propels migrants from the countryside to the city. This movement is a result of a maelstrom of decisions, individual yet also historical and collective. This story is an old one, and one that remains potent as an explanation for individual and social change, not just in China but also in India, the United States, or any number of other nations.[7] This narrative of change from the dying rural past to an active urban future was a logic that Dongtan was trying to upend with its grand dreams of sustainable development.

Although the language of sustainable urban and ecological development that animated Dongtan depends on pastoral/romantic views of nature, it is not just a redux of an imagined simpler (and romanticized) peasant past. Rather, Chongming Island was the "staging ground" for the "bold new" eco-future. Chongming was officially anointed as an "eco-island" in Shanghai's development plans.[8] How and when this transformation was proposed fascinated me, in part because I myself knew so little about where I was ostensibly "from." A genie had come to the island promising ecological nirvana, and I wanted to know more before it all changed.

The stories of Dongtan, in other words, are about managing and mythologizing Shanghai's hyperurbanization amidst worldwide anxieties about two major—and interlinked—transformations: the changing global economic order and the problems of climate change. Over the past two decades, the rise of China as the world's factory has changed the way the rest of the world lives and consumes, as the world became addicted to cheap toys, clothes, and food. At the same time, Western consumers are increasingly wary of the costs of that addiction—playing with toys drenched in lead paint and ingesting dangerous medicines, milk, and tainted food. The world also faces global environmental problems on a scale never before seen—population growth, water wars and drought, energy problems, and a vast accumulation of waste of all kinds. The tension between China's rise as a global power and its contribution to catastrophic environmental change is coming to a furious head. Of all the world's environmental problems, climate change is perhaps the most frightening, and the forecasts are indeed grim. Increasing urban populations and the cultural changes as to what constitutes a basic standard of living will tax energy and natural resources beyond the capacity of the planet. In this context, Dongtan can be understood as a part of an emergent "ecological Shanghai" discourse, with implications for policy and practice. This discourse is shaped by international actors in response to global pressures and in a national context, but operationalized in the local landscapes of the island and in the region.

More than mere technocratic policy response, the rise of Dongtan and Shanghai's ecological discourse must be understood through the larger social and cultural reimaginings of scale. If there is any phrase that represents both environmental problems and the call to action in the past three decades, it's the injunction to "Think Global—Act Local." On the most basic level, this approach connects thinking and acting. For many, this slogan effectively connects individual action with collective impacts or change. Less obvious but no less important, thinking globally and acting locally also demands that people more fully comprehend the complex scalar relationship between the local and the global.

Scale "maps" onto the fundamental political, environmental, and social problems that have preoccupied environmental activists and scholars over the past three decades, including the intersection of the local and global spheres, intensifying urbanization and pollution around the world, but particularly in the global South, and the increasing awareness of environmental pollution among individuals and communities in many locales. Significant environmental problems, from the loss of biodiversity to air and water pollution and habitat degradation, require interdisciplinary analysis and methods to analyze complex processes at multiple scales.[9] Cultural and political geographers generally focus on scale at the levels of the bodily, urban, regional, national, and global, while others focus on local, gender, or household scales. Ecological scale consists of both temporal and spatial dimensions. Ecologists generally agree that there is no single correct scale for ecological research, that cross-scalar and interdisciplinary analysis is necessary for ecological investigation, that ecological change is historical, and that scale raises metaphysical, epistemological, and ontological issues.[10] Ecologists focus on grain and extent, where *grain* refers to the smallest unit of measurement employed to study some phenomenon, and *extent* denotes the overall dimensions over which observations are made, including both space (area) and time (duration) in a given study area.[11]

The interplay between space and time is also what makes scale a key analytic term for humanists and cultural critics. Environmental activists, writers, critics, and artists engage pollution across space and time using imagination and cultural ideas. One scholar writes, "Spatial arrangements are made in everyday practices among people and other life and are tapped into broader processes such as time, imperialism, global economy, ecology, evolution and *memory*" (italics added). Imagination is a key resource in responding to environmental problems since "literature commonly layers environmental spaces with memories and seek to dream up other worlds."[12]

Scale as an increasingly prominent analytic tool is intimately connected to intensifying conditions of globalization, specifically capitalist economic development and related ideologies of neoliberalism, privatization, and deregulation. Scale and globalization are linked in part because of how the increasing movement of pollution and peoples and the concomitant ineffectiveness of environmental regulation (at multiple scales) are connected. The failure to address climate change is arguably linked to analytic problems related to scale. For example, a significant percentage of industrial pollution in China is a result of production for consumers in the United States, Europe, and Australia, but this pollution crosses the Pacific, landing in the western United States. (I'll discuss this phenomenon in chapter 1.) How should this pollution be measured? National terms? Global? Pacific Rim? The geographer Nathan Sayre suggests that some of the difficulties in confronting global warming are a function of the unique scalar qualities of climate change, including the temporal realm. He writes: "Temporally, the grain is likewise infinitesimal: that split second at which a chemical reaction occurs in combustion, photosynthesis, oxidation, decay, etc. But the extent is very long: once a molecule of carbon dioxide or nitrous oxide enters the atmosphere, it remains there for more than a century; most other greenhouse gases persist for one-to-several decades."[13] Nations such as China and India also use temporal dimensions in their political arguments against international treaties to regulate carbon emissions; they argue, in effect, that countries in the West have historically contributed greater carbon emissions and have a "head start" on economic development. Environmental problems often "cross" or jump scales, and there is a "spatial mismatch" that can occur in discussing an environmental problem between the scales of environmental pollution and its political regulation—across both space and time.

Thus, at its very core, the failed promise of Dongtan, indeed of eco-cities writ large, can best be understood as a scalar problem. On the one hand, large promises are made—a demonstration project in one place is meant to represent a daring new approach for an entire nation. Dongtan was evoked as a new phase of development, one that took ecology seriously, and which foretold a different pathway for the Chinese nation. Dongtan was a curious reimagining of E. F. Schumacher's "Small Is Beautiful," and his call for "smallness within bigness." In Dongtan, however, the bigness is the power of Shanghai, as well as a representation of a new "frontier" of Chinese environmentalism. Using a multiscalar approach illuminates my focus on ecological Shanghai discourse through its complex analysis of scale as both spatial and temporal practice.

Dongtan is as much an expression of imagination, historical memory, and anxieties about the future as it ever was a specific development project. The eco-city project arose in response to increasing awareness of the problems posed by climate change, but it was always meant to signify greater cultural and ideological meanings beyond the specifics of Dongtan. A multiscalar lens allows for a deeper political, cultural, and historical analysis across space and time, and the case study of Dongtan and of ecological Shanghai writ large opens a wider lens for environmental debates and social anxieties in the city, and within the region, the nation, and the world.

## PROPHESIZING ECO-SHANGHAI

On the drive out to the Dongtan wetlands, I passed a large billboard with three large photos of birds, and an exhortation to "Protect Bidrs [sic], Love Dongtan and Develop Eco-Shanghai." Protecting birds and loving Dongtan are tied to the project to "Develop Eco-Shanghai." What is this so-called eco-Shanghai? How does Shanghai's version of urban sustainability, its vision of an eco-Shanghai, reflect a set of what I call eco-desires? How are Shanghai developers, urban planners, and politicians, aided by global architectural and engineering firms, integrating ideas about sustainability into their own urban futures? Those "dreams" have broader political, ideological, national, and cultural contexts. Is that dream—that the future of the Chinese city is to be found in the rural—possible? Put another way, can the eco-future be engineered? Where and how? How could Dongtan have been touted to be the site of China's eco-urban future? Why did Dongtan fail so spectacularly, and what does its failure mean? What are the local impacts of global Western fantasies about the presumed solutions to environmental crisis?

Understanding eco-Shanghai demands that we know a bit about Shanghai. To some, Shanghai is like Timbuktu: a place that people know, but don't know why they do. In the historian Jeff Wasserstrom's phrase, the "Shanghai of the mind" has a long, illustrious history in the U.S. and European contexts.[14] Shanghai is simultaneously a sacred birthplace to Chinese communism and to modernism. In his influential *Shanghai Modern*, the cultural and literary scholar Leo Ou-Fen Lee identifies 1920s and 1930s Shanghai as the home of China's most important writers, performers, and intellectuals, strongly influenced by the city's urban consumer and commercial culture.[15] During the tumultuous 1930s in the midst of civil war, Shanghai was one of the world's largest cities, with one of the most active ports, accounting for more than half of China's national trade.

Regardless of Shanghai's past, a recent exhibition at the New York City-based Skyscraper Museum lays out the importance of Shanghai to the world's urban future.[16] The exhibit proclaims that Shanghai, home to three of the world's ten tallest skyscrapers, "is surely China's *prophecy* of the urban future. . . . If New York was the 20th Century's city of the future . . . is Shanghai the New York of the 21st Century?"[17] Whether or not Shanghai is indeed a prophecy of the future, it currently claims the world's fastest train, longest underwater pedestrian tunnel, and tallest hotel, as well as the world's highest swimming pool and longest laundry chute.

And even though I'm a New Yorker born and bred, I am stunned by the size and volume of the high-rises in Shanghai. It's not so much their height, but their width, sheer volume, and density. In a single development there are often fifteen to twenty massively wide buildings, a Bronx Co-op City every few blocks. In New York, building construction is often hidden behind fences. In Shanghai, the temporary housing for the migrant construction workers from the countryside is itself five stories high. The migrant labor force building Shanghai's high-rises and new highways is visually omnipresent, even if politically and culturally disenfranchised.

Part of this notion that Shanghai represents both China's and the world's urban future is due to scale and population. Shanghai has a population of more than twenty-three million in 2012. Shanghai's official population puts it in the top-ten ranking of world cities, and including the migrant population would certainly place it in the world's top five. Shanghai is a BIG city—whether measured by population size, economic output, or cultural impact—and now it looms large in the emergent discourse of ecological development.

Shanghai is the wealthiest city in China, as befits its proud history as the country's economic powerhouse. Unlike Beijing and Xi'an, Shanghai has no grand imperial past; its rise in the nineteenth century was as a commercial enterprise directly resulting from colonialism. From its forced opening by the British after the humiliations of the Opium Wars, Shanghai was divided into colonial concessions where Chinese citizens had no legal rights. Between 1853 and 1937, colonial Shanghai was, for all intents and purposes, an occupied world city.[18] Shanghai's global cosmopolitan outlook came to an abrupt end with the Japanese occupation and the Communist regime that followed, which effectively closed China to the outside world. After the Communists took power, Shanghai entered a long era of tension with Beijing. One Communist Party newspaper sneered that Shanghai was "a nonproductive city . . . a parasitic city . . . a criminal city . . . a refugee city. It is a paradise of adventurers."[19] The historical differences between Shanghai and Beijing, as alternative power bases proffering different models of development and with fundamentally different urban and political cultures, are also at play in the stories of eco-Shanghai and Shanghai's intensive modernization.[20]

In reaction against its long dormancy, Shanghai has been in a frenzied rush to claim its place among the great and wealthy cities of the world. Shanghai's rise in the past three decades has been extensively chronicled.[21] What is less well understood is the centrality of *ecological discourse* to its urban development policy—most clearly displayed at the Shanghai World Expo. Just two years after the global spectacle of the Beijing Olympics, China again took the world stage with the Shanghai 2010 World Exposition. Shanghai 2010 was the first world's exposition held in China, and only the fourth held in Asia, of the almost fifty held since the mid-nineteenth century. Publicity materials for the World Expo explained that the official slogan, "Better City, Better Life," was meant to represent "a powerful and lasting pilot example of sustainable and harmonious urban living." This ideological equation of sustainability with harmony exists in political contexts, as the cultural critic Chris Connery writes, where calls to harmony in practice have particular ramifications, such as suppression of "unharmonious" peoples and projects.[22]

Dongtan and Chongming's eco-development and the emergent discourse of eco-harmony require an understanding of the island's relationship to Shanghai. The relationship between the island and the city was transformed in 2010 when the world's longest bridge and tunnel opened, connecting Chongming Island to Shanghai. The ideas and images of the "ecological" that shape the promotion of Dongtan eco-city and Chongming eco-island also are key to Shanghai's urban development, specifically in plans to suburbanize the city's edges. As Shanghai responded to intense development pressures in its historic core in the 1990s and further extended its reach and impact throughout the region, ecological discourse became prominent in the city's suburbanization policy. In a city historically defined by colonialism and Chinese exclusion from foreign settlements, Shanghai's urban growth plan in the 1990s called for nine major real estate developments to be built in the so-called national styles of foreign nations, often with an ecological edge. The plan, called "One City, Nine Towns," intended to address Shanghai's overcrowding in the central city, was imagined and designed by a group of well-known international architects.

Shanghai, like the greatest world cities of the most powerful nations, stands as both exemplar and exception. Shanghai has always had a complex relationship to the outside world because of its unique population and political history. [23] It has always been different and it stands alone, crassly commercial, decadent, haughty, and critical. But the story of eco-Shanghai does indeed tell us something about China at a crucial time when forces of nationalism, global economic development, and environmental issues are colliding spectacularly. Transnational finance has already radically restructured the urban landscape in Shanghai and in the other explosive-growth cities of China, particularly in their skyscrapers. The restructuring of the urban landscape looks more and more ecological in its form, but it is no less transformative.

To paraphrase Wasserstrom, Shanghai, like New York, is a very good place to think about global ecology and urban change.[24] It is also a very good place to rethink modernization in order to reimagine American modernity at the end the American Century. Having grown up in Manhattan's Chinatown (and being one who saw the World Trade Center towers fall), I view Shanghai's erecting megahigh towers at breakneck speed as resembling a pageant or a historical reenactment of American history in its moment of ascendancy. It's like watching Chicago before its 1893 World's Columbian Exposition. It's a chance to watch urbanization and modernization moving full-speed ahead—in real time. It's a surging city where giant drills work through the night and a store can be torn down, rebuilt, and restocked in a single day, converted from a clothing store to a bookstore in the blink of an eye. The planning historian Thomas Campanella, in *Concrete Dragon*, writes about the

> bewitching consonance between the American urban experience and the transfiguration of China's cities today. . . . China's drive, energy and ambition—to be powerful and prosperous, to be a player on the global stage—it's more than a little reminiscent of America and its youth. . . . We were China once, and Europe was us. In spirit at least, China's like the US of a century ago—punchdrunk with possibility, pumped and reckless and on the move. Americans invented the modern metropolis and the world looked up to us with wonder . . . (of course, much of this ended badly). . . . Just as it once crossed the Atlantic, the urbanism of ambition has crossed the Pacific concrete dragon.[25]

But rather than being a pure echo of the past, the urbanism of ambition also has a green face to it, befitting an age of climate crisis. That Shanghai's prophecy, its gift to global urban development, has a green veneer needs serious interdisciplinary analysis that takes space and time seriously. This analysis is given rather short shrift in an era in which global anxieties about pollution and about ecological disasters related to climate change are as high as they have ever been in human history.

## THE URBANISM OF ECOLOGICAL AMBITION:
### DEFINING ECO-DESIRE

The World Expo, the One City, Nine Towns projects, and Dongtan are ecological fantasy islands, whether they are actually built or merely imagined. These are places where fantastic futures are made concrete and "green." But these are not the only fantasies that captivate me. The historian John Findlay uses the term *magic lands* to characterize the expansion of the U.S. western city after 1940. In a very different cultural and historical context, Shanghai's eco-cities, eco-islands, and eco-developments have been given almost magical status as the "solution" to global environmental problems. This book comes from my own quest to understand these fantastic spaces and magical belief systems—which seem newly ascendant—as cultural and planning discourses, including breathless invocations of development without ecological cost! China is the world's eco-villain! Eco-cities are the answer! Sustainability = profits!

What's newly prominent is the role of *ecology* in this utopian branding of the future, to borrow from the sociologist Miriam Greenberg's analysis of sustainability branding in postcrisis New York City and New Orleans.[26] What defines eco-Shanghai is the branding of the urbanism of ecological ambition. For instance, the gigantic Shanghai Tower, set to open in 2014, is intended to be the second tallest in the world, and its "green" features are a key part of its innovative design (these include nine indoor gardens and a design for increased energy efficiency). A cynic can view the prominence of ecology in Shanghai as greenwashing; an optimist, as the only answer to future shock. To me, the life stories of people I know and the places I visited help to give the grand plans on Chongming Island and in Shanghai partial grounding in people's lives and the places they inhabit.

What are the ideological functions of globalizing sustainability discourse? What kind of cultural work does ecology perform and in what political contexts? To learn more about "eco-Shanghai," I asked Dongtan's planners and those working on similar eco-development projects in Shanghai about their projects. This book starts in Dongtan as an exemplar "eco-city." But, at the same time, eco-city development is not unique to Dongtan. In other parts of China, in the United Arab Emirates, South Korea, India, and the United States, eco-city development is flourishing as the scale and scope of environmental damage becomes clearer to more people and nations throughout the world. The goal of eco-cities—to forge place-based pathways to environmental change—does not come without contradictions or complications. Eco-cities reflect the values and ideologies of their creators. Elsewhere, I have written about the similarities between Dongtan and

Masdar eco-city in the United Arab Emirates.[27] These similarities are not surprising given the transnational and technocratic visions that guide the projects, as well as the politically authoritarian contexts in which they emerge. These complications and contradictions of eco-desire have been vastly underanalyzed; those who could perform this analysis have been blinded by a desire for feel-good projects in an age of climate crisis.

This book shares the impulse to find eco-solutions but refuses to advocate the wearing of green blinders in the process. It begins by analyzing discourses of the ecological development of Chongming Island in historical and regional terms. I then turn to eco-themed suburban real estate developments around Shanghai, and finally, to urban and ecological discourses at the World Expo. Collectively, these sites reflect the "eco-modernization" discourse of Shanghai, through the lens of what I call "eco-desire." In the course of my research, I looked at official plans, state exhibits, and promotional videos; walked around a range of eco-themed real estate developments and the World Expo; and listened to voices of some people with no particular stake in Shanghai's new eco-future.

I define *eco-desire* as the fusion of desire, projection, profit, and fun in certain top-down versions of eco-development. Eco-cities and ecological development are heavily influenced by ecological modernization discourses, a set of concepts used to analyze environmental policies and institutions developed to solve environmental problems in a capitalist society.[28] Central to the concept of ecological modernization is the idea that ecological crises can be overcome through technological advancement. For proponents of ecological modernization, ecological crises are overcome via the efficiency of the market through economic growth and innovations in technology. Critics of ecological modernization argue that these ideas inevitably lead to proposed solutions that ignore concerns about political governance and the distribution of ecological burdens and that favor corporate sustainability schemes.[29]

My articulation of eco-desire borrows from the anthropologist Lisa Rofel, who argues that desire does not stem from a lack of material objects but instead is the productive force that creates neoliberal subjects unleashed by the capitalist machine.[30] Culture is the medium that creates the "desire" of neoliberal subjects in China to know, speak, and interpret China's postsocialist reality. Discourses about ecological Shanghai are, crucially, about local, national, and transnational environmental desire simultaneously. Drawing on Xuefei Ren's study of transnational architectural production in urban China, I analyze ecological desire through the transnational frameworks of its production by global actors and its consumption in the symbolically and materially rich world city of Shanghai.

Sustainability discourse in Shanghai—or at least in the projects discussed in this book—is a Potemkin village, using the image of ecological desire as its tenuous base. The current impulse to build eco-cities (ecological features in cities as well as literal eco-cities) in Shanghai is not an attempt to solve its urban and environmental problems but rather an attempt to make Shanghai feel less "not-ecological." Using these case studies, I argue that the current impulse to build "eco-Shanghai" is an effort doomed to fail, containing the seeds of its own failure. These ecologically themed developments are not serious attempts to solve Shanghai's dire environmental problems. Neither do they represent major infrastructure or environmental investments (with the important exception of the World Expo). Taken collectively, these projects are literally attempts to build an "anti-Shanghai," a space that will somehow be both rural and urban, Chinese and cosmopolitan, natural and artificial. These fantasies of integration and the grand plans to build and imagine places such as Dongtan cannot be understood outside of the cultural yearning for "harmony" within an authoritarian political system that can impose its vision and its will—to varying degrees of success—on local communities and landscapes.

These case studies are ideologically circumscribed and imaginatively rendered, yet they exist not solely in the realm of abstraction. Rather, my interest lies in how desire, branding, and images of ecology in Shanghai get translated into material realities that shape actual landscapes. Although their impact is not necessarily large in terms of acreage developed or units of energy consumed, their power is broader than any single quantitative measure. These fantasy islands represent a cross-current of powerfully swirling impulses in a particular place and time, *about* time and place, which have larger implications as the world careens and lurches in response to economic, ecological, and climate crises.

Each of these sites—Dongtan eco-city, Chongming Island eco-development, suburban real estate developments, and the World Expo—reflect how eco-desires function thematically and differently across the range of projects. In the cases of Dongtan and the suburban developments, the central eco-desire is the revaluation of ecologically pure landscapes from undervalued rural space to economically valued real estate. At Dongtan eco-city, Chongming Island was the locus for the magical and profitable fusion of fun, environmental concern and respect, and business, specifically tourism and real estate speculation. In the case of Chongming Island, eco-desire is closely tied to its island status as a "liminal place" or a "threshold to other worlds and new lives."[31] Chongming as a model "ecological" site for Shanghai's development reflects a metaphor, an imaginary "island" of ecological virtue in a city and a world defined by narratives (and the reality) of environmental chaos and decline.[32] These projects represent a yearning for moral and political order in a world threatened by chaos.[33] Across all the sites, but most sharply at the World Expo, ecological Shanghai is the fullest expression of techno-utopian eco-desire, or the ideology that posits that technology, engineering, and built solutions can provide the pathway out of environmental destruction.

Ultimately, these projects represent desires that are neither particular to the project at hand nor unique to the Chinese context. The primary eco-desires are about the wish to "have it all," defined as making money, having fun, and helping the environment. The desires that these projects represent are those of green or sustainable capitalist discourse in the Chinese political context, which suggests that capitalist means are the best solution to environmental problems.

## WHY AND HOW TO STUDY ECO-DESIRE

Multiscalar and interdisciplinary analysis is not just a methodological imperative but also a political one in environmental studies. Taking scale (of both time and space) seriously is important in terms of how problems are analyzed, understanding the roots of problems, and the possible policy outcomes to manage environmental problems. Using multiscalar and interdisciplinary analysis also explains in part why and how an American Studies urbanist and environmental scholar began to consider studying China.

I'm also interested in global cities and the globalizing discourses of environmentalism, having grown up in New York and researched its environmental justice activism and urban environmental policy. Most of my research has focused on "bottom-up" environmentalism and how politically and culturally disenfranchised populations use environmental and health-based concerns to gain political power and to enact social change. The projects I survey in Shanghai are the polar opposite, focusing on the elites within a city and embedded in transnational firms that exercise a huge amount of power in shaping physical landscapes, neighborhoods, and whole communities. To me, understanding the bottom up and top down, across cultural and international contexts, is fascinating, in that both approaches reveal important insights about how places, peoples, and environments are imagined, managed, and contested.

In the interdisciplinary field of American Studies, we study stories, places, and the circulation of ideas as well as material objects. In the contemporary moment, American Studies is also a good vantage point from which to study China. The storylines of dominance and hegemony about

"America" and Chinese ascendance on the global stage are complex and have both racial and historical dimensions. Nationalism, competition, and political and economic ideologies have shaped U.S. and Chinese foreign and environmental policy in the era of global climate change and the economic transformation of the past two decades. Thus, I'm interested in the stories that get told about the sources and meaning of global environmental problems and the kinds of fears they address. In the United States, these fears are about being left behind, and the broader economic implications of the globalization of manufacturing. In China, these stories are in part about national and urban optimism about the country's rise, and also about its vulnerabilities, environmental and otherwise.

In the United States, "China anxiety" has a long and vexed history. In writing about the symbolic role of China in the United States, the prominent Chinese American playwright David Henry Hwang has suggested that competition between the United States and China will continue to intensify, and that ultimately Americans will experience a new round of "Yellow Peril" rhetoric echoing the nineteenth-century anti-Chinese attitudes and policies that culminated in the 1882 Chinese Exclusion Act, the first racial exclusionary immigration law in the United States.[34] Signs of this resurgence are already visible in the U.S. cultural landscape.[35] Reactions to "Chinese pollution" become a mechanism through which we can analyze how the United States culturally makes sense of our changing historical and political power in a moment of global environmental, social, and economic crisis. As the journalist Donovan Hohn notes in an investigative article about contaminated toy production in China, "something changed" in American attitudes toward China in the late 1990s as a result of the growing trade deficit. China, Hohn writes, "began to cast a shadow and a spell over the American imagination . . . . We no longer know what to make of China: Is it our ally or our enemy? Our rival or our döppelganger? A repressive Communist dictatorship or the new century's new land of wealth and opportunity?

In a way, thanks to China, we no longer quite know what to make of ourselves."[36]

What, then, to make of these new Chinese forays into eco-city development? Here I examine political and cultural discourses that construct China as simultaneously the world's worst polluter and its best hope in the context of global climate change. I agree with those who argue that those interested in environmental problems and solutions must take China into account, if only on a pragmatic level. China's impact on the world, particularly in environmental issues, is simply too big to ignore. China is cast in the role of the laboratory for social and engineering innovation to address the world's environmental challenges. The cultural politics of global climate change discourses matter, as does the question, *Why now?* In 2006, China exceeded the United States in total carbon emissions, although its per capita consumption is far lower. It's no surprise that the problems associated with global climate change gained new attention in the very years in which China overtook the United States as the world's leading contributor of carbon emissions.

In part, the construction of the "Chinese pollution" problem is a cultural one, with particular rhetorics at work. The idea of "Chinese pollution" serves several purposes simultaneously in helping both the United States and China make sense of their national ecological and political imaginaries.[37] While corporations based in China, Europe, and the United States salivate about the prospect of the rising purchasing power of the Chinese middle class (a billion new consumers!), environmentalists (within China and from the Western industrialized world) shudder about what the actual, on-the-ground impacts of the associated production and consumption will look like. And the very real question of how to manage these complicated and often contradictory pressures around economic development, nationalism, and environmentalism are clearest with regard to climate change, where China, along with India, has vigorously opposed global attempts to deal with the crisis, from the Kyoto Protocol to the Copenhagen Accord.

Using Shanghai as my case study, I capture what eco-desire looks like at one particular time and place, to develop a concept that will have applicability beyond the specific case. Let's turn now, first, to the broader cultural debates about environmental issues in the U.S. and Chinese contexts.

# CHAPTER ONE

# Fear, Loathing, Eco-Desire: Chinese Pollution in a Transnational World

In 1983, when I visited China, I was an obnoxious American saddled with a bowl haircut. I was also the literal embodiment of my parents' triumphant return to a country they had long ago left, since everyone approvingly told my parents that I was a good "Fai Zai" (fat boy). Everyone was wearing communist outfits—blue jackets, hats, and dark pants. I had little interest in the endless parade of extended family or the historic sites and instead obsessively played with my handheld video game. At Tiananmen Square, I turned the game on for the umpteenth time. In it, Mickey Mouse carried a basket. He was supposed to catch eggs rolling down four chutes—the eggs came down faster and faster, until three broken eggs ended the game. Slowly, a crowd of a hundred curious people gathered round—they had never seen a video game. Someone said (in wonder) that in America they can even waste eggs in a game! Nothing about the lives of these spectators seemed to connect with my own existence in the United States, especially not that someone thought those rolling eggs were *real*, a symbol of affluence and waste. Nowadays, that video game would be made in China, and not a single stylish person (much less a crowd) would bat an eyelash.

China's privileged urban youths are increasingly obese from fast food and their own excesses of "screen" time. The China I saw then, populated by the monochromatic masses, is now the world's economic powerhouse. The title of one popular business book warns that the United States will become "China's Bitch," shocking in its profane title but not in sentiment. My own relationship to these national and global transformations is complicated. As an American consumer, I can't help but notice that almost everything I buy is from China. It's virtually impossible to consume otherwise.[1] I can also track social and economic change through "stuff." Those early trips meant my parents bringing large suitcases full of consumer goods then unavailable in China to friends and family. Recent trips in the past decade have completely flipped the equation. Now my parents start with empty suitcases, which when they return are filled with stuff: towels, socks, and cheaper clothes with strange English phrases randomly printed on them, and the higher-end clothes for the global export market, complete with well-known brand names and expensive price tags, that they buy at a fraction of the official "price."

The growth of Chinese manufacturing and other global economic changes have been well documented, as have their environmental impacts. The *New York Times* columnist Thomas Friedman, in his *Hot, Flat, and Crowded: Why We Need a Green Revolution—and How It Can Renew America*, explicitly calls on nationalism—driven by fear of China as our main competitor—in arguing for greater American investments in green technology. He writes: "as an American I want to make sure that my country is in the lead. . . . America wins! America wins! America wins! If Only."[2] I envy Friedman's enthusiasm and boosterism; if only I could share it. Friedman admires China's can-do spirit while writing of the State Council ban on plastic bags in 2008 (the Council is the highest level of state power, composed of the premier, state councilors, ministers, and so on):

If only . . . If only America could be China for a day—just one day. *Just one day!* . . . [A]s far as I'm concerned, China's system of government is inferior to ours in every respect—except one. That is the ability of China's current generation of leaders—if they want—to cut through all their legacy industries, all the pleading special interests, all the bureaucratic obstacles, all the worries of voter backlash, and simply order top-down the sweeping changes in prices, regulations, standards, education, and infrastructure that reflect China's long-term strategic national interests—changes that would normally take Western democracies years or decades to debate and implement. . . . What would be so bad? China? Just for one short day?[3]

Friedman admires the increasing attention that the Chinese Communist Party (CCP) has paid to environmental industries, particularly the 2004–2006 project known as "Green GDP." This project was an effort to create an environmental yardstick for project evaluation and to recalculate gross domestic product to reflect the cost of pollution. Friedman writes, "This could be the greatest show on earth."[4] He exemplifies the Western fascination with the "good" side of China's political authoritarianism: admiration of its ability to implement sensible environmental policy by fiat, with no consultation with communities or process to hold up beneficial environmental policies, investments, and practices. He's right; Green GDP *would* have been a big deal if it hadn't been almost immediately scrapped as a political nightmare (adjusting for pollution reduced red-hot growth rates in some provinces by 3 percent).[5]

I call Friedman's attitude "eco-authoritarianism," and it is a highly developed form of eco-desire. Western environmentalists can be captured by this eco-desire, convinced that the ecological ends justify the authoritarian means. But aren't environmental problems and solutions supposed to transcend nations? After all, pollution from Asia, particularly from China, moves, often across epic distances, traveling across the Pacific Ocean to the western United States. On some days, a third of the air pollution over Los

Angeles and San Francisco can be traced directly to Asia.[6] This pollution is in the Sierra Nevada mountain region, in the iconic Yosemite National Park all the way up to Donner Summit and northward.[7] Scientists liken the movement of polluted air to a "ribbon" covering the entire Pacific Ocean basin bent back and forth.

In theory, we're all on this sinking planet together. In practice, defining what the environmental problems are, where they stem from, and what the best ways to solve them are immensely complicated questions that can end up replicating and amplifying geopolitical, cultural, and racial struggles and anxieties writ large. Within the United States, our greatest ecological desire is to fixate on China as the focal point of the vast majority of global pollution, and thus displace our own responsibility for global environmental damage. After all, for the past century, the United States was truly "number one," to quote Friedman, not only in carbon emissions, but in many pollutants. At the same time, influential architects, environmentalists, and others in the United States fervently believe in the fantasy of China as the "go-to" place where great green things happen on a vast governmental scale. Contrast Chinese environmental policy with what the American environmental sociologist Andy Szasz calls the contemporary U.S. obsession with "Shopping Our Way to Safety," or environmentalism through individual consumption of things such as bottled water, buying or growing organic food, and the use of nontoxic materials.[8] That is not to say that Chinese middle-class consumers don't also increasingly drink bottled water, eat organic, and use "natural materials," but there is a difference in the national character and investments, both literal and cultural, in environmental policy and action.

China is our psychological displacement and doppelganger, our enemy and our salvation. It is home to the world's first "solar billionaire," and Chinese companies represent 47 percent of the market share of solar panel installations in the United States, dwarfing the 29 percent market share for American companies.[9] China is also the world's largest market for wind energy.[10] Yet, China's investments in green technology are also seen as a cause for alarm by elected officials and trade bodies in the United States. For example, the U.S. International Trade Commission imposed tariffs on Chinese solar panels of 24–36 percent, accusing Chinese solar manufacturers of dumping cheaply made panels.[11] In the United States, our ecological desire is defined by an ecological blame-the-victim game. We focus on China at the moment when its carbon emissions surpass ours and ignore that our per capita rate is far higher. And it's not just about carbon. In 2004, according to a World Bank Report, China surpassed the United States as the world's largest waste generator.[12]

We fear China and its pollution; at the same time, we are defined by our envy of the power of authoritarian government to make positive environmental changes. In contrast, Chinese eco-desire takes a related, but somewhat different form. I suggest that Chinese eco-desire is based on three closely linked factors: technocratic faith in engineering, reliance on authoritarian political structures to facilitate environmental improvements, and discourse of "ecological harmony" between man and nature.[13] The rest of the examples in this book—Chongming, Dongtan, suburbanization, and the World Expo—are examples of these factors at work.

In China, the shape that eco-development takes is a direct result of the authoritarian political structures that promote and enable large-scale planning—though these "big" plans for improvement often lead to significant environmental devastations, most notoriously (but not only) the Three Gorges Dam.[14] Contemporary Chinese environmental policy is defined by the tendency to build on an epic scale. In political scientist James C. *Seeing Like a State*, he explains what it means to "see like a state."[15] In the twentieth century, large-scale plans for improving the human condition often went spectacularly, and sometimes violently, wrong (examples include compulsory ujamaa villages in Tanzania, collectivization in Russia, Le Corbusier's urban planning theory in Brasilia, the Great Leap Forward in China, and agricultural "modernization" in the tropics). Scott explains how and why these plans share a literal and political perspective. Attempts to make a society legible and to arrange the population in ways that simplify state functions create the conditions of their own failure, especially as these utopian plans and projects disregard the experiences, worldviews, values, and desires of their purported beneficiaries. These episodes of state-initiated social engineering share key elements: administrative ordering of nature and society, high modernist ideology (including a valorization of rational design through urban planning and manipulations of temporal/spatial context), authoritarianism, and a weak civil society.

Contemporary eco-authoritarian practices—like the eco-city and eco-development trend in China—are a milder, greener version of the plans discussed in Scott's *Seeing Like a State*. These schemes don't lead to the deaths of millions. But they are similarly doomed to fail in ecological or social terms. Authoritarian political structures by definition inhibit strong civil society. That explains why, even though China has very strong environmental legislation on the books, it's often not enforced.[16] Scott's theory of "seeing like a state" is useful in that far too many environmentalists wear blinders when it comes to the contemporary eco-city.

Understanding his theory of "seeing" means that we instead focus on issues of power and power relations. Unlike climate skeptics, climate change activists and sensible policymakers understand the urgency of global environmental problems. This urgency can sometimes lead to a willful blindness to the negative consequences of projects that are proposed to address climate change but end up creating or exacerbating other social injustices.[17] Chinese eco-desire is also in lockstep with American eco-desires, which hold China as both the environmental pariah and salvation in a fun-house distortion of our own environmental hopes and insecurities, paradoxes and failures.

This chapter lays out both the realities and the discourses around Chinese pollution that set the political and ideological contexts for Dongtan eco-city, Chongming Island ecological development and planning, ecological suburbanization, and the World Expo. Climate change is the primary environmental and policy context. In other words, climate change is a "metanarrative" that structures policy decisions.[18] The desire to address climate change can dovetail with a willful blindness to the failures of projects that purport to advance environmental aims. When describing Chinese pollution, I'm not talking about it solely as a discursive phenomenon. Chinese pollution is real, it's systemic and huge (and growing), and it hurts Chinese populations the most intensively (only 1 percent of Chinese urban residents breathe clean air, and estimates of early deaths attributable to air pollution are in the hundreds of thousands per year) even as its impacts are regional and global in scope.[19] That said, "Chinese pollution" must be understood not just as an environmental and scientific problem to be solved by engineering and technology, but also within broader cross-cultural, comparative, and political frameworks.

I give a brief history of pollution in communist China as a way to show the linkages between contemporary environmental policy and development and the recent past. In other words, the frameworks and discourses of Chinese "environmental solutions" and "ecological harmony" in the post-reform era are directly related to these earlier periods. Both this history and contemporary policy changes are important in shaping the broader discursive landscape upon which eco-cities are being built in China, as well as the recent environmental casting of the Beijing Olympics in 2008. I then turn to an overview of Shanghai's environmental problems as a way to situate the city's recent forays into ecological development.

## CHINA: THE NATION RUNS BLACK

In 2007, the *New York Times* ran a series of investigative articles under the banner "Choking on Growth." Focusing on a series of devastating contemporary environmental disasters in China, the series highlighted the social and environmental costs of economic growth and the rampant political corruption that destroyed a variety of landscapes and habitats, and their costs to human and nonhuman populations. From the burgeoning water crisis, to the hundreds of thousands of early deaths from the polluted air (often triggered by poor fuel standards in a transportation system centered almost entirely over the past three decades around automobiles), the toxic and chemical pollution that contaminated Lake Tai (the third largest body of fresh water, which sustained two million local residents), the extinction (or near extinction) of rare Yangtze River species (the Baiji dolphin and large freshwater turtles), wastewater contamination, and illegal drugs used in the farmed fish markets, the picture was grim and largely devoid of hope.

To longtime China watchers, "Choking on Growth" offered no real surprises. In her book *The River Runs Black: The Environmental Challenge to China's Future*, the foreign policy expert Elizabeth Economy documents the ruinous environmental costs of China's economic development in flooding, desertification, water scarcity, and dwindling forest resources. In *Mao's War against Nature: Politics and the Environment in Revolutionary China*, the international relations scholar Judith Shapiro argues that CCP rule laid the groundwork for the contemporary landscape and politics of Chinese pollution. She documents how closely intertwined the abuse of people and the abuse of the natural environment were under Mao. These abusive programs included population control policy in the 1950s, the building of the first big dams, the Great Leap Forward, "grainfields in lakes," wetlands destruction, and the forced relocation of urban youth.

This war on nature, or seeing nature as the enemy, is not unique to China; in many ways it came out of the U.S. World War II context of military research, especially the postwar growth of pesticides.[20] What is arguably unique is the large scale and destructive impacts of this Mao-era war. My own parents, like virtually everybody in China at that time, were directly affected by Mao's war on nature. My parents remember banging pots to keep the sparrows from landing in order to kill these pests through sheer exhaustion, and they experienced the famine triggered by the Great Leap Forward. My father was forced to relocate to the countryside, and those memories explain why he still won't eat carrots, one of the few foods available during those turbulent times.

The traumas of Maoist China have been well told, and my parents' experiences are not exceptional. Far less understood is how much these traumas under Mao were directly caused by his war on nature, and what the continuing legacies of this war are in contemporary Chinese environmental and urban development policy. Contemporary CCP's ecological development can't be separated from the historical and authoritarian context, no matter how attractive it may be for some in the West to imagine China as an environmental savior. Shapiro argues that the long, dark "shadows of Mao" continue to hang over China's environmental policy, in the case of the Three Gorges Dam—the world's biggest dam, power plant, and consumer of dirt, stone, concrete, and steel, which displaced 1.3 million people (and led to major environmental problems like landslides and flooding). This influence continues in projects now coming to fruition: the three-decade-long massive urbanization policy and other huge public works projects, like an epic sixty-two billion-dollar plan to move twelve trillion gallons of water from the south to the parched north; in campaigns to develop the western frontier; as well as in the unrelenting obsession with building the tallest, biggest—and, now, most sustainable—buildings. These plans are less of a direct attack on nature than that against the sparrows, but they are nonetheless motivated by similar impulses. These include an obsessive technological control of natural resources, masked now in part as sustainability discourses, as well as the belief in large-scale monumentalism.

While this war on nature may have begun under Mao, it is only in the post-reform period that the environmental costs of Chinese pollution have truly gone global. This transformation is largely due to technological advances in manufacturing and transportation (and their impacts across vast distances), changing multinational corporate practices, and ascendant globalizing ideologies of privatization and neoliberalism. Taken together, these technological, political, and ideological shifts have functioned to essentially make China the "factory" for the world. The cultural question of the impacts of Chinese pollution reveals as much about the problems of Western consumption as of Chinese production. This question begs another: how much "Chinese pollution" belongs to China, if a large percentage of the pollution produced is for the international export market?

According to the International Energy Agency, more than a third of China's carbon emissions come directly from making products for foreign consumers.[21] How, then, does it make sense to talk about "national" pollution data when the catalysts for this pollution in the Chinese context are, in large part, Western corporations producing goods for European, U.S., and Australian consumers (though of course also for a significant and growing Chinese middle class)? Not only is China the "world's factory," it is also, some argue, its smokestack. For example, the growth of China's industrial economy must be understood in inverse relation to Germany's, which has seen its carbon emissions decline by 19 percent since 1990 as a significant percentage of its industrial production has moved offshore to China.[22] Similarly, calculations of British carbon emissions leap if output within China for British factories is counted as U.K. rather than Chinese emissions.[23]

Of course, the growth of manufacturing and the impact on rural-to-urban migration within China are closely linked. Urbanization is closely tied to economic growth. Currently, 70 percent of Europeans and North Americans live in urban areas, while only 40 percent of the African and Asian population is urban. According to a 2008 Chinese Academy of Social Sciences report, China's population was 1.3 billion with a 45 percent urban population, and it is expected to reach 70 percent by 2050. Another estimate has China's urban population expanding from 572 million in 2005 to one billion by 2030. Put in another context, in twenty years China's cities will have added 350 million people—more than the entire population of the United States today. According to one estimate, by 2030 China will have over two hundred cities with more than one million inhabitants (compared with thirty-five in Europe today).[24] You can already see this explosive growth in Shenzhen, in southern China, home to China's first special economic zone and its largest factory region. Here, the largely rural population of 350,000 in the early 1980s exploded to an "official" population of more than ten million in 2010 (the "true population" is millions higher) and it now has the world's fifth highest population density.[25]

China has indeed exemplified the economist Joseph Schumpeter's process of "creative destruction" as a political and economic force, destroying far more of its older urban fabric in its twenty-year building binge than any other nation has done in peacetime, far surpassing the losses, human and physical, of urban renewal in the United States.[26] By some measures, this urban rebuilding constitutes the largest destruction of property in human history. As the cultural critic and literary scholar Sheldon Lu suggests, "Chai-na (literally, 'tearing down!') is indeed the proper name for contemporary China, as we witness the destruction of old buildings," often on a massive scale.[27] The example best known to outsiders is the destruction of the old *hutong* neighborhoods in Beijing before the Olympics.[28] In the contemporary Chinese city, the spirit of the master builders Robert Moses and Baron Haussmann reigns supreme, but on a scale that far exceeds the physical and cultural impact of Moses in New York or Haussmann in Paris. The destruction is not contained within a single city or traceable to a single powerful planner or bureaucrat, but instead has been unleashed by the full force of the CCP itself as national policy, practice, and ideology.

Although there are clear links between the environmental history of China under Mao and contemporary environmental change and urbanization, what is truly unique about current-day China is the speed, scale, and scope of the pollution produced, which hits the local workers and communities the hardest. The environmental destructiveness that comes from manufacturing is especially intensive in high-tech (as opposed to traditional) manufacturing. Traditional manufacturing is dirty in its own way, but different in type and health impact. The air pollution in Shenzhen has roots in manufacturing, coal power plants, auto emissions, and chemicals released into the air from production processes. In 2003, Shenzhen had 131 days of smog in the year as coal power plants were not equipped to remove smaller particles such as sulfur dioxide (which merge with $H_2O$ particles in the atmosphere and create black acid rain). This pollution is so strong that it burns through car paint and hurts human skin. Factory pollution and the population increases have transformed the water to a highly polluted waterscape, as the economy has transformed from one based largely on freshwater fishing to a highly industrialized one.

The scale, speed and scope of China's boom have been well-documented by journalists, researchers, and artists. The Canadian Edward Burtynsky photographs quarries, recycling yards, factories, mines, the Three Gorges Dam, and Shanghai's urban destruction and renewal. The documentary film *Manufactured Landscapes* follows Burtynsky to China as he photographs its manufacturing and industrial revolution. The film opens with a ten-minute single shot of an immense factory floor more than a kilometer long. Burtynsky's photographs of the recycling yards capture epically high mounds of electronic waste scoured by women and children in search of materials for reuse and resale.

Much of U.S. "e-waste" (monitors and cell phones, for example) is sent to China, where this waste leaks lead, cadmium, mercury, chromium, and polyvinyl chlorides. These are known to have negative health effects, from brain damage to kidney disease to mutations and cancers. Activist groups like the Basel Action Network and Greenpeace, along with mainstream environmental organizations like the Natural Resources Defense Council, have been working on this issue over the past two decades, but serious problems persist.[29] One news segment documented a southern Chinese town named Guiyu, where women were heating circuit boards over a coal fire, pulling out chips and pouring off the lead solder. The town has the highest levels of cancer-causing dioxins in the world. Pregnancies were six times more likely to end in miscarriage, and seven out of ten kids have too much lead in their blood, a condition that leads to major brain and developmental problems.[30]

China is central to global environmental discourse, policy, and practice, understood to be the central component to any serious ostensible "answer" to the global environmental crisis. Those interested in global pollution have to take China into account, given the sheer scale of pollution produced there. Policy rationale, paranoia, envy, and fuzzy boosterism compete for space on the "China-watching" stage, jostling for influence within China, and among the cosmopolitan and technocratic elites. The broad international cultural consensus is that the "action" is taking place in China, especially in terms of building projects. Part of this is purely economic. China's growth created an economic surplus used to build infrastructure (as I detail later, some U.S. and U.K. architecture and engineering firms have more than 40 percent of their staff based in China). This perception of "action" is not just economic, but ideological. The Chinese government has used domestic "soft power," focused as much on events and buildings, as it has on its official foreign policy. And Shanghai, in particular, rests on its soft power, specifically in relation to its skyline.[31] In architecture, planning, and contemporary art, China is the new frontier, the utopian future where anything can happen.

China is, in other words, what the "West" was to the United States in the nineteenth century or, even earlier, what "America" was to Europe in the eighteenth. These frontiers are the peripheries unchained from the social and cultural strictures of their centers, and freer in their manipulation of the landscapes around them. These frontiers are also where the exploitation of powerless people ran rampant in the relentless search for wealth. Friedman, in admiring CCP investments in Green GDP-ism, exemplifies this impulse to understand China as the "New World," liberated from old limits and social structures, as well as the fear that China will pull ahead, leaving the United States in the proverbial dust, much as the eastern United States was left behind as the western United States grew, especially during the Gold Rush era.

But is Friedman's description of China's green investments as "the greatest show on earth" mere hyperbole? Not if you look at the numbers. Recent changes in Chinese environmental policy have led to a significant growth in capital investments in "building green." For example, at the Seventeenth National Congress of the Communist Party held in Beijing in 2007, President Hu Jintao coined the new term *shengtai wenming*, or an "ecologically harmonious socialist society."[32] He argued that China "must pursue comprehensive, balanced and sustainable development . . . and build a resource-conserving and environment-friendly society . . . so that our people will live and work under sound ecological and environmental conditions and our economy and society will develop in a sustainable way." This speech signified the first time the CCP had highlighted ecology, putting it explicitly on the Party's agenda. Hu explained: "The emergence of shengtai wenming is a global revolution related to the mode of production, lifestyle, and the concept of value. It is an inevitable global trend. It is a new choice for human society after agricultural civilization and industrial civilization."[33] He called for a broad new awareness of shengtai wenming to "be firmly established in the whole of society."[34] That same year, in his "State of the Union" address, Prime Minister Wen Jiabao made forty-eight references to the environment or pollution.[35]

Being put on the Party agenda makes all the difference. After all, all land in China is owned by the central government, although local municipalities lease development rights. In China, no major development happens outside the Party system, to the consternation of other nations which cry foul at the unfair advantages of state sponsorship. Although the political and academic debate in the past two decades in Western Europe and the United States has been about the impact of privatization under neoliberal doctrine, in China, the split between public and private entities is largely irrelevant. Simply put, the distinction between private and public in China is not the same as it is in the West. And these national development and land-use strategies and policies have favored controversial actions. For example, much industrial development in China takes place on lands that were formerly rural, and forced land conversions remain highly contentious.[36]

After the 2007 announcement of shengtai wenming, these public-private entities began major capital investments in environmental industries, including green building and the environmental protection industry.[37] One of the public-private entities is the Shanghai Industrial Investment Corporation (SIIC), the client for Dongtan eco-city, which I discuss in the next chapter. Since the beginning of the twenty-first century, China's environmental protection industry has grown at an average annual rate of 17 percent, far outstripping the rest of the economy.[38]

Growing awareness that international concern about Chinese pollution was significant and that the unchecked pollution highlighted by the *New York Times* series "Choking on Growth" was no longer palatable made international and national concerns synergistic. What that means in practice is complicated, but the main point is that around 2007–2008, major environmental changes were afoot at the national CCP and government levels. For example, China issued "China's National Climate Change Program," the first policy document about climate change in China. This document clarified China's goals and principles in dealing with climate change.[39] In 2008, the Chinese Ministry of Environmental Protection was established to centralize the duties of environmental protection and strengthen its law enforcement power, in part because of a growing recognition at the national level of the importance of environmental protection to economic development.[40]

Whether these policies trickled down to the provincial level or were adopted in the realm of individual environmental practices by consumers or average citizens is another story entirely. Sometimes, provincial governments actively worked to thwart ambitious national environmental goals like reducing energy consumption.[41] At the same time that there was a new government focus on green buildings, the World Bank estimated that 95 percent of new building construction in China did not meet energy-efficiency standards.[42] In other words, many new buildings lack insulation and are energy inefficient. This lack of insulation is a huge factor in climate change, as buildings constitutes a large percentage of carbon emissions (in the United States, almost 39 percent of carbon emissions comes from buildings).[43]

The Ministry of Environmental Protection also became responsible for examining and approving what in English is roughly translated as "trial eco-provinces, cities, and towns" and *shengtai wenming jianshe shidian*, a phrase roughly translated as "ecological civilization trial sites." These trials began in 2008.[44] Around this time, fourteen provinces started to construct "eco-provinces,"[45] 150 "eco-cities," and eleven "eco-counties" that are named national eco-counties.[46] What defines an eco-county or an eco-city? On paper, what defines an eco-county, eco-city, or ecological civilization site is often defined by highly bureaucratic language.[47]

There is often a large gap between what is on paper and what happens in practice. Thus, these "ecological" terms are often quite meaningless on the ground. That is why in the hyperpolluted Lake Tai region, the whistle-blower Mr. Wu, who reported on the chemical companies polluting the lake, was outraged when his city was named a "Model City for Environmental Protection."[48] The picture on "eco-cities" is even more vague. The general understanding is just that these cities should exhibit "environmental protection," result in "energy savings," and bring about the "*harmonious co-existence* of humans and nature."[49] With few quantitative standards and indicators, different places build their own eco-cities based on their particular activities, understandings, and imaginations.

Consider, for example, another prominent eco-city project, the Sino-Singapore Tianjin (Zhong Xin tianjin shengtai chen) in Tianjin, a city in northern China. This project is a strategic cooperation between the Chinese and Singaporean governments to improve the living environment and build an "eco-culture" through a green transportation system, drinkable water, and green buildings.[50] By 2020, this project will house 350,000 people in a low-carbon, green environment in an area half the size of Manhattan, built on dumping grounds for toxic waste and barren salt flats abutting one of the world's most polluted seas. As of March 2012, sixty families had moved to the site, which will also be a hub of green technology and creative industries. In sharp contrast to most "eco-development" and eco-city development in China, one-fifth of the housing in Tianjin will be subsidized for low-income workers.[51]

At the same time, policy interpretations of "sustainable" development in China are relatively narrow, focused on "managing" natural resources in an era of unchecked growth. Where sustainability discourse in the United States includes a "third pillar" or "third stool" of equity alongside the familiar pairing of ecology and economy, such an approach is virtually impossible (with the notable exception of Tianjin) in the Chinese national, political, and local contexts. The question of equity is largely off the table from the CCP policy perspective, but at the same time it is also reinforced through the elevation of the repetition of "harmonious elements" (man/nature) in ecological development. Harmony, of course, in contemporary Chinese state discourse, is akin to suppression of "unharmonious elements."

At the same time, ordinary Chinese citizens have responded with vigor to the cacophony of environmental disasters, risking great personal and professional danger in questioning the status quo of development at all costs. The journalist Jonathan Watts, a longtime environment correspondent for the *Guardian*, interviewed hundreds of nomads, philosophers, businessmen, conservationists, scientists, lawyers, and farmers across the vast expanse of China's regions and ecosystems in his exhaustively chronicled book *When a Billion Chinese Jump: How China Will Save Mankind—or Destroy It*. In it, he documents the tidal wave of grassroots protests against chemical plants, waste incinerators, and other pollution sources, which he suggests show considerable concern for environmental health. In recent years, high-profile environmental protests in a number of different cities have succeeded in protesting and blocking incinerators, copper smelting, and coal-fired plants.[52] It is crucially in this political context of government fears of discontent that state-level, top-down adoption of environmental rhetoric and policy must also be understood.

## ECO-DEVELOPMENT WITHOUT DOWNSIDES

The disjunct between the dream of eco-development and the complicated reality exemplifies the ecological desire for eco-development without downsides. This green (capitalist/sustainable) dream in China has a fraught recent history. The "ecological civilization" discourse and increasing capital investments dovetail with the land grab of real estate developers, who get cheaper lands and enjoy favorable policies if their development plans fall under the rubric of "ecological civilization." For example, SIIC is involved in six other "eco-city" plans in locales far away from Shanghai.[53]

The country's highest-profile eco-village, at Huangbaiyu, which began in 2001 in northeastern China, was designed by the well-known American "green" architect William McDonough,[54] in conjunction with an organization run by Deng Nan, the daughter of Deng Xiao Ping, the former leader of China. With a proliferation of first glowing and then damning publicity, the project failed in large part (according to its former resident anthropologist Shannon May) because of the lack of understanding of the local rural Chinese contexts into which the imaginings of global sustainability were projected by McDonough, his Chinese allies, and the local developers.[55] Although more than forty houses were built, they remain empty. The price of these houses was far beyond local residents' economic means. Garages were built for many new complexes, but not one local family at the time owned a car. Many peasants refused to move into the new houses because the yards were too small to raise domestic animals, and even worse, the houses were too far from the fields that were the sole source of the villagers' income. McDonough turned his firm's attention away from China's eco-projects, and Huangbaiyu is no longer listed on the company website.[56]

Despite the many difficulties in the recent history of eco-city and eco-village development in China, ecological images retain their *ideological* power with the government and with elites, and with those who serve their needs, especially in the biggest cities, Beijing and Shanghai. By those criteria, the 2008 Olympics in China's capital city, Beijing, was literally ground zero for China's green dreams.

## GREEN DREAMS, GREEN MASKS:
## ECO-FANTASIZING THE BEIJING OLYMPICS

I have suggested that the problem of Chinese industrial pollution as a result of production is also a global problem of consumption and demand. The problem depends, at least in part, on how to measure accountability, when production and its environmental costs are intimately linked to the problems of resource extraction, production and manufacturing, and global consumption. These debates about the global character and contexts of "Chinese pollution" generally get subsumed under the burdens of cultural representation, as my colleague Mike Ziser and I have written elsewhere.[57] Take, for example, the global media concern over the impacts of Chinese pollution, which reached fever pitch in the 2008 American news coverage of the Summer Olympics in Beijing, an episode that serves as a potent example of this repurposing of environmental discourse to geopolitical use. NBC's early coverage of the Olympics focused on the extreme air pollution produced by Beijing's factories, construction sites, and motor vehicles.

Ostensibly a story about the health of high-performance athletes, the unmistakable effect of the drumbeat of "Chinese smog" reports was to correlate Chinese geopolitical threats with environmental threats. When the world-record holder in the marathon, Haile Gebrselassie of Ethiopia, declined to compete in the Olympic marathon in order to preserve his lungs, the news coverage was intense, as it was when the U.S. bicycling team arrived in the Beijing airport wearing black masks designed to filter out particulates they claimed might affect their performance. During the Olympics themselves, various Western media outlets made coverage of the atmosphere a major part of their narrative line about the Beijing games. The Associated Press set up an air monitoring station on the Olympic Green. Media webpages sported widgets that kept a running record of air quality—a new stream of information incongruously positioned alongside the familiar stock, bond, and commodity tickers.

To counter the well-documented problem of Beijing's atrocious air pollution, the Bird's Nest and the Water Cube built for the 2008 Beijing Olympics both use "nature" as a model for balance, "harmony," and functionality (see figure 1). Both were also engineered by Arup, the firm behind Dongtan.

Analyzing the elements of eco-desire embodied by the Bird's Nest raises similar intriguing questions about the relationship between architecture and politics. The first is the central meaning of the organic and the natural. Patterned after traditional Chinese ceramics, the building is meant to evoke, according to its designers, a "porous . . . and a collective building, a public vessel."[58] The design serves as a sort of architectural preemption of criticisms from Western observers primed to draw conclusions about China's autocratic government from its Olympic façades. The stadium casts an ironic glance in the direction of the West's habitual reference to the organic as the touchstone of design (and also to the orientalizing habit of ascribing naive

Figure 1. Bird's Nest, Water Cube. Photo by A. Alerigi, Creative Commons License

naturalism to Eastern cultures).[59] The second is about the relationship between this question of openness and the ethics of working with a politically authoritarian regime.

In response to the U.S. film director Steven Spielberg's pulling out as artistic advisor to the Olympics to repudiate China's inaction on Darfur, the Swiss architects of the Bird's Nest, Herzog and de Meuron, wrote that it was in fact their *responsibility* to engage in the hope that their stadium might embody and even perhaps promote the idea of freedom. For instance, the design is such that visitors can choose their own random paths. According to de Meuron, "We wanted to do something not hierarchical, to make not a big gesture as you'd expect in a political system like that but [something that for] 100,000 people [is still] on a human scale, without being oppressive. It's about disorder and order, apparent disorder. It seems random, chaotic, but there's a very clear structural rationale."[60] Herzog adds that the design was aimed to support the "Chinese love" of public spaces, offering a "playground." They make a clear distinction between "creating a building that fosters a country's ideology—say, Albert Speer's work for Hitler—and one that seeks to transform it."[61]

But is there such a clear distinction between craven handmaiden to dictators and determined enlightener? Herzog and de Meuron's disavowal of Albert Speer, Hitler's favorite architect (called by one historian "the architect of the Devil"), aims to counter those critics who liken the 2008 Beijing Olympics to the 1936 Olympic Games and their explicit promotion of Nazi ideology. But despite their disavowal of Speer, the comparison is inevitable, if only because his son, Albert Speer Jr., designed the Beijing Olympic Park under the guise of a "green" facelift.[62] At three times the size of Central Park, the 2,864-acre site incorporates the China National Garden and ecological sanctuary. He designed a sixteen-mile-long north–south axis that connected the center city with the Olympic Village, the Forbidden City, and a new railroad station in the southern section of Beijing (the Water Cube and the Bird's Nest lie on opposite sides of the axis). One writer highlighted the connections between the father and son: "Speer's Berlin was to have been a nexus of monumental arches and grand boulevards, a capital to end all capitals. Speer Jr.'s blueprint for Beijing is equally monumental, the kind of large-scale urban concept possible only under a totalitarian regime."[63] In the run-up to the Olympics, more than three hundred thousand residents lost their homes, and the historical hutong neighborhoods made way for new apartment block housing. As many writers and residents have documented and lamented, the Beijing Olympics created a monumental physical landscape that not only has little space for ordinary people, but has actually actively destroyed a vital urban fabric in hundreds of neighborhoods around the city.[64]

The well-known Chinese artist and political dissident Ai Wei Wei offered his critique of design and Olympic totalitarianism. He worked on initial designs for the Bird's Nest with Herzog and de Meuron but resigned before the opening ceremony. He disavowed it in an attack on the "disgusting" political conditions under the CCP. He called the Bird's Nest and the general use of art/architecture for propaganda purposes a "fake smile" used to hide the dark side of China's political system and lack of true freedom. When asked about what China was trying to hide, he replied, "There are too many things. The whole political structure, the condition of civil rights, . . . corruption, pollution, education, you name it."[65]

Herzog and de Meuron's naïve insistence on their ability to "change China for the better" through their "organic" and "nonhierarchical" design concept stands in sharp contrast to the post-Olympic reality of the Bird's Nest.[66] The Bird's Nest is currently a largely abandoned and decaying site, home only to a small winter activities park.[67] The Olympic Green is now the site of a "Green Dream Park," what one visitor called "the worst theme park ever known to man." The "Green" component of the park is to "promote awareness of climate change and environmental protection" through do-it-yourself activities.[68] One visitor describes the experience:

> If you've ever seen those North Korean documentaries which showcase bizarre attractions completely empty of people, this one comes frighteningly close. . . . Upon passing through security (beware terrorists!), an eerie scene awaited us: 90s era Gameboy music on repeat, and a desolate park, other than a dance troupe, who seemed like they were randomly hired to dress up in animal costumes and do something strange on stage. . . . What about those do-it-yourself activities you ask? . . . [You can] decorate a vase and put a seed in there, and to pay to make a tie dyed piece of cloth. . . . The only free activity we found was a claw crane. But it wasn't filled with stuffed animals, but instead with cans—and yes, beer cans too. If you manage to successfully get a can (we didn't), you can insert it into yet another machine which will give you some coins in return.[69]

Put together, the Bird's Nest, the hysteria over pollution, and the Olympic Park show just how ecological images are a central, albeit highly contested part of the China/Beijing/Olympic story. The official story by the CCP seeks to represent Beijing and China as a whole as a clean, green, developed, and highly organized place. This national context matters greatly in understanding why and how Shanghai sought to keep up to, and at, the "ecological" cutting edge, primarily through the 2010 World Expo, as discussed in chapter 5.

## WHITHER ECO-SHANGHAI?

If Beijing is notorious internationally for its haze, with pollution so bad as to be visible from space and occasionally to shut down airline flights, what precisely are Shanghai's major environmental problems, both real and perceived? As one of the world's largest cities, its sheer size means that it faces a rather typical set of urban development challenges. The population density and growth expectations have major land-use implications. The major environmental issues in Shanghai are related to housing, water and air quality, and transportation and land-use planning. Due to its soft soil and decades of groundwater pumping, the city has sunk more than six feet since 1921, a problem that is not unique to Shanghai but is particularly extreme there.[70]

Shanghai's low-lying coastal nature is a major vulnerability with sea level rising because of global warming. According to recent news reports: "During the past years, the city has suffered more extreme weather, missed rain during the normal wet season and seen a temperature hike almost four times higher than the global level. . . . Because global warming is heating up the sea, local fisheries are expected to see their business drop."[71] But the biggest risks are silting, flooding, and the destruction of wetlands (which used to protect the city against flooding) in order to create more land to support the city's growth rate through land development and construction.

What is also special about Shanghai, as opposed to a "typical" Chinese city facing development challenges, is its unique status in China as a cosmopolitan place and a central interface with global capitalism and the workers who service it. Thus, it is perhaps no surprise that one policy and market response to climate change was to develop a carbon emission rights trading program in mid-2012, involving two hundred major local polluters.[72] Although some scholars have critiqued carbon trading markets on the grounds that using market mechanisms is just a reiteration of the problem itself, Shanghai is moving full-speed ahead with its carbon trading market.[73] With Shanghai's special status also comes special attention to the quality-of-life issues that its privileged residents (including the native-born Shanghainese and the global transnational elites) demand.

Overcrowding, poor housing conditions, and residential restructuring are some of the major environmental problems facing Shanghai. Housing has been, and is still, a major problem in Shanghai, whether defined by density or in urban redevelopment policy and practice. In Shanghai alone, redevelopment projects in the 1990s displaced more people than thirty years of urban renewal in the entire United States.[74] In 1985, the average population density in downtown Shanghai was 40,000 persons per square kilometer, but in some areas the density has risen to 160,000 persons per square kilometer. One official survey found that 1.8 million households were living in overcrowded conditions, including more than two hundred thousand households in dwelling units with less than two square meters per person.[75] During the 1990s, tens of thousands of households were "rehoused" each year, a result of three major reforms in housing: the upward adjustment of rents, increased investments by the private sector in housing, and urban restructuring at the local district level.[76] Authorities acknowledged in 2009 that between 70 and 80 percent of petitions submitted involved forced evictions in the name of economic and city development.[77]

Under the first phase of land reform (1979–1987), Shanghai was one of the first cities to experiment with separating land-use rights from land ownership and allowing for the transfer of land-use rights to foreign investors.[78]

Urban land reform is a primary function of state revenue generation, with major social costs for residents. In other words, the goal to promote urban growth is largely "disconnected from the interests of residents living on the land."[79] At the same time, the scale of relocation has produced "property-based activism" as residents seek to negotiate the best deals for their particular housing situation.

Like Burtynsky, the photographer Greg Girard documents these changes in his *Phantom Shanghai*. Girard says that he makes "photographs that show what a place, *this* place, looks like when it's used in this way. Here is Shanghai's *lived-in-ness*, the vanishing evidence of the hard flow of time through this city."[80] Both Burtynsky and Girard document the beauty of destruction and the juxtaposition of so much destruction with large-scale high-rises under construction. Their typical image is of a house in rubble, with mounds surrounding it, looking utterly alone, with a new fifty-story apartment building just above. The science fiction writer William Gibson writes in his preface to *Phantom Shanghai* that Girard's photos represent "the actual vanishing, the hideous twentieth-century urban hat trick itself . . . the line of dawn rushing through desert, causing stones to explode."[81] The planning historian Thomas Campanella argues that the human collateral and psychological costs of the craze for new building projects in China is immense. He calls it domicide, or the "emotional, psychological and social trauma caused by the deliberated destruction of home by human agency in the pursuit of specific goals."[82]

The sheer number of people relocated for urban redevelopment in Shanghai is immense, but the meaning of this dislocation for the inhabitants is not well-known outside of the city. These changes are often hugely unsettling, especially for the older generation. My own family left Shanghai in the 1950s, not to return until the 1980s. When my parents first returned, many places from their youth hadn't changed much at all, while others had already disappeared. The first places to change were near the historic core, one of the first focal points of major urban redevelopment. My mother grew up a block from the famed Bund, in what is now a fancy department store in the famous Nanjing Lu shopping district, equivalent to New York City's Times Square. My grandfather worked as a horse veterinarian at the Shanghai Race Club, long a symbol of Western decadence, racial exclusion, and British imperialism, symbolically "cleansed" after the Revolution as the "People's Square." Because of his association with the racetrack, my grandfather left for Hong Kong, and his family soon followed. After three decades away from Shanghai, my mother tracked down her schoolmates, all of whom had grown up within a block of her. None of them still lived in the area, the last among them pushed out during the 1990s rehousing boom, and my mom's apartment building is now the site of a fancy department store.

One exception is my mom's best friend's brother, who still lives in the apartment they grew up in, in a building designed by a French architect. Behind the façade and the bustle of tourists on their way to the Bund, he still lives with his wife and teenage daughter in a single room about ten feet by twenty feet, using one of about fifteen cooking stoves out on the communal hallway, and a single toilet and shower for the fifty residents on that floor to share. If Girard and Burtynsky revel in the large-scale sadness of old buildings tossed out, my mother's friend's experiences indicate perhaps why some Shanghainese are a bit more unsentimental about relocation and change, especially if it means more money, a little more privacy, and cleanliness.

For the younger generation who lived their entire lives in the context of such constant destruction and construction, the piles of rubble and migrant workers living in the buildings they are paid to take apart are their norm and their reality. One of the best documentations of this reality is called *Growing Up with Shanghai*, a series of soundwalks with young Shanghainese who were born and raised during the rapid modernization of their city in the 1980s and 1990s.[83] This series of sound recordings follows Shanghainese young people along an hour-long walk, with the sounds of the city in the background, reflecting on their memories of change. It's a remarkable historical document of a city that often claims to decry nostalgia, despite the disclaimer of Terence Lloren, who said when he initiated the project that it is "not meant to have any educational or historical significance."[84]

One of the interviewees, named "Bobby" in English, grew up on the same street as my mother. His reflections revealed the magnitude of the urban change: "Ever since Dong Hai Shang Du was rebuilt in 1992, everyone around here has great expectations [for success]," but most businesses failed there. Why? According to Bobby:

> When I asked my grandparents about it, they told me that during the Cultural Revolution, the Dong Hai Shang Du used to be a row of shops. In front of these shops there could be a lot of Pi Do Hui [gatherings where people were publicly criticized for their beliefs] and many innocent people . . . were wrongfully accused. . . . Some couldn't take the humiliation and slander and many of them would commit suicide by jumping off the roof of the Dong Hai Shang Du, and their spirits won't go away. That's why, in this particular location, no matter what business is here, it won't survive. Even big businesses like McDonald's couldn't last for over two years.

Bobby's recording also points to the layers of sadness and violence hidden behind the façade of go-go commercial culture in the city. Despite great pressures against them, a small number of housing activists and lawyers have resisted relocation, to their great peril, including jail time.[85] Perhaps the rush to change and to obliterate the past is a response to this sadness and to the traumas of urban historical and cultural memory in the face of such extreme and brutal development.

Shanghai's urban development policy in the past three decades—tear down (Chai-na), instead of rebuild—is in some ways an extension of the city's long-standing view of urban change. The intensive building boom also has environmental impacts, and shrinking green spaces weaken the city's ability to absorb carbon dioxide.[86] Shanghai's historical golden age and raison d'être is its commercialism, facilitated, of course, by its contact with rivers and the seas.

This water, a source of wealth, is now a symbol of the city's pollution and its potential flooding in the face of global climate change. Water quality in local rivers is a major problem. The Huangpu River is the source of most of the city's water supplies and also the location of a huge port, while functioning as a water transportation system and a sink for much of the city's industrial discharge. Eighty percent of the delta landform on which the municipality is located is drained by the Huangpu River catchment, a complex interlocking network of canals, drains, minor watercourses, and rivers. Groundwater is generally only about a meter below the surface.[87] Most water bodies in Shanghai are moderately to very severely polluted, contaminated by toxic substances such as phenol, cyanide, mercury, arsenic, and chromium.[88] Some describe the Huangpu River as "a chemical cocktail" of raw sewage, toxic urban wastes, and huge amounts of industrial discharges.[89] Industrial discharges, domestic sewage, and non-point-source pollution are the three main sources of wastewater discharges and polluted effluents. In addition, livestock waste and agricultural runoff are a major problem. Recently, the city has invested heavily in water improvement. There are still major problems, though, such as the leakage of phenol (an acid used to make detergents) from a cargo ship and, most recently, the discovery of thousands of pig carcasses in Shanghai's drinking water, dumped by pig farmers upstream.[90]

Shanghai also has major air-quality problems, even though its air is not as bad as Beijing's. Concentrations of sulfur dioxide ($SO_2$), total suspended particulates (TSP), and lead are far above healthy levels in the urban districts.[91] These levels of particulate air pollution from energy and industrial processes in Shanghai were, about a decade ago, among the highest in the world. Major industrial sources (power plants, large iron and steel works, and chemical works) consume large amounts of coal and contribute greatly to emissions, smoke, and dust in Shanghai. Industrial emissions of heavy metals and toxics are also significant contributors to air pollution in Shanghai. Although the air is getting cleaner, coal still accounts for a majority of the energy used in Shanghai.[92] Just how clean the air is depends on what data are used. For example, the Shanghai Environmental Protection Bureau uses air-quality information depending on particles of 10 micrometers, not the smaller 2.5 standard that is most harmful to human health, especially of the young and the elderly. Therefore, the U.S. consulate in Shanghai began issuing its own pollution statistics as an "unofficial resource" for the expatriate community living in Shanghai.

The transportation sector is also a major contributor to air pollution and carbon emissions, specifically the auto infrastructure. The number of motor vehicles increased at a staggering rate in China beginning in the 1990s. On the production side, the forty-two thousand cars produced in 1990 jumped to 2.3 million in 2003.[93] According to the *Financial Times*, in 2013 China produced more cars than Europe (at more than nineteen million). The problems stem not just from the growing size of the motor fleet but also from lax emission standards and poor road infrastructure. In the past, ambient lead levels from leaded gasoline (banned in 1997) have also been a major concern. Until recently, the motor vehicle fleet was fueled mainly by leaded gasoline.[94] Despite better controls on fuel quality and emissions standards, the sheer volume of the increase of vehicles in Shanghai generates substantial carbon emissions. Conservative estimates of greenhouse gas emissions from Shanghai's transportation sector show emissions quadrupling by 2020, while high scenarios project a sevenfold increase.[95] To give context for the already completed highway construction, Robert Moses constructed some 415 miles of highway in the New York metropolitan region in his entire career. Shanghai has built well over three times that amount in the 1990s alone.[96] At the same time, the urban subway has grown from virtually no miles to the most track miles in the world.[97]

In addition to transportation, Shanghai produces a huge amount of solid waste daily. In 1994, the city generated thirty-five thousand tons of solid waste per day, equal to 12.5 million tons per year, with two-thirds of this waste generated by industry and one-third by households. Although industry historically reused a large percentage of its wastes, disposal remains a major problem. The wastes consist principally of heavy metals, organic waste, waste acids and alkalis, calcium carbide residue, toxic sludge, and various organic chemical compounds.[98] In the early 1990s, 40 percent of the waste was barged along canals and rivers to two poorly designed landfills. The rest was either disposed at 410 unofficial stockpile sites or dumped, often into waterways, although new infrastructure has vastly improved the situation.[99] But by 2000, the amount of waste in Shanghai had increased dramatically, with a significant amount burned in incinerators that produce extremely toxic ash.[100]

These complex environmental and land-use challenges in Shanghai have been dealt with in very particular ways. The city is getting cleaner and the environmental picture is brighter, in part due to state-centered investments in infrastructure and the use of heavy carrots and sticks to induce better efficiencies in its residents.[101] Using other measures, however, the environmental picture is much more mixed, with the prognosis for improvements murkier.

CONCLUSION

This chapter focused on the conflicting realities, desires, hopes, and dreams surrounding "Chinese pollution" in the United States and in China, and how they all influence the emergence of eco-Shanghai discourses. Laying out the environmental history of Chinese pollution helps us to understand the contemporary realities and discourses around "Chinese pollution" at the Beijing Olympics and in CCP policy. These political and cultural contexts for Shanghai's ecological development put what is happening in Dongtan eco-city, the Chongming Island eco-developments, ecological suburbanization, and what occurred at the 2010 World Expo within broad webs of meaning, desire, ideology, and investment.

The "why now?" question may seem fairly obvious: international and national awareness of global climate change and environmental destruction such as species extinction, water shortages, and air pollution as a result of the growth of manufacturing in China is increasing. But the answer to the "how?" question is not so obvious. What is the "form" that the solution of the real and perceived crisis of Chinese pollution takes? In China more generally, and Shanghai in particular, the answer is manipulations of the built environment, through eco-city building, and "high-tech solutions" that promise both environmental benefits and economic growth. This green capitalist approach, cloaked in technocratic and technological solutions, is not unique to China,[102] but it is onto China that the American desire for, and revulsion against, the authoritarian structures needed for such ecological development are projected.

In other words, desire *always* animates ecological development. But whose desire, and to what end, is a mélange of fantasies, money, and dirty politics, as much as it is about shiny, clean, fantastically green "eco-cities" for the future. Ecological development in Shanghai is as much influenced by U.S. ambivalence about Chinese manufacturing as it is by local, regional, and national politics. It is shaped by global design, architecture, and engineering discourse and practice, as well as by the actual eco-systems that surround the complex and quickly changing urban landscape that is the Shanghai megaregion. The next two chapters explore the Dongtan eco-city project more closely, as well as the island context of Chongming within the broader regional context of Shanghai.

# CHAPTER TWO

# Changing Chongming

*Have you tasted homemade cheese? Have you smelt the fragrance of the hay in the barn? If not, take a walk from the Energy Center to the international eco-farm. The eco-farm is located at the North and next to the modern agricultural district. It consists of a Sino-Italian eco-farm, a Sino-German eco-farm, a Sino-Japanese eco-farm and Dongtan Taiwan folk Village. . . . [P]eople will be able to visit four different places: the Florentine village of the Sino-Italian eco-farm, the picturesque architecture of the Sino-German eco-farm and the Hokkaido buildings of the Sino-Japanese eco-farm. They will also experience the aboriginal appeal of the Taiwan folk Village. . . . While appreciating this beautiful vista, as relishing the local fruit, vegetables, locally produced sausages, cheese and beer and hearing oral music, visitors will find themselves back in the good old days of the past, as well as in the 21st century. And all this just in Shanghai.*

    *Zhao Yan and Herbert Girardet,* Shanghai Dongtan: An Eco-City, *194–195*

*A foreign power has invaded. Battle and devastation are spreading their stain ever more widely. The innocent are dying and no one is immune from the touch of violence.*

    *Timothy Brook,* Collaboration: Japanese Agents and Local Elites in Wartime China

The epigraphs to this chapter describe the same place, Chongming Island—the first as fertile fantasy, the latter as a land beset by wartime terror. The description of Chongming Island as a smorgasbord of nations and tastes was published to both celebrate and imagine the glorious eco-future in Dongtan. The second epigraph is from a history of Chinese collaboration during the brutal Japanese occupation in the late 1930s and early 1940s.

This juxtaposition unsettled me—neither of them fits what I thought I knew about the island, the place where my father was born and about which my mother constantly chided him. According to the "Chongming Club," an online forum for Chongming locals living off-island, mostly in Shanghai, my mother's attitude toward my dad's island roots remains pervasive in contemporary life. One laments, "They, Shanghainese, all look down upon us Chongming people and call us peasants." Another adds: "Why do we love Chongming so much? Because we have taken enough Shanghai people's supercilious looks."[1]

My Chongming associations were significantly different from the ecological vision of pastoral beauty (and I also have never associated anything remotely Chinese with cheese). Dongtan intrigued me, and it challenged me to learn more about a place that only ever existed in my life as the proverbial "old country" in my family's own journey from China to the United States. What I learned is that Dongtan is not the quixotic or mad rendering of a utopian environmentalist or a plan generated by a graduate eco-design class, but the apotheosis of years of interventionist planning from the highest levels in Shanghai and by the national Communist Party, culminating in a 2004 visit to the island by China's president Hu Jintao. On this visit, he expressed his desire "to construct [Chongming] into the first-class eco-island in the world."[2]

A year later, the U.K. prime minister Tony Blair and Hu Jintao attended a ceremony in London, where Arup, a global planning, engineering, and design firm, and Dongtan's principal investor, the Shanghai Industrial

Investment Corporation (SIIC), signed an agreement to expand their existing partnership to plan and develop Dongtan and several other similar eco-cities.[3] SIIC is one of China's largest real estate developers, and one of the first Chinese companies listed on the Hong Kong Stock Exchange. Arup is not well-known to the average person, although it has helped to build several iconic structures, including the Pompidou Center in Paris and the California Academy of Sciences in San Francisco. In China alone, Arup built Rem Koolhaas's China Central Television (CCTV) headquarters, as well as the Beijing Olympics Bird's Nest and Water Cube. These three buildings constitute China's contribution to contemporary global architecture.

Dongtan was planned for a population of fifty thousand by 2010—the year was originally chosen to coincide with the world expo. Growing to five hundred thousand by 2050, Dongtan was supposed to usher in a new era of green approaches to urban design, holistic economic and business planning, and sustainable architecture and infrastructure (including 95 percent of its energy from alternative and renewable sources, and 90 percent of the waste to be recycled). Early glowing profiles of Dongtan from 2006 and 2007 described the plans as "bold" and "forward-thinking." In the halcyon days, before political and technical obstacles stalled the project, Western journalists cheered over the techno-utopian promised land. In an age of climate and environmental anxiety, journalists and the global elites sought good news, and Dongtan eco-city promised a positive and potentially profitable pathway out of climate chaos. A 2007 article on Dongtan in *Wired* was typical of the early press coverage in devoting considerable attention to the broader political forces within Shanghai, and within Arup, that collectively led to the growth and ambition for the plan.[4] The press coverage at the time took on faith both the positive language and Arup's vision and skill to "design cities that work better—not just as grids or transport networks or skylines but as *ecosystems engineered* from the start to foil gridlock, energy waste, pollution, even economic inequality" (emphasis added).[5] Arup would come up with the "rules and standards" to "deliver a city."[6] But the tide soon turned. The early wave of positive coverage, which focused on its boldness and vision, was followed by critical articles that labeled Dongtan an "eco-Potemkin." *The Economist* reported in 2009 that its demise was a direct result of political corruption by the plan's proponents.[7]

To better understand the visions and desires that undergirded Dongtan and the conditions that led to its ultimate failure (the subject of the next chapter), we need to look at a whole suite of factors that shaped it. These include why and how eco-fantasies take the form of eco-cities, and the question of whether an eco-city can be an "ecosystem engineered." But one major factor, which got almost no attention in the media coverage of Dongtan, was the basic geographical fact of where it was located. Chongming Island has gotten short shrift in the breathless evocations of a dawning of the ecological New Age that Dongtan represented.

This chapter corrects this omission by asking, How did Chongming Island, long considered a rural backwater to Shanghai, become the temporary locus of the world's cutting-edge fantasies about technology and sustainability? What does it all mean to local residents? These questions matter, even though the Dongtan project failed. In fact, these questions are intimately connected to the story of Dongtan, although few analysts of eco-cities or journalists writing about the topic think about Chongming at any length. Although Dongtan may never be built as initially imagined, ecological development and planning on the Chongming Island continues unabated, as it does elsewhere in China and in other ambitious eco-city proposals. The discourses that saturate Chongming and eco-island development set the ideological contexts for the eco-city. Both eco-cities and eco-islands imagine a pure and unpolluted ecological space that functions as the clean counterpart to the polluting city—in this case, Shanghai. Discursively, the idea of "ecological places" is an old one that depends on spaces of purity and cleanliness. This notion of purity contrasts sharply with insights from the fields of urban ecology in the environmental sciences and the social sciences, which do not distinguish between ecologically pure human spaces and polluted ones.

Part of this distinction between pure and polluted is evident in the language used by Dongtan planners. One Arup planner told me simply in describing the inspiration for Dongtan: the project was always "about the birds."[8] Another described Dongtan as dealing with issues of rest and unrest, and another encapsulated it as "about harmony."[9] This chapter focuses on the histories and stories of Chongming and its people, while the next chapter focuses on the transnational architects and planners who are reshaping the island in fundamental ways using these notions of eco-desire in their reimagining and development plans.

Dongtan helps me to understand my family's journey from the island and to understand this place that my family once called home. Why and how did Chongming become the ecological cutting edge? How are historically degraded and culturally negative representations of rural spaces being reworked into clean, healthy, and ecological places in the context of Shanghai's urban development? There *is* no Dongtan without first understanding how eco-desire is operationalized and imagined on Chongming Island. Put simply, Chongming does the ecological heavy lifting for the Shanghai region, just as Dongtan concentrates ecological virtue on the island itself onto its eastern shore.

## FROM BROTHELS TO BIRDS

Chongming has always been defined by ecological and social change, primarily in the active migration flows between the island and the mainland. Radical change of a different kind has rocked Chongming as it has the rest of China in the past three decades. Most dramatically, it was transformed in 2010 from an island accessible only through boats and ferries to one connected to Shanghai through new infrastructure like bridges and train routes. These connections have created completely new visions and stories. The bridges and tunnels themselves conjured and imagined the narratives and hopes about the island's future, graphically illustrated through planning documents and project descriptions.

Chongming is a pretty agricultural landscape of farms, trees, occasional wandering livestock like goats, numerous two-story new houses, and decrepit old apartment blocks. *Chong* means high and *Ming* means unrestrained and far-reaching, and thus *Chongming* denotes the broad flatland above the water. Two sandbanks in the estuary emerged out of the sea in the Tang Dynasty (A.D. 618) called Dongsha (East Sandbank) and Xi'sha (West Sandbank). Soon afterward, six households of fishermen became the earliest residents.[10] Historically, Chongming was administered as part of the Jiangsu province to the north, but since 1958, it has been part of Shanghai city.[11]

Chongming Island grows ever larger each year at an increasing rate because of environmental damage upstream. Deforestation, a result of rapid economic development over the past half century, has led to increased silting. The island doubled in size between 1950 and 2005 and is currently about three hundred square miles. The island's wetland area was listed as a nationally protected area in 1992, and in 2001, it became an "important bird area" listed under the Ramsar Convention on Wetlands.[12] Although best known as a passage area for the critically endangered black-faced spoonbill, Chongming's wetlands also provide passage for the spotted greenshank and winter grounds for the hooded crane.

Chongming County has thirteen towns and three villages, with a population of approximately 700,000 locals and a "floating population" of people from other regions of approximately 111,000 (including thousands displaced by the Three Gorges Dam project who chose official relocation to Chongming). The Han are the majority ethnic group, along with minorities of Mongolian, Hui, Man, Zhuang, Bai, Yi, Chaoxian, Uygur, Buyi, Hani, Tujia, and Tibetan.

Chongming people have a "glorious revolutionary tradition," including anti-Japanese combat and peasant rebellions, and the island was an incubator of early grassroots Communist Party organizing. One government website extols this revolutionary history: "During the long period of revolutionary struggle . . . Chongming people contributed their lives for the revolutionary cause of the Chinese People." Part of this "revolutionary struggle" is documented in one of the few English-language studies of Chongming. Timothy Brook's *Collaboration: Japanese Agents and Local Elites in Wartime China* explores the meaning of resistance, complicity, and collaboration against the backdrop of the Japanese invasion of China in the 1930s. Chongming Island is his final case study and the one chapter focused explicitly on resistance. He provides important basic information about Chongming: the swampy north shore, the modest commercial value of the agricultural economy, the network of canals, dikes, and seawalls, the regular destruction of this infrastructure from typhoons, and the minimal industrial sector comprising two cotton-spinning mills.[13]

This wartime history explains why Chongming Island was the recently proposed site of a memorial to Japanese atrocities. During the occupation, the military tested comfort stations here to which the soldiers were supposed to direct their sexual urges, later rapidly expanding their use throughout Asia. More than two hundred thousand comfort women were used for sexual slavery for the Japanese military, and there were more than one hundred comfort stations in Shanghai alone. The largest among them, where five hundred women were regularly raped, is now a bank building. In the past decade, the building boom, including the expansion of "greenbelts," eradicated many of these sites in Shanghai.[14] When the Japanese descended on Chongming Island, soldiers created havoc, including:

> looting property and rounding up women for sexual service. Those unfortunate to get caught were dragged to makeshift brothels, though some were raped in the open air. . . . The youngest, who was bayoneted by the soldier who penetrated her, was an eleven-year-old girl in the town of Changxing,

the granddaughter of a prominent gentry family. The eldest to be raped, and who then committed suicide by drowning, was a grandmother on Jiangyuan Lane in Chongming city.[15]

Chongming Island had three comfort stations, and in 2000 a Chongming comfort woman filed a high-profile lawsuit against the Japanese government demanding compensation.[16] The brutality and sexual violence of occupation was not unique to Chongming, but the island was where Japanese soldiers were quarantined if they were found to have venereal and other sexual diseases. Thus, the Chongming comfort women were particularly vulnerable to sexual diseases in addition to the traumas of wartime mass organized rapes.

My father was born in 1939 on Chongming Island in the midst of the Japanese occupation, and my grandfather was head of a local businessman's association, like the collaborators that Brook writes about during this violent period of Chinese history. Until I went back in 2009 to meet my extended family, most of what I knew about Chongming and my family could only be gleaned from two faded pictures. The first is of my father as a wide-eyed toddler, being held by his father, next to his pregnant mother (two months before her death in childbirth) and her parents—the prosperous merchant and his wife sitting next to him, both with arms crossed. I can't make out my great grandmother's bound feet from under her clothes. The other picture apparently was taken at the same time—full of other aunts and cousins, whose names, histories, personalities, and identities are largely lost to me. My great-grandfather was landed gentry, a well-off merchant who owned a large grocery store in Chongming's main town. His wealth is evident in the photo itself (having a photograph taken was still relatively expensive) and in the fact that he had another name reserved for rich elders. The joy in the photographs (taken on December 8, during the Laba Rice Porridge Festival) belied the brutal reality that the Japanese were in control of the island while resistance fighters were burning telegraph poles and destroying bridges.

This violence is largely buried in official documents about Chongming's history and future. Instead of looking back to the violent past, the Chongming government, like boosters anywhere, focuses on the optimistic stories of growth, potential, and development. But even that optimistic story can be hard to tell by the numbers. Contemporary Chongming is defined by a negative population growth rate and relatively low economic activity. Politically, Chongming is part of the Shanghai municipality, but strong cultural, economic, and linguistic divides persist.[17] Chongming Island occupies 20 percent of Shanghai's total land area but contributes only a tiny share to the city's GDP. There are different economic and social challenges on the island. Chongming residents, for the most part, skew on the old side, and there are very few young people among the current farmers (and the farm laborers are imported from nearby regions). Most who are still farming are old, weak, sick, disabled, and female (Lao, ruo, bing, can, fu).[18] Chongming youths who can do so leave the island to get educated and work in Shanghai, and few return to live permanently, though many come to visit often, particularly on the weekends.[19]

Nowadays, Chongming and Shanghai officials are trying to change the island's status, from a sinkhole that ambitious people escape to a site of dynamic investment opportunity. The key to changing the relationship of dynamic center to dragging periphery is to extol the island's natural and ecological assets. Change on Chongming is a result of a complicated matrix of marketing/branding and fiscal investment through land and real estate development. Initially, development is primarily conceptualized in infrastructure terms, mainly improving the transportation connections to the island.

Thus, a key part of Chongming's development depends on transforming perception—to value "nature" and, more important, to find some way to profit from it. In "Shanghai's City Plan 1999–2020," government planners positioned Chongming as the site of Shanghai's sustainable development, green industry base, tourist and recreation base, and the "model ecological place" in the twenty-first century.[20] In 2003, it was officially declared an "ecological island" by the Shanghai government, which meant that development activities that conflicted with the protection of the environment were prohibited.[21]

The idea that Chongming is a key focal point of Shanghai's urban and economic development is not new. But the specific terms of this development discourse have changed over time. In the 1980s, Shanghai chose Pudong over Chongming Island as the site of the city's new center for global finance and trade. Pudong, now the site of Shanghai's iconic skyscrapers, was at the time a poor farming region like Chongming. But the intensive development and hypermodernization of Pudong in the 1980s and 1990s serves as both a model and a warning for Chongming's contemporary development.

In other words, Shanghai's policy focus and economic investment for Chongming promises great change. But the *form* of that change is what is currently under debate. As the next chapter shows, Shanghai is explicitly rejecting the high-rise Pudong model of global finance for Chongming by extolling the unique ecological and natural features of the island as its chief argument for social and ecological development.[22] At the same time, the comparisons and competition between Pudong and Chongming remain, to a far lesser degree, in the multiyear drama and intense speculation around which area would be the site for mainland China's first Disneyland. Pudong was named as the site of the future Disneyland in 2009, but Chongming did get a compensatory tourist attraction, a miniature version of Michael Jackson's Neverland ranch, which opened in 2010. According to one of the Chinese investors who reproduced Neverland at a 1:17 scale, "By building a Neverland here in China, we want to pay tribute to [Michael Jackson] and at the same time offer the Chinese people an outlet for expressing their love towards him." Shanghai Neverland will have "Chinese characteristics to have it blend in with the local environment."[23]

The features that made Chongming Island historically "backward"—its natural and rural character, open space, underdevelopment, and lack of industry—are now considered the island's main economic virtues. The ecology and beauty of the island is—now—the source of its natural capital. The concept of natural capital, taken from Hawkens, Lovins, and Lovins's influential manifesto,[24] undergirds Arup's Dongtan plan. The idea is that under industrial capitalism, nature is perceived as abundant but without value. However, new contexts of scarcity of natural resources transform this historical, economic, and cultural view of nature. Thus, companies and governments that can recognize this paradigm of valuing natural capital are positioned to profit in the contemporary political climate.

Ecological economics is widely used in the theory of the development of the eco-city. It conceptualizes how physical nature is transformed: first from nature to ecological functions, and then to production and consumption/leisure functions. This transformation takes place through the advancement of techniques of measurement and quantification, which becomes part of an ideological construct that assigns an equivalent economic value to nature.[25] This process is central to the development of techniques that measure the ecological function of an ecosystem.[26] In the context of the eco-city, the relevant ecological functions are those that maximize energy efficiency and minimize pollution of water, air, and land. The measurement of ecological functions in terms of economic inflows, outflows, price, demand, supply, and market and nonmarket natural resources illustrates how the ecology of eco-cities is designed and promoted as economic function rather than as a complex intermingling of the social with the natural, what political ecologists and radical geographers term "socio-nature."[27]

The large-scale promotion of the eco-city as the technological solution to urban and international environmental problems is the center of much attention in global environmental discourse. A recently published World Bank report titled "Eco$^2$Cities" promotes the integration of what it calls a "one system approach" to urban planning and urban living through the development of eco-cities. The term *Eco²Cities* refers to ecological and economic cities, which the World Bank defines as "cities that create economic opportunities for their citizens in an inclusive, sustainable, and resource-efficient way, while also protecting and nurturing the local ecology and global public goods, such as the environment, for future generations."[28] The World Bank report recommendations reduce complex urban problems of governance to a rationalist economistic approach, anchored by corporate operations as a model of urban governance.[29]

The work of the ecological economist Erik Gómez-Baggethun on the commodification of ecosystem services outlines how shifting views of nature are tied to particular economic ideologies. He argues that "the conceptualization of ecosystem services suggests that the trend towards monetization and commodification of ecosystem services is partly the result of a slow move from the original economic conception of nature's benefits as use values in classical economics to their conceptualization in terms of exchange values in neoclassical economics."[30] This transformation of ecosystem services has taken place through the valuation of nature in terms of ecological functions translated into a cost-benefit model.[31] The cap-and-trade approach to reducing carbon emissions as a policy response to climate change is the prime example of this concept.

In short, debates about creating economic value out of nature are part of the ideological context of eco-city development in Dongtan, which illustrates the fracture between the purported goal of developing a city that is ecologically sound, and the reality of urban sociopolitical complexity on the ground. Eco-cities are lauded as a solution to reduce fossil fuel emissions—a space denaturalized of social, economic, and political processes but, rather, focused on technological advances and utopian qualities.

Nature's newfound value also has, for Chongming, a place-based and gendered dimension.[32] One resident claims that Chongming is "Shanghai's illegitimate child" and, thus, its "secret garden." Chongming's seductive potential lies in its position more closely aligned with (feminine) nature, and antithetical to the hyperurban and highly capitalized economic (masculine) "engine" that is Shanghai. Chongming Island is Shanghai's secret garden, ripe for development, waiting ecstatically for the technology and tourism that will at last reveal Chongming's charms to off-island visitors seeking an "experience" with nature, albeit a version of nature heavily mediated through technology and engineering. It is this mixing of female nature with masculinist technology that transforms historically degraded rural spaces into highly desired ecological places. While rural spaces remain poor, ecological sites retain the virtues of rural spaces (i.e., clean environments) while increasing their value (i.e., investment capital opportunity).

These changing ideas about "nature" explain why Dongtan on Chongming is the right project in the right place—at least, according to its various champions and a significant number of environmentalist, architects, and other professionals, both in China and internationally.[33] This view dovetails with the local government's attempt to develop Chongming Island as an eco-friendly tourist destination. Another major factor is the changing national language and policy about improving rural spaces and environments. Dongtan's boosters thus also implicitly reference policy and language around "quality."

Quality, or *suzhi*, includes physical, psychological and cultural attributes, and the quality of consciousness.[34] The government's fear is that China is populated with too many "low-quality" people, defined in both moral and educational terms.[35] *Suzhi* was used in the 1980s in reference to population management and was later given prominent attention in 1997 when Jiang Zemin gave a talk at the Fifteenth Congress of the CCP. At this meeting, the private sector was raised to the same level as the state sector in the socialist market economy. To do so, Jiang explicitly called for more "high-quality people." For its part, the national government describes quality not just intrinsically but hierarchically; in other words, suzhi is understood to be higher in the city than in the country, in Han areas than in minority areas, and in the economically advanced areas than in "backward" regions. (This spatial hierarchy is not unique to China; it echoes Lenin.)

On the international level, the CCP policy is to increase and improve the "quality" of the Chinese people. Both government policy and the popular perception in China is that peasants' anti-market position and their traditional feudal consciousness are symbols of low quality that simultaneously constrain their economic development.[36] In this context, Dongtan's focus on uplifting rural lives through technology and engineering aims to increase the economic activity on Chongming Island as well as its quality, through a moralistic discourse of improvement and increased engagement with the market and modernity, best represented by Shanghai.

### ISLANDS: ISOLATION OR IDYLL?

Based on its own development plans, Shanghai city is improving and changing Chongming in direct and literally concrete ways, most obviously in October 2010 with the opening of the Changjiang Tunnel-Bridge Expressway, the world's longest bridge and tunnel connecting the Pudong area of Shanghai to eastern Chongming Island (near Dongtan). That bridge and tunnel is an engineering marvel—consisting of an 8.9 kilometer (5.5 mile) tunnel between Shanghai's Pudong area and a small island, followed by a 10 kilometer (6 mile) cable-stayed bridge to Chongming Island (see figure 2). It was built with a cost of 12.6 billion yuan (1.85 billion U.S. dollars). International bridge and tunnel aficionados celebrated the opening, joining the official State celebration that included dancers, bright balloons, numerous statues of Haibao (the Shanghai World Expo's mascot), and requisite smiling politicians.[37] The tunnel boasts the world's largest diameter of its kind, but this epic project is not unique within China, home to four of the world's longest-span cable-stayed bridges.

Figure 2. Chongming Bridge. Photo by Smyth, Creative Commons License

Twentieth-century China was full of stories of transnational builders and engineers who remade the nation in their own interests and images. For example, builders and engineers associated with the American Red Cross built thousands of miles of roads in China in the 1920s, and U.S. automakers helped expand this system, in part to increase their market share. One of the first major highways in China was built by a Hong Kong–based developer and Princeton-trained engineer named Gordon Wu, who designed it expressly in the image of the New Jersey Turnpike in the 1990s.[38]

Bridges and major infrastructure are more than mere technical and engineering marvels. Terry Hill, Arup's chairman, claims that "engineering is more than a profession—it's a way of thinking about the world."[39] What then, is the "way of thinking about the world" in Chongming's new infrastructure? What is thought, sought, and attained with the Changjiang Tunnel-Bridge Expressway is power and control over the vagaries of nature, mastery of time over space, and a world where cars win over boats. It symbolizes a practical and predictable world where passage to Chongming Island is no longer subject to the whim of the weather (bad weather could stop boats for up to many hours and sometimes even days). Control and transformation go hand-in-hand for the engineer, which explains why many of the leading political figures in communist authoritarian states (including Hu Jintao) are engineers.[40] Americans like their politicians to be self-made men; communists like theirs to be engineers. A sympathetic profile of the founder of the maker of the world's largest tunneling machines (the company that tunneled from Shanghai to Chongming) quotes his admiration of Dongtan, "if it's green, no problem. I could live there." His admiration for Dongtan is unsurprising: "Dongtan was a city after his own heart. It was designed by engineers, and built by the world's fastest growing superpower. It was perfectly made, admirably efficient, yet not so different from the villages that Europe built a thousand years ago."[41]

But what does it mean that a contemporary Chinese eco-city is meant to evoke and improve upon European villages from a thousand years ago? And what does it mean when an island is no longer an island? The historian John Gillis, in his account of island cultures and their impact on the global world, suggests that "islands evoke a greater range of emotions than any other land form. We project onto them our most intense desires, but they are also the locus of our greatest fears. We feel extraordinarily free there but also trapped. Associated with pleasure, islands also harbor pain."[42] This pain, isolation, and loss of connection disappears when islands become linked to their mainland. Paradoxically, he notes that non-islanders project the feelings and perceptions of pain, isolation, and anxiety onto island residents and island spaces. In practice, islanders themselves are, by necessity, personality, and trade, the most well-traveled and cosmopolitan people in the world. This observation is certainly true of Chongming and even of my own family. Chongming men have a strong and proud history as maritime men—from the rank and file to famous admirals in the Chinese navy. My grandfather was a merchant who transported goods between Chongming and the Shanghai waterfront, keeping houses in both places, and who served as a steward in the 1950s after he left China. My father improved upon his father's station at sea, becoming a navigator based out of Hong Kong in the 1960s.

To combat the perceived island isolation, powerful economic forces and technological changes emanating from the mainland have propelled an orgy of bridge and tunnel building around the world, nowhere with greater enthusiasm than in China. The past thirty years have seen more islands connected by bridges, tunnels, and high-speed ferries than in all of previous recorded human history.[43] Gillis suggests that "remoteness is the product of a relationship between two places but these places are unequal to one another. Today, powerful mainlands bestow remoteness on relatively powerless islands."[44] What was a five-hour boat ride for my dad in the 1930s became a forty-five-minute car ride over one of the world's largest bridge-tunnel spans. This change is a perfect illustration of the geographer David Harvey's "time-space compression."[45] He defines time-space compression as a key feature of postmodernity and of late capitalist development through which technologies accelerate or demolish spatial and temporal distance.

In other words, bridges and tunnels are *not* neutral technological or transportation infrastructure, benevolent gifts bestowed upon a grateful populace. Rather, bridges and tunnels reinforce and reinscribe geographical and political hierarchies that have mainland cultures and economies increasing their control and power over islands. And although bridges and tunnels may alter the status and accessibility of an island, islands remain islands, thus reinforcing the German sociologist and critical theorist Georg Simmel's observation that "in connecting two things we simultaneously underline what separates them. . . . [I]nsularity and connectedness are but two sides of the same coin, their meaning forever entangled."[46]

Contemporary bridge-building in China echoes the age of iconic bridge-building in the United States, from the mid-nineteenth-century Brooklyn Bridge in the East westward to the grandeur of the 1937 Golden Gate Bridge on the Pacific Ocean. The symbolism of bridges was a big factor in Shanghai, which decided to go with the Nanpu Bridge as the first linkage infrastructure between the two sides of the river, the Puxi and Pudong, although tunnels were cheaper to build. Campanella points out that tunnels were "not photogenic. They strike no heroic silhouette against the sky. A bridge on the other hand, is a proud and soaring thing that makes for great publicity shots at tourist brochures."[47] Calling such bridges "eye candy," he describes the folio, titled "Bridge of the Century," published to celebrate the completion of Shanghai's epic bridges, as evidence of the city's "infrastructure pride."

On a practical level, the question then is: what did it mean to make Chongming Island accessible by bridge and tunnel to Shanghai? Not much good from an ecological standpoint. In the weekends that followed the 2010 bridge opening, more than one hundred thousand day-trippers from Shanghai visited Chongming, including the sensitive wetland areas. Within a month of the bridge opening, local authorities limited visitors to the wetlands amidst concerns about their environmental impact.[48]

The other part of government infrastructure planning is to connect Chongming to Jiangsu in the north. The completion of that project makes Chongming the midway point in a new superregional corridor, raising land values and housing prices on the island to match Shanghai's phenomenal real estate prices, and bringing wetlands protection into greater conflict with urban and tourism development.

More frequent connections to the mainland also have serious ecological consequences in terms of invasive species. Chongming Island's two main invaders, with no natural competitors, are *Spartina alterniflora* and *Solidago canadensis*, both of which originated in North America (the former was brought from the U.S. Atlantic Coast to protect the marshes in 1979, while the latter was introduced as an ornamental plant in the 1930s).[49] In an interesting reversal of the biological invasion discourse that focuses on the Asian carp taking over the Great Lakes, the United States is the source of Chongming's greatest invasive species threats.

In many ways, what happened to Chongming Island after the bridge was built is not geographically or historically unique to China. After all, nature tourism was a key factor in garnering political support to begin the U.S. national park system in the mid-nineteenth century. Visitors to Yosemite brought back tales of grandeur, and painters like Albert Bierstadt promoted the idea that epic landscapes were "America's cathedrals" (sometime literally painting a cross on epic faces of cliffs, valleys, and dramatic sunscapes). The paradox of destroying nature by opening and expanding access is an old conundrum, of which Chongming's developers are well aware. In fact, Dongtan's proponents explicitly cite the Everglades as its model, despite the evisceration of the wetland ecosystems once opened to development in southern Florida.[50]

Is Chongming ready for these changes? When I drove around in August 2009, a couple of months before the bridge opened, my cab was the only car on the brand-new super highway. My cabdriver thought I was nuts for wanting to go out to visit the wetlands. But I served as a built-in audience for his musings on his hometown. Our two hour long drive gave him a chance to point out the local high school, which sends its graduates to prestigious universities like Fudan in Shanghai, and Beijing University. He pointed to the new apartment block real estate developments that dotted the island, especially reveling in sharing the prices that struck my traveling companion as more suitable for downtown Shanghai than rural Chongming. On our ride, livestock occasionally ambled onto the road, and old people often stopped and stared. I passed occasional slogans calling for Chongming to fight climate change, and lots of old people walking. As a very young man living in the largest town on the island, my father would go only once a year to visit his grandmother in the island's interior, walking more than seven hours to get there.

Those almost empty roads that I experienced on the way to Dongtan in the summer of 2009 are already gone. Just months after the bridge opened, the highways on the island were, not surprisingly, noticeably more crowded with cars. And my 2010 bus trip to Chongming was indeed spectacular, especially the long ride over the bridge. It is an epic view with an aesthetic payoff, though at what ecological and social costs is not clear.

## LOCALIZING IDENTITIES, DEBATING DEVELOPMENT

Given the official Shanghai policy to develop Chongming Island as a "model ecological place" and its handing off of much of the master planning of the island and various eco-development projects to global firms (as discussed in the next two chapters), what are the general reactions of Chongming residents to Dongtan and their island's development? Of course, there is no singular voice with which the islanders speak.[51] The easiest reactions to track are probably those of highly educated, highly technologically adept youths, many of whom have left the island. These youths express their feelings, thoughts, ideas, happiness, and anxiety about their hometown through the Chongming Club. In this online forum, they call themselves "Chongming people" (Chongming ren) or "indigenous" (tuzhu min). This strong Chongming identity, in fact, has been reinforced by Chongming's "second-class" status based on the long-held stigma of Chongming being a poor, alien island. This stigma is, paradoxically, a source of pride. As one indignant "voice" states, "Why do we love [our hometown] so much? Because we have taken enough Shanghai people's arrogant looks. They look down upon us Chongming people." "Hometown is beautiful in everybody's heart. Chongming is my hometown and her position cannot be changed in my heart. I can speak even better Shanghai dialect than Shanghai people, but it will not change me as a Chongming person. In Shanghai, I will speak loudly to tell friends that I am a Chongming person!"[52]

For some off-island Chongming locals, the island's ecological development plans generated new identities as a source of pride. Many online forum participants expressed this yearning for their hometown to gain long-denied and deserved recognition. As one person wrote, "Although Chongming is less developed . . . ten years later, we believe that there will be a splendid Chongming in front of us." Another argues that contemporary plans for development are "more mature and more suitable to play international games. If Chongming was chosen to be developed ten years ago, the result would be like the development of the Shanghai city—a still forest and a concrete city—which did not have the consciousness of building an eco-city. So I am very proud of being a Chongming person." Most simply, one writes, "Chongming is not only worth living in, *it is also a place that has a dream*" (emphasis added).[53] In other words, ecological language has infiltrated the local discourse of "dreams" for some island residents. The ecological development ideology has become the normalized, everyday language since Dongtan endorsed an imagined eco-future for Chongming island.

At the same time, this "dream" is not universally accepted. The ambiguity lies in the government's limited communication with locals about the meaning and impact of ecological development on their lives. The fifty-four-year-old former peasant Tai'an Ding moved into a new apartment in Chenjia town after his land was confiscated for the development project. He was confused by the concept of the "eco-city." Although his new apartment is classified as an "eco-building," his new home neither uses renewable energy to provide electricity nor was constructed with any special eco-standards. Ding said, "For us, ecology means living in a greener area, some places have trees."[54] Another example is Shen, a peasant from the Tieta village of Chenjia town whose land was confiscated in 2006. His household was one of the thirteen hundred to be moved into an "eco-building." He said, "This is just a normal residential complex. I do not know the meaning of the so-called eco-city." But he knows that living in this eco-city means that they now have to pay monthly electricity and gas fees, as well as go to a supermarket to buy food and vegetables. In fact, most of the land from the three villages of Chenjia town was confiscated for the development of the Dongtan eco-city. Peasants were granted a township household status and guaranteed a subsidy of 290 yuan (forty-two U.S. dollars) per month. However, just two years after they were moved, this subsidy was canceled without any explanation and many of the former peasants are still unemployed. Still others complained about the top-down character of the project, which does not put local perspectives at the center of the planning process. As one person asked on the Chongming Online Club, "Why can only the so-called professors, professionals, and the political leaders speak [for Chongming]? Why have they not listened to our indigenous ideas? Only we have the real speaking rights."[55] Others complain about the lack of resources for tourists.

On the other hand, this language of ecology is a very specific index of social and economic development. Material prosperity is not only the precondition for building the eco-city, it is also the goal. This economic focus on eco-development is clear in the debates on the Chongming Club, which centered around "What is meant by ecology?" These ideas were furiously debated in an online forum held with Chenlei Peng, the Party secretary of Chongming County. Most of the participants urged the government to accelerate the development process. For example, one Chongming resident said, "It is a great idea from the central government to build Chongming into an eco-island. However, it is hard for Chongming to rely on itself. I think it needs more special care from the Shanghai city and the government. . . . In recent years, I noticed that some professionals have suggested that Chongming can be built into an offshore financial center. This is a great idea and it is suitable for the definition of Chongming being an eco-island."[56] Thus, while some did express their desire for protecting the fresh air, unpolluted water, and precious birds, the more significant factors for Dongtan and its ecological development are the possible benefits to the residents' economic lives, changes to their stigmatized image, and possibilities for increased social capital.

In general, the emerging consensus on the Chongming Club is that the local economic development planning process is too slow and largely ineffective. They criticize government officials for not knowing how to develop Chongming adequately. One laments, "I heard about the Chongming plan when I was in primary school, but I am more than thirty years old now and Chongming still does not have a clear plan of development. I don't know whether I would be lucky enough to see the day when Chongming people can go outside conveniently and won't need to worry about [their financial problems] when they are old. Chongming is like a poor child without parents' and grandparents' love and care. [I] am very disappointed with the leaders of Chongming county who [hardly] fight for Chongming; I am also disappointed with some leaders from the city too, and I am angry with the interest groups [who took advantage of Chongming]."[57] They attribute these problems in part to political and historical factors (including competition with other localities and regions) and not mere incompetence. In many ways, the island's slow development is also attributed to the lack of political sophistication of the islanders, who are cowed in the face of all the attention on them in the past decade. One Chongming development watcher commented that "the island people who have been enslaved for thousands of years are already used to isolation and scolding."

My own extended relatives who still live on the island share this mix of deep local pride and profound skepticism about Chongming's development schemes in general and about Dongtan in particular. Wu Jia, the eighty-three-year-old family matriarch (she is the niece of my step-grandmother) is a case in point. Born and bred on Chongming, she is a proud woman, incredibly strong and bossy, yet friendly, befitting the school principal she once was. After the communists took control, her husband was sent to the island and served as a high-level local government official for many years. When Wu Jia picked me up at the ferry terminal, she insisted on getting in the cab of only someone she recognized, peering closely at the face of each driver—local provenance clearly matters. She decided it was better to take the bicycle cab to save some money, and then chided me for slipping the driver an extra 1RMB (15 U.S. cents). Like others on the online forum, Wu Jia and her family are proud of the attention that their island is finally garnering. Given their deep stake in local institutions, they clearly feel that their island's time has come. Yet, when asked if they would live near Dongtan (or even come with me to visit), they laughed riotously. *Why? What's there!* Having never been to the eastern edge of the island in their lives, they lived lives that were intensely local. *Nothing out there! No shopping, no doctors, no life. Crazy talk!* Even island peripheries, it seems, have peripheries.

The Tunnel-Bridge Expressway, the exalted symbol of technology and modernity, is itself highly debated on the Chongming Club. Generally, opinion is split between those who directly benefit and those who think the project is inconvenient, because they live on parts of the island that are far from the bridge (principally those on the western part of the island). The bridge ends in Chenjia town on the eastern part of the island, and those living in the west face an hour-plus ride home once on the island (this contrasts with the ferry system, which had multiple points of entry on Chongming Island upon leaving Shanghai). One sign at the ferry ticket office orders people to speak Mandarin, and not their local dialect when buying tickets.

Chenjia is adjacent to the Dongtan conservation area, and is set to become one of four "relaxation towns" serving visitors hoping to experience an idyllic rural lifestyle or visit the wetlands. Those in the cynical camp scoff at the benefits of the bridge, which they say is largely inconvenient and irrelevant to them and "just for tourism." Still, others extol the benefits of the bridge with pride: "Chongming people finally stood up. I love Chongming, I love my beautiful hometown." Others celebrated their "liberation" from the tyranny of Yatong (the boat company). One comment used the bridge fee to confirm the long-held suspicions that Chongmingren have about their status to Shanghai: "Why do they charge a bridge fee? . . . Chongming has been subordinated for a long time. Phone calls were charged a long-distance service fee if you call central Shanghai. Many schools used to refuse Chongming students."[58] In this estimation, the bridge fee is another slap on the face for the island, representing Chongming's continuing subordinated status to "supercilious" Shanghai.

CONCLUSION

The debate about the Chongming of the future is well represented by another odd juxtaposition, different from the one with which I started the chapter. The photo is from a history of the island, which highlights its traditional industries of fishing and maritime activities. This "past" contrasts greatly with another image I saw on the island in 2010, in which a white male bicyclist leans over the tagline: "Bring the World to Chongming, Take Chongming to the World" (see figure 3). More than likely, the bicyclist has driven his bike over the bridge (which has no bike lane) so that he could ride amidst the natural, supposedly untouched beauty of Chongming Island.

Understanding the fierce debates about Chongming Island's overall development among some locals is important to understanding that ecological development on Chongming cannot be reduced to a cynical ploy of corporate and government masters to completely create eco-desire. In other words, the corporate logic of the planners and developers aligned with the local politicians' agenda to generate heated debate and drive new cultural and ideological investments in the discourses of environmentalism and development. Although different segments of the island population are sharply divided by interest, geography, and generation, they are all generally aware of Chongming's development debates and the centrality of ecological

Figure 3. Tour of Chongming. Photo by
author, 2010

discourse to them. The online conversation, primarily engaged in by young
off-island educated elites, is not centered on whether Chongming should or
should not develop its economy, but, rather, *how* to develop the eco-city
fairly to benefit all the islanders.

When the attention of the world briefly focused on Dongtan, journalists
largely skipped over Chongming Island to rave about Dongtan's techno-
utopian features. But skipping over Chongming takes Dongtan out of important debates: about how to fully represent ecological dreams *of* and *on* the
island and its residents, the role of the island vis-à-vis Shanghai, and the
sublimation of its violent past. Chongming Islanders are used to this neglect,
and largely tired of it. They are demanding new rights, drawn from the sense
of social belonging that the bridge (along with the Internet) has brought to
the island.

# CHAPTER THREE

# Dreaming Green

*Engineering the Eco-City*

I knew I was getting close to Dongtan when my taxi passed three large wind turbines (bird-lovers hate turbines because birds meet grisly ends in the gigantic blades). The Japanese-built blades turned slowly, cutting through the humid and thick air. My parents had insisted that their friend come with me. Intensely hypersocial, she helped me get through the meals with my father's extended relatives, mediating expertly between my Shanghai and their Chongming dialect. After lunch, my father's first cousin's son walked us to his shiny black car, apologized for not taking us to Dongtan, and got us quickly to the cab that drove us to the marshy landscape.

After an hour of driving, I understood why he didn't come. It's really, really far away from the main towns. The bored guard at the gate and the local man who promised a more "exciting" rural experience in exchange for money were the only people there. I walked on a raised wooden walkway about a quarter mile above the wetlands, and, after about fifteen minutes, finally and excitedly saw a single big white bird. Here, on these wetlands, the glorious Dongtan eco-city is imagined as inhabited by five hundred thousand people by 2050. But as of December 2013, Dongtan has not been built and its future prospects look grim.

In *The Concrete Dragon*, the planning historian Thomas Campanella discusses how contemporary Chinese cities are remaking themselves in six ways: speed, scale, spectacle, sprawl, segregation, and sustainability. He regards the first five in decidedly ambivalent terms but he holds out sustainability, represented by Dongtan, as an optimistic coda. He was not alone in believing that Dongtan might improve on existing Chinese urban development policy and practice. Unfortunately, Dongtan's realities have not lived up to the hopes and dreams of its boosters. What Campanella and others could not (or would not) see was that Dongtan itself was not the antidote to the problems of urban development in China but rather their culmination.

Despite the ubiquity of the bird pictures on Chongming Island, Dongtan eco-city is decidedly not driven by bird-lovers (domestic and otherwise), who would by and large prefer no development so as to preserve the unique wetland habitat. Bird-lovers rarely dictate land-use policy and practice. Dongtan is, first and foremost, a political and economic development project in which the client, the engineers, the architects, and the politicians (on the island, in Shanghai and Beijing, and abroad) have financial stakes and larger goals that sometimes conflict and other times mesh.

This chapter discusses the rhetoric and promise of Dongtan and its ultimate failure. Dongtan rose from nothing, reached a political peak, and ultimately was never built. Why and how did Dongtan boosters think this eco-city project on this island ever made sense? What are the geopolitical fears and desires that influenced the project? What were the cultural and ideological roots of Dongtan and the many reasons for its ultimate failure? Does it have an afterlife? What were—or are—the culture and politics at work in Dongtan? Why was so much invested (both literally and ideologically) in the dream of Dongtan eco-city? In part, the answers stem from Chongming's status as an "eco-island" and Dongtan's as an "eco-city," reflecting the desire to identify and concentrate "ecological places" as the solution to burgeoning environmental and climate crises. This ideological construction of the eco-island and the eco-city assumes that ecological places are those in which a particular conception of nature dominates, especially those places that are devoid of large numbers of buildings and people. This construction of nature draws on particular notions of wilderness in which people are largely absent.[1]

Dongtan and these particular iterations of the eco-city do indeed reflect a "quest" (the term Arup uses in its press release) and dreams. But these quests are for profit and image-making, not for sustainability. In other words, eco-desire in and for Dongtan is mobilized by planners, engineers, real-estate developers, and politicians to fuse discourses and nature images with economic development and profit-making. The dream is green—but of cash, not ecology. Both ecology and money-making are inextricably linked: eco-desire as investment strategy.

Arup contended that the project failed owing to local contingencies and politics. But Dongtan was never just a local affair and it was always more than mere technical or engineering marvel. Rather, Dongtan was always a fiercely ideologically contested and constructed cultural project in which the dreams and politics of eco-desire run deep. This desire—that ecological and economic good can be one and the same, rather than in conflict—is dominant. That's why the story of Dongtan is worth recounting and analyzing. It represents what some call green capitalism, with greenwashing elements.[2]

But neither *green capitalism* nor *greenwashing* do full justice to the central role of stories and imagination that *dreams* and *desires* imply. Dongtan's lack of uniqueness paradoxically signifies its importance. Many (if not most) huge and experimental architectural projects fail, in China and elsewhere.[3] That's the name of the game in high-stakes global architecture. But the claims that were made for Dongtan were so grandiose and pathbreaking that it's important to understand what was going on, even if it never came to be. A corollary of this "green dream" is a worldview that posits the solutions to global environmental crisis as fundamentally about engineering, technology, and architecture. This worldview imagines profit-making as a necessary by-product of these innovations. These desires are enshrined in national government policy and practice, as well as by transnational architecture and engineering firms of which Arup is typical, not exceptional. In other words, although the project failed, there are still many lessons that can be learned from it, even if those lessons are not the ecological ones that the proponents sought to teach the world.

These transnational eco-desires are captured by procorporate, heavily technologically mediated eco-city fantasies articulated by global planning, engineering, and architecture firms, which have an especially strong presence in China. In this chapter, I look closely at two firms that have a particularly strong hand in Dongtan, and on Chongming Island and Shanghai more broadly: Arup (the Dongtan planner) and U.S.-based Skidmore, Owings and Merrill (SOM, in charge of Chongming Island's master plan). These firms' vision is arguably easier to dissect than that of their investors.[4] Their worldview is clear in their public materials, including the press releases their public relations staff writes, interviews that the planners, engineers, and project managers give, and the books they publish. These actors have a disproportionately strong impact on shaping the transnational environmental discourse in the global imaginary, visions that have real-world impacts on local landscapes and communities. The same group of firms that develop ecocities also build world expo pavilions and Olympic parks. One reason ecocities resemble one another is that they share not only ideologies but also builders.

Eco-desire also works on another level for international architectural and engineering firms, in their investment, both capital and psychological, in eco-authoritarianism. As one Arup staff member writes in a book documenting the firm's influence on contemporary Beijing, "China today represents a test-bed for progressive design. It offers a *new freedom* to build in a way that many Western societies have not experienced since postwar development" (emphasis added).[5] In the epic drama that is China's urbanization policy in the past two decades, international architecture and engineering firms based in the United States and Europe are dominant players, and their largely uncritical embrace of this "new freedom to experiment" depends on an authoritarian state structure. Arup's desire to build green, and build big, allows the firm to psychologically screen out the unsavory by-products of its projects. These include the forced relocation of local populations and the longer-term social and economic transitions that Arup's projects trigger.

Arup's privileging of engineering solutions is not surprising. Its influence is arguably "bigger than any single architect," having engineered "a significant sampling of the greatest—and greenest—buildings of their time."[6] In 1946, Ove Arup, a Danish designer, engineer, and philosopher, founded the firm, which played a key role in the building of (according to one critic) seven of the ten greatest buildings of all time.[7] Arup's contemporary practice focuses on the increasing significance of the "environmental agenda in architecture."[8] Arup is increasingly focused on environmentalism as a technological problem that can be overcome through its laserlike focus on engineering calculations. As its founder Ove Arup said, "The engineer uses the law of economy and the tools of mathematical calculation to engage with the universal and in this appeals to the intellect. By contrast, the architect, by his arrangement of forms gives us the measure of an order which we feel and thereby affects our senses and emotions."[9] The "evolving relationship" between architects and engineers collapses the Cartesian divide between the intellect and the senses, the mind and the body, although some argue that ecological architecture is a return of modernism itself rather than its evolution. As the designer of the Beijing Olympics' Water Cube argues, "the era of architects as the sole authors of the building is coming to a close. . . . [T]he creative powers of engineering are just as important in contributing to a work of architecture."[10]

Arup's vision of sustainability enacts a technocratic praxis, in which the engineer is god, but a good god committed to design, sustainability, art, and connection, an approach that the firm calls *total architecture* or *unified design*.[11] The vision is seductive, particularly in the context of climate change. As one notable Arup engineer explains, "Sustainability brings people together around a common theme. This is a critical time for society and its relationship with the planet's eco-systems. The moment is right for radical thinking. 'Unified design' is the mechanism by which to get to the next step: to understand how we can minimize human impact and maximize human opportunity."[12] The problem, which Arup judiciously ignores, is that discourses of "unified design" have particular national contexts of political authoritarianism. This governance structure enables the big projects to be proposed, and its particular contexts do not necessarily dovetail with Arup's benevolent vision, however seductive that vision might appear to outsiders.

As I mentioned in chapter 1, China's first major eco-village, at Huangbaiyu, failed due to lack of understanding of the local context. Here, the perspectives of local residents in areas proposed for eco-development in China collided with the goals of the global eco-architects/planners. Architecture is littered with similar stories of so-called visionaries trumped by the intransigence of small-minded locals or corrupt officials, or so the story is often told. There are key differences between Huangbaiyu and Dongtan. Huangbaiyu was a real inhabited place, while Dongtan was a newly proposed city. Huangbaiyu was a rural place touted as an "eco-village," whereas Dongtan was supposed to be an "eco-city," befitting its proximity to Shanghai. Last, Dongtan's development is more focused on lifestyle, consumption, and fun than Huangbaiyu's, which was focused more on uplifting the lives of the impoverished local residents. But, ultimately, what both projects share is a cultural politics in which these sites are projections of global fantasies of what an "ecological life" and "experience" looks like in a rural Chinese context.

## TRANSNATIONAL FIRMS AND THE MARKETING OF
## SUSTAINABILITY: ECO-CITY 2.O

The story of Dongtan, and of its particular iteration of the "eco-city," is in part a tale about the increasing entanglement of transnational architecture and engineering firms with sustainable urban development and planning. On Chongming Island alone, Arup's Dongtan plan was just one of more than sixty development plans proposed between 2000 and 2005.[13] The complete list is a veritable Who's Who of big global firms and big plans, almost all of which engage the ideas and language of sustainability as their central grammar.

Their collective version of eco-cities is grounded in real-estate development and branding, not in the traditional U.S. roots of ecological cities or in ecotopian discourse. The eco-city is linked to ecotopia, first depicted in Ernest Callenbach's 1975 novel. The eco-city and ecotopian ideas were developed at roughly the same time in the wake of the environmental movement in the United States coming out of the 1960s counterculture. The journalist Jeremy Smith reflected on Callenbach's *Ecotopia*, which he calls a "hippie-dippie relic."[14] In the novel, Callenbach's narrator is a journalist who in 1999 travels to Ecotopia (roughly, Northern California, Oregon, and Washington), which had seceded nineteen years earlier from an ecologically decadent United States. He gets to Ecotopia via high-tech magnetic propulsion train. A matriarchy now runs the government and male bonding rituals thrive. The narrator goes native, convinced that the secessionists were right, seduced by their open mating practices and a love affair with an Ecotopian woman. Smith notes that much of what seemed improbable in Callenbach's time (e.g., recycling) is now standard practice.[15] One scholar of literary ecotopias suggests, "Utopians remind us that purposeful choices can be made and that there is a prospect of a better or cleaner future. . . . [U]topias keep ideals alive and can offer hope through futuristic visions."[16] Others argue that "utopianism of one form or another, in the positive or the pejorative sense, permeates all environmentalism."[17]

Richard Register first coined the term *eco-city* in his 1987 book *Eco-city Berkeley*, in which he cites the significant influence of Paolo Soleri. Soleri, an Italian architect, named his dream community in Arizona "Arcosanti." Arcosanti was built based on his vision of the fusion of architecture and ecology, which he called *Arcology* (1969). Soleri began to build Arcosanti in 1970 (and it is still slowly being built more than four decades later, funded through the sales of bells and visits to the site).[18] "Ecotopian" ideas have changed dramatically in contemporary life, but they still retain some shreds of connection to and influence of their countercultural roots in the Bay Area and Arizona.

For instance, Smith describes the continuing impact of *Ecotopia* on contemporary ecological development, specifically in the Treasure Island Sustainability Plan. The Sustainability Plan was to build Treasure Island, in Northern California's Bay Area, into the "greenest city in the United States" (although the project ran into difficulties in early 2014).[19] In 2010, it became part of a $1.7 billion proposed deal with China Development Corp., the Chinese national railway and Lennar Corp. to construct 12,500 homes, both as a string of high-rises on Treasure Island and as village developments at the former Hunters Point Naval Shipyard in San Francisco. The Chinese intended to use the project as an entry into more development deals in the United States. Smith does note the major differences, principally the big money involved.[20] Callenbach's ecotopia was small-scale, sexually free, critical of science and modernity, and skeptical of capitalism. Small-scale economies and countercultural practices, not corporate capitalism, were seen as the answer to the problems of environmental destruction.

Despite the symbolic and historiographical links between eco-cities and ecotopias, contemporary eco-city builders eschew them. Dongtan's project head at Arup, Roger Wood, rejected the utopian label: "*Utopianism* is too strong a word. Dongtan is *necessary* for how people need to live in the future when resources are limited. We need 'appropriate' models of transport and energy."[21] Arup's disavowal of utopianism and embrace of technocratic language is not surprising, as the term *utopian* (or *ecotopian*) generates ambivalence among engineers and mixed reactions in different political and historical contexts.

This reaction is particularly intense in China, where utopian ideas and political revolution have a different cultural valence. Within the contemporary West, *eco-utopianism* is often perceived as a dirty word, irrelevant and dreamy, raising embarrassing memories of baby boomer self-absorption. In rejecting utopia/ecotopia, Arup staff focuses instead on the hard-headed pragmatism of their technical work. For Arup, their role in alleviating the global environmental crisis is to do what they've always done best: to find innovative engineering and technology solutions. The language of "appropriate models" leaves little (acknowledged) space for dreams and stories, while expertise and specialized knowledge rule with rational and sometimes totalizing force.

Nonetheless, Arup's descriptions of Dongtan are themselves redolent of the utopian label they run from. Rather than ecotopianism, they revel in their own version of techno-utopianism. Embedded in this worldview is an admiration of all that is technical, rational, and efficient. According to one profile of Arup's then-deputy chairman Cecil Balmond, "engineers build cities—the rest of us just live in them."[22] To paraphrase, engineers and architects build eco-cities—the questions are whether anyone will live in them, why or why not, how they will be built, what they look like, and what values they embody.

In their writings, Arup staff celebrate their role in the "iconic and monumental projects commissioned to support the Olympics," and the firm proudly boasts that more than 25 percent of its staff is located in China.[23] Arup is not alone in its view of China as its best customer, one of the few countries in the world with the money and the chutzpah to dream—and build—big. China, in other words, is where the world's big engineering and architecture and design firms have firmly pegged their proverbial hammer and nail. *Solutions for a Modern City: Arup in Beijing* proudly recounts, "As China's political and cultural capital, Beijing has become a focal point for many of these changes and is booming. . . . One firm, above all others, is closely linked to the striking transformation taking place in Beijing today. That firm is Arup."[24] Thus, Dongtan is best understood within the broader political and architectural climate in an era in which the state is attempting to monumentalize the coming Chinese Century.

## IMAGINING DONGTAN: "THE QUEST TO CREATE A NEW WORLD"

On the face of it, Dongtan differed in a significant way from Arup's other major China projects, such as the Bird's Nest and Water Cube. It is also not, like the Shanghai Tower, an epically high skyscraper. The Shanghai Tower, currently being built in Pudong as China's highest building (and the second highest in the world), will join the Jin Mao and World Financial Tower as a long-planned trinity. Its innovative double-skin façade creates better insulation and energy savings (up to 24 percent, meaning lower construction costs). The Shanghai Tower, designed by the American architect Art Gensler, was recognized by U.S. Commerce Secretary Gary Locke in May 2010 as an example of how China and the United States are working together to "give a glimpse" of the future of green energy. The building is organized as nine cylindrical buildings stacked one atop another. The spaces between the two façade layers create nine atrium sky gardens. Rainwater is supposed to be collected for the air conditioning and heating systems, and wind turbines are supposed to power the building.[25]

Dongtan, by contrast, is flat. It is not a megaskyscraper but rather is conceptualized as a "blank slate" that could be the anti-Pudong or the anti-Shanghai. Dongtan is the ecological mirror of the megaskyscraper landscape that characterizes Shanghai. But the Shanghai Tower and Dongtan are not as different as their architectural renderings would imply. Both depend heavily on technical and engineering innovations to deliver not just environmental benefits, but an entirely new experience of the "green future."

This focus on "experience" is clear in a seductive storyline and a rapturous vision of Dongtan. When Dongtan was announced, SIIC and Arup coproduced a 227-page bilingual, lavishly photographed promotional book titled *Shanghai Dongtan: An Eco-City*. This book, written by Herbert Girardet and Zhao Yan, literally illustrates the desires of the planners, architects, and investors regarding the world they hope to create.[26] *Shanghai Dongtan: An Eco-City* tells a relatively simple story, one that sets up villainous trends (pollution and urbanization), their victim (the birds), and the saviors (who utilize the best that science/technology, architecture, and planning have to offer). The opening pages show, on one page, a map of the region (and an unnamed yellow line running from Shanghai over the water to Chongming, through the island close to the eastern edge near the Dongtan site, and then west to the central island, and up to Jiangsu) and, on the facing page, a brief political history of the project.[27] The aim is to create a "new world," but before the new world can be created, the planners and investors must first pose an important question—what is the problem that Dongtan is supposed to fix?

The book sets up Dongtan as the "natural" (that is, commonsense) answer, but ignores a number of unstated questions: What happens when a city of five hundred thousand is proposed on ecologically sensitive wetlands where there is no present human population to speak of?[28] What happens when an island like Chongming is connected to the surrounding city and regions of Shanghai and Jiangsu? How can catastrophic environmental change be avoided? Rather, the book answers its own central question for the client and the planner (and journalists and Western environmentalists): Is it possible to propose a city of a half million people and promise no ecological harm?

The answer (yes, in case you had any doubt) is evident in the focus on the experiences and benefits to the imaginary residents of, and visitors to, Dongtan and to the "environment" itself, specifically the birds. These benefits constitute the central transnational and corporate desires in the Dongtan project, to imagine a massive development that not only does no ecological harm, but actually produces environmental benefits. These hopes undergird the central desires underlying Dongtan: that a built environment can be at the cutting edge of technology, sustainability, and modernity through a profitable lifestyle transformation. In Dongtan, nature is improved through technology. In some ways, this transformation echoes Levi Strauss's arguments about cooked and raw images, and specifically Marxist analyses of how nature images are deployed as ideologies in advertisements.[29] In other words, the nature of Dongtan wetlands is "cooked" to create a new symbolic order of Dongtan eco-city that improves on the *nature of nature* in Dongtan.

Additionally, Wood added that Dongtan was intended to "provide employment" for local impoverished fisherman and that Dongtan was planned to be a mixed-income city rather than a wealthy suburb of Shanghai.[30] But when I asked him whether there would be any specific provision for a mixed-income population, he admitted that was not to be. In the book, images of birds form the backdrop to these stated questions: "Do we want Dongtan to be a city with a large number of high-rise buildings? Should we simply follow the usual steps of urban-industrial development? Ought Dongtan's economy be allowed to develop at the cost of its environment? Should we forge ahead in an unsustainable way?"[31] Rather than replicating Pudong's skyscrapers, Arup argued for building Dongtan on fundamentally different premises.[32]

*Shanghai Dongtan: An Eco-City* combines a number of different genres— part policy manifesto, part coffee table photo book, travel brochure, and, ultimately, science fiction tome. First, it begins with a poem set against an image of natural calm: "It started as a sand bank / Then it grew into an island / Soon it will hold the world in awe / And what is it? / It is Dongtan."[33] The opening section is filled with gorgeous full-page photographs of the island's natural beauty. These include pictures of riverbanks, goats, oxen, butterflies on a field of sunflowers, and, last, a single spoonbill. This section is book-ended with another epigraph, which reads, "With a timescale of seven years / we will / explore a new possibility of urban development / a new way of life / new methods of production and more . . . / above all, it is a journey."[34] The so-called journey then proceeds as a series of quests.

First comes "Looking for Shanghai," followed by "Looking for Black-faced Spoonbill," and the third is "Looking for an Eco-City." In short, this section presents the problems that Dongtan is aiming to answer. The preamble to "Looking for Shanghai" makes this abundantly clear: "Too much of the world has turned to barren land where mankind has left its mark," the text superimposed over the image of a desiccated landscape. "Looking for Shanghai" represents the local equivalent of "mankind's mark" as a series of photos of individual skyscrapers next to one another. This cutting and pasting of photos of individual skyscrapers rejects the possibility that the hyper-urbanized landscape itself is a panorama. This section also cuts and pastes highways (88) and street crowds and cars (90) in a manic visual that is aimed to produce a sense of fracture and chaos reminiscent of the movie *Blade Runner*. The problem, the authors of the book argue, is pollution, and urban alienation, combined with the scale of China's modernization.[35]

The problems posed by Shanghai's urban alienation are immediately followed by the presumptive solution, titled "Looking for Black-faced Spoonbill," which extols the "natural capital" of the landscape.[36] In short, the first two sections ("Looking for Shanghai" and "Looking for Black-faced Spoonbill") visually and rhetorically set up the problems—intensive urbanization and the starkly different pathways to development. The answer to both, the book argues, is in the third section, "Looking for an Eco-city." This section contains a number of graphs and computer-generated renderings of Dongtan's development.

This section of the book reads a lot like a genre I call high-tech eco-geek. Environmentalists have long sought to improve environmental conditions through technology. But where the 1960s U.S. version coming out of the counterculture and alternative communities focused on low-tech solutions (like building your own windmill) in Stewart Brand's *Whole Earth Catalog*, this new iteration depends on the complexity that only computer systems and technical expertise can render. Although technology is often the source of environmental problems, this discourse focuses on the virtues of high-tech solutions to environmental crisis aimed precisely at generating these visceral responses: *I didn't know we could do that! That'd be cool!* It's like the Jetsons turbocharged in the face of climate change.

From the pragmatic and scientific, *Shanghai Dongtan: An Eco-City* moves into what reads like a real estate investment brochure, with images of residents, almost all of them whom are white, exercising with a beautiful waterscape as the aesthetic backdrop. The "we" and "I" here taking this "Imaginary Journey" are visibly white and, more often than not, blond. Here, the text reads, "in 2020, we boarded a pleasure boat that brought us from downtown Shanghai to the Nangang Port of Dongtan, which was the starting point where the city began to grow. . . . [O]n the wide embankment embracing the port on both sides, I saw guesthouses, hotels, restaurants and stores scattered here and there with people under wide parasols sipping their coffee."[37]

The target market for Dongtan eco-city is not the actual transnational financial elites who come to Shanghai to work and play. According to Wood, Arup's goal for Dongtan is "a Chinese City for the Chinese." Despite this language, the images represented are not primarily of Chinese residents. Transnational elites (imagined as white) signify a politics and set of aspirations.

Whiteness represents not only Western modernity but also, more precisely, an advanced, developed, and privileged social position and lifestyle in China. The image of whiteness is widely commercialized and dispersed through printed magazines, newspapers, and TV commercials to represent the aspirations of Chinese viewers to a so-called higher social status and better life.[38]

In that sense, improvement of various stripes is a *process*, not merely a project or a place. This journey through "space" and "time" is subtitled "An Imaginary Journey to 2020,"[39] where the subjectivities and experiences of the imagined Dongtan resident and visitor continue to take central stage. The we/I are "a little tired," but fortunately a large variety of transportation alternatives are possible: foot, boat, horseback, solar-powered vessel, and "of course, hydrogen-powered trolleybuses, cars and motorbikes." The journey continues here, to the Dongtan science and education zone, where the protagonist looks "back in history seeing a vast sea in the place I had just been through." From this orderly change of scenes, this imaginary protagonist comes to the world-famous natural wetland where "a large flock of seabirds glided past in front of him in the direction of the city, with the clamour of a thousand flapping wings. He accepted this clamour in silence while looking up at the sky at the dark silvery flashes reflected by the wings." Fortunately, the protagonist is not alone to enjoy this grandeur. A stranger with a telescope reveals that "every time he sees bird flocks passing by, he can't help holding his breath in awe." After the awe-inspiring moment, the protagonist puts his bike on a bus and works his way back to the port, where he runs into "large numbers of people, some taking the walk on a fisher's dock, some on their way back from the sea, some tasting the newly fished seafood, some angling in private. Among them are . . . an excited crowd of foreign tourists over from Shanghai ready to see this world famous eco-city with their own eyes."[40]

Tourism, appreciation, excitement, and awe come to signify the imagined future of Dongtan and, by extension, Chongming Island. In short, the natural landscape and the intensive real estate development are imagined as a mini-Vancouver or Hong Kong, where the natural beauty of the waterscape is an engine of improvement and betterment, with an associated and inexorable real estate development, leading to rising land values and skyrocketing housing prices.

## DONGTAN DISAPPOINTS

So why, given the tremendous amount of energy, resources, and excitement, did Dongtan eco-city fail? Arup contends that the Dongtan project is "dead" but that the fate of Dongtan is not in its hands.[41] The most frequently offered explanation is, unsurprisingly in the contemporary Chinese context, political corruption. In 2006, when Dongtan's construction was set to begin, Shanghai's then–Communist Party secretary (and its former mayor from 2001 to 2003) Chen Liangyu was arrested and ultimately sentenced to eighteen years for bribery and abuse of real estate transactions. For accepting bribes, the former director-general of SIIC Wang Guoxiong was sentenced to life in prison, and SIIC's finance director Li Yizeng was sentenced to fifteen years in jail. Arup was not involved in those cases. After Chen's arrest in September 2006, many large construction projects were immediately put on hold pending further review. Since that time, however, many other projects' permits have been renewed and completed while Dongtan and those most identified with Chen have languished indefinitely.

The other major reason given is that there was "confusion" about who was to pay for the project, Arup or SIIC. This explanation sounds ridiculous, given that the two major players have a great deal of experience in both financing and building big projects. Dongtan's failure is tied to several factors specific to that project and the land in question. One of Dongtan's former designers, Shanfeng Dong, said, "China's current city statutes are suitable for the previous decades when China was still in its industrial development period. There is a lack of basis for constructing eco-cities."[42]

Another problem was changing government policy related to farmland management and development. In order to assist SIIC in the wake of the financial crisis in 1998, the Shanghai government gave SIIC permission to develop Dongtan. The central government began to tighten its policy in managing farmland, however, and took back the local government's right to issue land-use permits. The policy requires that if one square kilometer of farmland is used for development, the locality must reclaim an equal amount of land, which Dongtan's planners did not account for.[43] Yet another factor was conflict between the Chongming local government and SIIC. Although SIIC has the right to use Dongtan's land, ownership still belongs to Chenjia town.[44] For example, the Chongming county government was eager to speed up the development of Chenjia town and began to invest in infrastructure, public transportation, confiscation of farmland, and relocation of the local peasants.

As one local peasant, Yong Liu, recounted, his family used the money from the compensation for land confiscation to buy an apartment in the relocation area. They didn't have any other income after they lost their lands, however. One officer from Chenjia town's Agriculture Center said that the Dongtan project was carried out independently by the government and SIIC, which thus conflicted with each other (the local government's pace was much faster than the corporation's).[45] The last major factor was the changing personalities and leadership at SIIC. The chairman of the SIIC board, Laixing Cai, a founder and main supporter of Dongtan, retired in 2008. Shanfeng Dong and Jiang Li were two important members of Dongtan project who quit their jobs at Arup and joined SIIC, which promptly reassigned them to the other Chinese eco-city projects such as Langfang. The new chairman Yilong Teng was the Party secretary of the Higher People's Court, Shanghai. Teng considered the eco-city plan as a part of national strategy and thought it should be constructed at the political level, not the corporation's technological level.[46]

Despite these setbacks, in 2008 Arup announced that a scaled-down version of Dongtan was moving forward and that the international bank HSBC and Sustainable Development Capital Limited would be working on the financing of the real estate development with a new business model. Seeking to emulate the development of Harvard University and the Massachusetts Institute of Technology in Cambridge, a memorandum of understanding announced that a new research facility would ground the development of Dongtan eco-city: the Dongtan Institute for Sustainability.

The story of how Dongtan is represented as the ultimate promise to a whole host of environmental problems is itself instructive. Dongtan was always set up to fail, whether or not it was ever able to accomplish its original technical goals, in part because it was always meant to represent more. Dongtan was set up as an alternative, ecologically friendly narrative for the "Chinese City," and its failure from the perspective of the Western architects and engineers is that it got caught in politics that they could not control or understand. Although this explanation might technically be true, this narrative absolves the transnational architects and engineers of any agency or responsibility. This failure narrative posits their contribution as politically clean and technologically advanced, and has Dongtan derailed by complex national and regional politics. It puts their contribution on the technical side and cleaves off politics to the murky corrupt world of the Chinese, rather than acknowledging how technology, engineering, and politics were intimately woven together in Dongtan, in other Shanghai sites, and throughout China.

## SHANGHAI, SOM, AND SUSTAINABILITY FROM ABOVE

But we do know that Chongming Island's eco-development continues, despite Dongtan's failure, and ecological development (whatever that means) in Shanghai remains both powerful ideology and material practice.

There are literally dozens of development plans at various stages, many headed by international firms. The most influential architectural firm on Chongming Island and Shanghai is arguably Skidmore, Owing and Merrill (SOM). SOM developed Chongming's master plan to double the population living there. SOM's most famous projects include the site for the 1933 Chicago Century of Progress Exposition, Sears Tower, and John Hancock (Chicago), the Istanbul Hilton, and the National Commercial Bank in Saudi Arabia. SOM is also the builder of the Freedom Tower on the site of the destroyed World Trade Center, and the Burj Kalifa (the largest skyscraper in the world, reaching a half mile into the sky), which opened in Dubai in 2009 (and which stands, as of 2010, 95 percent empty, in an effective symbol of the postbubble global economic standstill).

Long associated with modernism, SOM's focus, like Arup's, is increasingly on "sustainability," including an award-winning design of the University of California–Merced campus, and the Treasure Island plan.[47] Even before the Chongming master plan, SOM had already left a major imprint on Shanghai, having built its (currently) tallest building, the iconic Jin Mao Tower, in 1999 and Xintiandi, one of the most well-known and early controversial redevelopments in China. In 1997, SOM's San Francisco office established the historic development concept for Xintiandi, implemented by Wood and Zapata (as discussed in chapter 4, the project displaced a large number of people and replaced them with a tourist-consumer destination). Akin to the redevelopment of Faneuil Hall Marketplace development in Boston or Baltimore's Inner Harbor project, Shanghai's Xintiandi represents a particular vision of urban and economic redevelopment that favors high-end customers and tourists.[48]

SOM's Chongming master plan imagines the island as a major center for shipyards and manufacturing of ship machinery, cranes, and other port equipment. The plan also focuses on Chongming's development as a recreation and tourism area. SOM's plan calls for the urban development of eight new cities, to cover 15 percent of the island. Each community will consist of walkable and accessible districts that will accommodate eight hundred thousand people to live and work. But, despite this ambitious plan, it has been put on hold. The main architect of the plan, SOM's Philip Enquist, critiques how the plan itself has been shelved by the Shanghai government.[49] Like Dongtan, the master plan has fallen by the wayside in the sea of complex internal local and regional politics, not always apparent to outsiders.

## CONCLUSION

What then can we make of the failure of Dongtan and the Chongming Island master plan? Are the various agents of these failures indicative of any larger trend? Is there any lesson that can be derived from their lifecycles? On the one hand, failure is not surprising, particularly in the context of experimental high-stakes architecture, only a tiny fraction of which is ever built. But, given all that Dongtan was supposed to be and the changes it was meant to usher in, what are the lessons? Arup's Peter Head maintains that despite Dongtan's apparent failure, its influence is nonetheless significant: "Dongtan showed that it is possible to develop sustainable cities, which encourage the use of public transport, recycle their waste, use natural ventilation in buildings and use large proportions of renewable energy. These cities will be clean, quiet, unpolluted and exist in *harmony* with the natural environment" (emphasis added).[50]

Dongtan failed to materialize owing to not just narrow political reasons but also a whole suite of broader cultural and ideological factors. The main problem is the ways in which the eco-city model itself depends on segregating nature and environment into a particular place, and the eco-city model's fundamental unquestioning acceptance of technology and engineering as the solution to environmental crises. That is, Dongtan's essential purpose is not environmental but rather to function as a pragmatic and technical solution to Shanghai's numerous environmental and political problems associated with urbanization and development.

Dongtan shoehorns Shanghai's ecological development into a particular place, at the same time that the transnational builders and engineers refuse to take off their blinders, despite their rhetoric about Dongtan as a "Chinese eco-city for Chinese people" or that Dongtan "was about the birds." It was neither, and worse. Instead, Dongtan was an engine for real estate development and regional transformation, to create economic value and enhance real estate speculation in the guise of environmental and wetlands protection. Transnational architecture and engineering firms cannot take Chongming Island seriously from the point of view of local places. In satisfying the demands of their clients, SIIC and Arup accept the basic calculation of a top-down and technocratic view of environmental development.

In other words, eco-Shanghai = Chongming Island = Dongtan eco-city. The more concentrated the ecological place, the less ecological responsibility the rest of Shanghai city must take for environmental standards more broadly defined. Some critics argue that Shanghai lost its chance from the perspective of environmental benefits during a decades-long building boom when environmental standards (on energy efficiency, for example) were, first, not built into construction codes, and then not enforced.[51]

One of the other major reasons Dongtan failed, and why I think most eco-cities as currently conceptualized are doomed to fail, is precisely because they don't take their own ecotopianism seriously. I am not a pessimistic critic of utopias. I like them, and might even consider living in one. But we need to study Dongtan with these questions asked by one scholar of literary ecotopias: "What can I learn from this utopia? What insights and practical wisdom can be gained from it? What striking contrasts are evoked by this utopia, to stimulate our imagination and possibly enable us to more clearly reflect on political issues? To what extent does it provide a useful and challenging way of solving existing problems? Is this utopia a source of original ideas, and does it indicate relevant ways for solving our modern social problems? Can the ideas from this utopia contribute to modern-day discussions and enrich political debate on a future sustainable society?"[52]

The relevance of Dongtan as utopia is to show the primacy of a top-down, highly corporate and technological eco-city, one that makes almost no mention of power. Dongtan as ecotopian site, and the worldview it represents, also ignores people and their differences: between rich and poor, urban and rural, local and migrant. The same critique is true for Dongtan and broader movements for ecological modernization and suburbanization in Shanghai, as we will see in the next chapter.

# CHAPTER FOUR

# It's a Green World After All?

*Marketing Nature and Nation in Suburban Shanghai*

> There is just one moon and one golden sun.
> And a smile means friendship to everyone.
> Though the mountains divide,
> And the oceans are wide,
> It's a small world after all.
>
> > Richard Sherman and Robert Sherman, "It's a Small World," theme
> > song of the Disney attraction of the same name, 1964

Whether or not significant development takes place at Dongtan, we will always have Thames Town to visit. Thames Town is a literal recreation of "authentic British-ness" located on Shanghai's outskirts. Built in 2001, Thames Town is an already decaying "English" village complete with Tudor-style pubs, corner shops, Edwardian houses, Canary Wharf, and Victoria redbrick warehouses—an amalgamation of hundreds of years of British architecture. The decay here is not mere metaphor but literal, in the "walk carefully or that panel of faux-wood that is already half off will fall on you" sense. The majority of visitors are young newlyweds who have come to take their wedding photos on a giant lawn in front of a huge Gothic-style church (based on an actual church in Bristol). Decked out in (white, red, and pink) wedding dresses and fancy tuxedos, pairs of young lovers patiently wait their turn to pose romantically in front of what is, in effect, a giant concrete stage set (the doors are padlocked). They come to take part in "exotic marriage customs," trailed by makeup artists and photographers.

Most non-Chinese journalists and tourists here paint Thames Town as an example of Jean Baudrillard's simulacrum, or as travesty.[1] They hold that Thames Town is "not a real city, yet a *built dream*, gripping powerfully into the imagination of the Chinese" (emphasis added).[2] Surreal images do abound in Thames Town: the faux cast-iron clock tower with four different (and equally incorrect) times on its four faces; the shop lady playing by herself in a toy store in a city without children; the unnamed statues of famous Brits (Clara Barton and Charles Darwin) amidst the ubiquitous eviction notices for nonpayment for electricity service. I visited it with my colleague Simon, a British-born architectural historian, who was as complimentary of the faithfulness of the reproductions of British architectural styles as he was horrified by the poor-quality construction. The mall across from the church was empty, filled with wires hanging from the water-stained ceiling and broken glass strewn across the floor. We met a well-off Shanghai couple who asked Simon, the "authentic" Brit, if Thames Town "was better." "Better than what?" Simon responded, answering that there was no "real Thames Town" in England. There was no place where Victorian houses were right next to the Docklands, where Gothic structures abutted Canary Wharf. The husband insisted, *"Isn't Thames Town better than England itself, because everything is new!"*

Thames Town cannot be reduced simply to a "built dream" gone horribly wrong, a singular example of bad taste, or a representation of different cultural assumptions about fake and real, new and old. Rather than Thames Town being an exceptional example to mock, it is, I suggest, a particularly apt manifestation of the powerful mobilization of "nature" and eco-desire in an era of contemporary Shanghai suburban development. The built dream, in other words, is partially green, a central component of contemporary Chinese suburban landscapes.[3] What matters for the green "dream" here is not just the Gothic church but also the lawn in front of it. Lawns have a curious logic and function, and environmental historians have examined what happens when the ideologies about the lawn get separated out from the particular (wet and rainy) ecosystems that spawned the ideal of the English lawn.[4] For one thing, in the western U.S. deserts, the ubiquity of lawns leads to wasteful water usage (outdoor water use often accounts for half or more of all residential water demand, especially in the hotter inland areas of California where population growth is now fastest).[5] In the postwar context of American suburban development, the lawn represented the glories of the single-family home, domesticity, and a "Father Knows Best" normative gender politics. One scholar of Western-themed suburban landscape argues that, at its heart, "traditional" Chinese architecture was focused on replicating natural landscapes, most famously in the imperial and private gardens of old historic dynasties. Thus, the move to "appropriate power" through architectural mimesis is not as much an anomaly as it first appears.[6] But, I would suggest, the form of that nature is historically distinct. Thames Town's lawns represent the eco-desire for green towns and open spaces that are held out as the antithesis of Shanghai.[7]

"Nature" and "nation" are conflated for particular ends in particular ways that connect concretely with Dongtan and the 2010 World Expo. Dongtan and Thames Town are also pragmatically linked through their political architect, as Thames Town was a central part of the "One City, Nine Towns" project associated with the disgraced Shanghai mayor and Party chief Chen Liangyu. Thus, the representation of nature that Thames Town embodies is a historical artifact of Shanghai's urban development and economic planning, through a process that began in 1994. One City, Nine Towns was not just any ordinary plan for urban development: in a unique cultural twist, each of the nine towns was modeled after a European nation or city. According to Shanghai planning officials, politicians, and their overseas designers, foreign visitors would be unable to tell "where Europe ends and

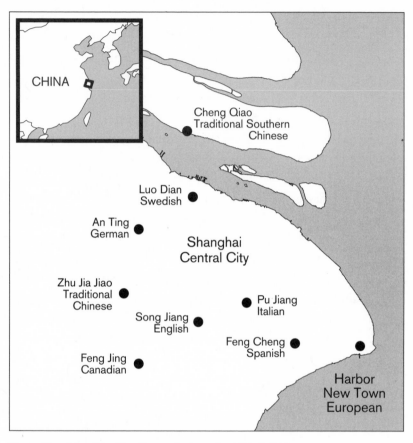

CHINA

Cheng Qiao
Traditional Southern
Chinese

Luo Dian
Swedish

An Ting
German

Shanghai
Central City

Zhu Jia Jiao
Traditional
Chinese

Pu Jiang
Italian

Song Jiang
English

Feng Cheng
Spanish

Feng Jing
Canadian

Harbor
New Town
European

Map 2. Map of One City, Nine Towns. Cartography: Michele Tobias

China begins."[8] The one city (Song Jiang, where Thames Town is located, is the city) and seven of the nine towns were built in the purportedly "authentic" architectural style of Western nations—England, Canada, Spain, Sweden/Northern Europe, Holland, Italy, and Germany—with the other two towns built in "Chinese" styles. Two of the towns (one of the Chinese towns, on Chongming Island, and the Dutch/Harbor New Town) were also particularly "environmental" in their building practices. Although not all of the towns are explicitly "environmental" in theme, what links all of them is a sublimated eco-desire.

The roots and the cultural implications of envisioning happiness and bliss as European have a long and troubled history in Shanghai, given the West's colonial domination and the history of the international concessions. According to project boosters, the plan represents a reckoning with this painful history, in a cycle of redemption and reconciliation, under the guise of suburban real estate development.[9] Foreign architects have been a central component of Shanghai's development practice, beginning with the international competition to design the high-rise Liujiazui central business district in Pudong.[10]

Architectural critics, in contrast, critique the One City, Nine Towns developments as neocolonial and the projects as theme parks (reserving their greatest bile for Thames Town).[11] Other scholars focus on the tensions between importation of foreign ideas and cultural adaptation.[12] When I describe One City, Nine Towns, I'm usually asked whether the towns are anything like Disneyland's "It's a Small World After All." This association is unsurprising, as both depend on a stereotypical view of national culture, one that paradoxically homogenizes in the act of celebrating difference. That particular Disneyland ride originated at the 1964 World's Fair sponsored by Pepsi. In it, each doll sang his/her own national anthem, but the discordance was overwhelming. To correct this discord, the song "It's a Small World" was written after the Cuban missile crisis to stress the importance of international unity.

In some important ways the One City, Nine Towns project is like "It's a Small World," but in one way it differs. What connects the so-called distinctive national cultures is that each town foregrounds a vision and ideology of nature and environmentalism through suburbanization. Verbally or visually

Figure 4. Deer at Thames Town. Photo by Simon Sadler

extolling access to green space, clean air, and healthy living through slogans or statues of faux Bambis eating grass (see figure 4), nature and ecology are conflated with nation-ness. Here, eco-desire is the fusion of nature and nation to represent a vision of transformation, modernity, and cosmopolitanism in Shanghai's suburban development policy in a particular historical and cultural moment. Eco-desire runs through the different towns in altered forms even where the town theme is not explicitly "environmental." Whether the focus is on clean air (Thames Town), low-carbon living (An-Ting), water (Pu Jiang), or eco-friendly houses (Northern Europe town), natural images and concepts are embodied and built into the national characters of these developments as a way to "imagine" the virtues of ecology in real estate development in a hyperurbanizing Shanghai.

What is at stake here? On the one hand, natural images represent an importation of ecological greenwashing in a real estate context, echoing

Dongtan. At the same time, the larger issues are much broader than the "taste" or theme park critique. Rather, what is being worked out through these projects is the ideological formation and construction of middle-class Chinese consumers within the new suburban vision. This vision and policy work synergistically to create new ecological subjects within a broader national, environmental, and social context, although whether economic land-use development and environmental "harmony" can coexist remains an unsettled and unsettling question.

Suburbanization and urbanization, in other words, are tightly interwoven in Shanghai. Suburban developments in Shanghai are part and parcel with "skyscraper" Shanghai, and representations of nature are one way in which to understand this relationship. To understand suburbanization in isolation from the global ambitions of the central city would be to misunderstand both suburb and central city. The relationship and reconciliation between suburb and city is managed through ecological desire, broadly defined, and set against a "national" and "global" stage. Understanding the how and why of Shanghai's One City, Nine Towns plan helps to set the stage for the 2010 World Expo, which I examine in the next chapter. Ideologies of nature and suburbanization are an important part of the moral discourse of the city's urban development agenda and practice.

## SHANGHAI SATELLITE CITY
## DEVELOPMENT IN HISTORICAL CONTEXT

The One City, Nine Towns project fits within the broader urban and historical context in Shanghai. Shanghai has a long and complicated relationship with satellite city development. In 1929, the Shanghai municipality created a new downtown Jiangwan area, and shortly afterward issued the "Construction Plan of a Big Shanghai." In 1945, the Shanghai government issued a plan to construct eleven satellite cities to relieve the population pressure of the central city, although they were never built. Satellite city planning effectively ended after the Communist Party took control in 1949 because the Party regarded cities as a colonial by-product of European-American capitalism, instead prioritizing rural development. As more and more people moved to central Shanghai, however, urban problems proliferated. In 1951, the Shanghai government started to construct new industrial areas in order to move the "dangerous and polluted industries" outside of the central city.

Despite relative inaction on official satellite planning, Shanghai continued to grow. Today, the Shanghai "urban system" is immense, with 230 centers, seven satellite towns, thirty-one county seats (designated towns), two industrial districts, 175 market towns, and fifteen farm market towns. As in the other largest cities of the world, getting from one end to the other can take hours. The Shanghai government turned its attention to urban planning and development in the 1990s in response to China's explosive global expansion and Shanghai's status as the financial center of the nation. Shanghai municipality articulated that "the central city districts manifest prosperity, the rural towns manifest strength," and confirmed that a central component of "The Tenth Five-Year Plan" was "One City, Nine Towns."[13] Collectively, the new city and towns were expected to house a total of a million or more newcomers by 2020. All of them were satellites of central Shanghai, and although most of the towns were entirely new developments, others were new developments in already existing communities. The "towns" and the "city" were planned as self-sufficient "satellite cities" where residents could live, work, and shop without having to travel into central Shanghai.[14]

In 2001, the State Council approved "Shanghai's Urban Plan (1999–2020)," which developed the new construction model.[15] In 2002, Shanghai clarified the primary goals and strategy of its urban planning and development: speeding up urbanization, modernizing agriculture, and transitioning farmers to city residents under the auspices of "three convergences" (industrial parks; large-scale agricultural operations; and farmers converging on towns).[16] The ultimate goal is to alter the concept (and relationship) between city and village, the central city district and the suburbs. The hope was to shape and control the expansion of the severely crowded central city, to grow the nine towns to stimulate the outlying areas, to shape industrial parks for employment purposes, and to attract residents from the central city to alleviate transportation and other housing pressures on the core.

In the 1990s, numerous polluting factories in the city center were closed down or relocated to the outer reaches of the Shanghai, freeing up central city land for urban redevelopment.[17] This trend is not unique to Shanghai. A key feature of "world city" development in the past two decades has been the relocation of manufacturing from the city core and the growth of real estate and tourism in its stead (New York City and London are exhibits A and B of this process). A key feature of recent urban and land-use planning has been the break between industry and housing amidst the declining influence of the *danwei*, or work unit. For decades, people's living and work contexts were one and the same, but this identity was weakened and broken under China's liberalizing economic policy. Thus, the new attention paid to environmental amenities is partially related to people's new ability to choose their housing and work locations in ways that radically changed from the advent of the Communist takeover in 1949 to the economic reform era in the past few decades.[18]

## STEREOTYPICAL NATURE/NATION

Under changing political contexts that reshaped the literal spatial development in Shanghai, its residents faced immense changes in the physical and ideological landscapes of the city. In this context, real estate development and land speculation increased dramatically. The role of American-style suburbanization is not unique to Shanghai. Market research in 2003 found that 70 percent of property developments in Beijing emphasized Western geographies and architectural motifs.[19] In particular, these developments were explicitly modeled on Southern California suburban landscapes. There

Figure 5. Thames Town Sign. Photo by Simon Sadler

are literally carbon copies of the same housing development in Rancho Santa Fe in San Diego, and in Shanghai, built by the same developer. But Chinese suburbanization is no mere echo of its American cousin. Chinese suburbanization is motivated less by racist antiurbanism and fear of crime than by the particular national context of real estate speculation.

One critic suggests that Thames Town "stands in stark contrast to what it is not. It is not the arterial multilane roadways or the congested, polluted urban sprawl. It is in the realm of make believe, a utopian town that offers its residents . . . an exclusive living space to begin a life of happiness and bliss."[20] Its unreality contrasts with the Song Jiang district's rich history as one of the main antecedents to contemporary Shanghai, one of the original sources of the region's "pure" Shanghai dialect and identity. When the Taiping Rebellion reached Song Jiang, the city was protected, not by a Chinese-led army, but by the ragtag Ever Victorious Army, led by the American Frederick Townsend Ward. In 1927,

Song Jiang was finally swallowed by Shanghai, putting an end to the Song Jiang prefecture, which had existed since the thirteenth century.[21]

Some argued that the one city and nine towns were effective symbols of the (in)appropriate role of the "international" in the context of China. "International" here stands as a code for both an architectural "style" and as a material practice, as the main architectural firm in charge of each town hails from the nation the town is said to represent.[22] Thus, Albert Speer Jr. (of the Beijing Olympic Park) designed An Ting (German Town). Augusto Cagnardi from Gregotti Architects in Milan designed Pu Jiang (Italian Town). Barcelona-based Marcia Codinachs was the architect of Feng Cheng (Spanish Town). The Thames Town project came from the Atkins Group based in the United Kingdom (which also did another project on Chongming Island, although not Dongtan); Stockholm's SWECO, which also is the lead architect for another major Chinese eco-city named Caifeidian, did the work for Luo Dian (known as either Northern European or Scandinavian Town).[23] Hamburg's Gerkan, Marg und Partner designed Harbor New Town.

The one notable exception to this pattern (home country/national development) is that the designers of the two "Chinese" towns are international firms with non-Chinese principals. Zhu Jia Jiao was designed by Ben Wood/Studio Shanghai (the designer of the famous Xintiandi project in downtown Shanghai) and the Chongming eco-town (another "eco-town" distinct from Dongtan) by the German firm Stadtbauatelier. Ben Wood, originally a Boston-based U.S. architect, is best known for the "cultural/entertainment" Xintiandi project, which redeveloped a part of central Shanghai into a more corporate version of itself with its traditional Shikumen housing. Xintiandi is complete with both a Starbucks and the First Congress of the Communist Party Museum.[24] It also led to an unhappy relocation of sixteen hundred families.[25] One profile admiringly calls Wood "Our Man in Shanghai" and explains his "formula" for part theme park, part history, part high-end consumption projects applied throughout his Chinese projects. In another, he says, "'They know me pretty well in this neighborhood, because I like to ride through here a lot,' . . . raising his voice to be heard over the growling motor. 'What they don't know,' he adds with a hint of regret, 'is that I'm also the guy who is going to make this way of life disappear.'"[26] Wood's Zhu Jia Jiao project, costing eighty million dollars, is "inspired by China's 13th-century water-town plans stitched together with picturesque foot bridges and semi-detached contemporary-style condos."[27]

From the original planning statements to the finished product, ecological images and rhetoric have been central to marketing these new international suburbias. The signs in An Ting, the town explicitly linked to Shanghai's auto production industry, call relentlessly for "Low Carbon: The Original Ecological German Style Apartments" (see figure 6). Thames Town signs urge residents to "enjoy sunlight. Enjoy nature. Enjoy your life and holiday" (see figure 5). Part of the distinctiveness of these developments aimed to attract buyers and investors is the value that ecology adds, in sharp contrast to the buyer's notions of what suburban housing can and should look like.

In other words, the One City, Nine Towns project depended on promoting a *stereotypical* nature in the form of the built (national) environment. Despite the concept of diversity of national forms and real estate development, what unites these developments is the crude cudgel of nature. In one typical speech before the Shanghai Suburban Investment Environment group titled "Shanghai Suburbs: Hot Land for Investment," one government official explained how the plan fit with the goals of Shanghai's suburban development. First, industry, population, and foreign capital would be transferred from the center to the periphery. Second, social services would be increased. Third, and most important, these new developments would stress ecology, described as "green agriculture, ecological environment construction, forest and water systems, eco-forest environment with humans and nature."[28]

The rhetoric is that given Shanghai's need to develop a radically new style of "ecological planning," it seemed only natural to "learn from foreign

典藏公寓现房呈现

low carbon
THE ORIGINAL ECOLOGICAL
GERMAN STYLE APARTMENTS

安亭新镇
ANTING

Figure 6. An Ting. Photo by author, 2009

countries' experience" in constructing unique towns so that, by bringing in top designers from Western nations, they bring the best of international ecological design. A key component of each town is to "use its comfortable ecological environment, different and unique styles of towns, and modern functions of the living [space] to attract people from the central districts." The fundamental operating principle is that "the basic infrastructure and public service should be relatively better than the city, and the ecological environment is better than the central city."[29]

In a radically new political and housing context in which people can "choose" where they live (after a half century when they could not), part of what tips the "choice" is ecology and nature, most and best associated with "international" designers. And, in a radical break with typical Chinese urban development and unlike central Shanghai, the plans would avoid the construction of high-rise buildings, focusing instead on low or multilevel architecture.[30] The renewed focus on the environmental benefits of cities, especially in light of energy usage, is gaining serious attention in books like Edward Gleaser's *Triumph of the City: How Our Greatest Invention Makes Us Richer, Smarter, Greener, Healthier, and Happier,* in networks like the Urban Climate Change Research Network, and in climate governance agreements at the global urban scale between mayors of cities across the world (i.e., through the World Congress on Cities and Adaptation to Climate Change).[31]

Suburbs have long been defined in the West as places of retreat from the pollution, density, and disease associated with urban life. Without industrialization in the nineteenth century, the Garden City movement would never have taken off in England at the dawn of the twentieth century. Fifty years later in the United States, car-driven suburbs exploded after World War II as predominantly white city-dwellers sought their own version of the American Dream, with a lawn and a white picket fence. In other words, the conditions of urban life are the problems that suburbia purportedly solves. From nineteenth-century Britain to postwar America to contemporary China: Shanghai's urban policy and suburban real estate development adopts a somewhat similar grammar of nature, comfort, and escape (or at least the 1950s version of American suburbia, before the realities of sprawl ruined the dream, along with the air). One major difference from the United States is that the Shanghai real estate and urban development model has typically depended on large-scale apartment complexes connected by transit, not the single-family home based on the car, although the One City, Nine Towns project deviates from this model.

These developments are indeed a successful Rorschach test for something—the difficulty of defining or evaluating "success." They are empty towns, devoid of people and commercial or street life, confirming critical opinion of them as simulacra (or the eco-Potemkin of Huangbaiyu). On the other hand, as a real estate investment venture they more than succeed. One employee of the Weimar villa sales site, Huajie Chen, told a reporter, "Most houses in An Ting new city have been sold. There are only 100 units that are not sold." The problem is that most buyers did not move in. Chen described the three types of buyers: employees of the local auto companies (whose primary residence is elsewhere, but who stay in Shanghai for business); businessmen from Jiangsu province (just north of Shanghai), who come to the villas only for holidays; and investors, who bet the houses will increase in value. Although the original plan was to attract thirty thousand people, the actual population was so low that the only kindergarten in An Ting could not open for lack of students.[32] The new city offers few employment opportunities, and drivers to Shanghai would face a forty-five-minute commute—there is not yet a subway to the central city.

The same dynamic (successful real estate venture but no residents) is also present in Thames Town, despite its relatively accessible location on the subway line with direct access to downtown Shanghai (this relative accessibility is part of why international critics have tended to focus on Thames Town: it's easier to visit). My colleague and I visited with a family friend who grew up in downtown Shanghai, the granddaughter of a Party general, a young woman who now attends college in the United States. She was initially excited by the Thames Town website but ultimately disappointed by the experience. When I asked if she would ever live there, she shot me a horrified look. When I asked if she would live there for free, she still demurred. Then, I upped the ante with a "what if they paid you to live there," and she still refused. The best comparison I can offer is that it's sort of like asking a born-and-bred Manhattanite if she'd consider the outer reaches of Staten Island—but a Staten Island in drag as a dilapidated "classic" English town.

So, despite the broad effort by Shanghai urban planning officials to "relieve pressure" in the central city by developing these towns, they have not appeared to succeed as a primary residence for many, although they have been successfully sold. In other words, the mobilization of nature in selling real estate has done at least part of its job, to create the natural capital, as in Dongtan, to justify the higher real estate prices in areas long deemed marginal to the central city.

## MAXIMUM SKYLINE, MINIMALIZED NATURE

Green and clean socialist living city
Technologically hygienic city
the healthy future garden-salad city.
An ordered oasis of high-tech corporations, Siliconed Valleys, and global
    investment zones.
A massive forestation and green infrastructure planning strategy,
corporate parks, urban forests, flowering roadside urban therapy.
A private Eden of commodified residential real estate and lush greenery,
intelligent homes, luxury, and class-differentiated scenery.
Pudong—one of China's first garden cities—planted in Shanghai's Tenth Five
    Year Plan[33]

One way to think about the meaning of Thames Town is that it is a totally normal example of shoddy construction in China. Although a building may look good, it falls apart or, in one particularly dramatic case, down. In June 2009, a thirteen-story new development in Shanghai fell down, killing one worker. Investigations pointed to the low-quality pilings used, and the poor placement of the dirt from the garage excavation next to a riverbank, which led to water seeping onto the site.[34]

For me, Thames Town's decaying buildings and the sideways Shanghai skyscraper remind me of Albert Speer Sr., not least because his son, Albert Speer Jr., is the architect of An Ting (German Town). In 1934, Speer Sr. proposed "A Theory of Ruin Value," which suggested that even in an empire's decline (as in imperial Rome), decayed architectural relics remain monumental and awe-inspiring. The practical purpose of this theory is to avoid modern materials in favor of natural materials. In practice, this meant for Speer Sr. that for grand Nazi buildings and sites he designed (such as the Zeppelin Field or party rally grounds, or the New Berlin, which was never built) "we planned to avoid, as far as possible, all such elements of modern construction as steel girders and reinforced concrete, which are subject to weathering. Despite their height, the walls were intended to withstand the impact of the wind even if the roofs and ceilings were so neglected that they no longer braced the walls. The static factors were calculated with this in mind."[35]

In other words, Speer's ruins were a symbol of the Nazi regime's grandeur. The theory was also, some argue, a product (or justification) of the reality of the lack of iron in wartime Germany.[36] The ruins of Thames Town and the sideways skyscraper are also a symbol of the brutal efficiency of capitalism and its search for cost-cutting at the expense of quality, a symbol, in other words, of a con. That confidence game is also a reflection of the superhot, irrationally exuberant Shanghai building boom, where prices have gone up beyond all economists' expectations: a bubble waiting to burst, which keeps stubbornly defying expectations that it will do so.[37]

Thames Town's decay and the sideways skyscraper are contemporary examples of *Shanghaiing,* a term that originally referred to the nineteenth-century practice of kidnapping men to work as sailors on American merchant ships for the China trade. Sailors were pressed into unfree labor by "crimps" with colorful names like Jim "Shanghai" Kelly, and Johnny "Shanghai Chicken" Devine, both of San Francisco. The term's meaning gradually expanded to generally denote kidnapping or engaging in fraud. The geographer and performance studies scholar Shiloh Krupar uses the phrase *Shanghaiing the future* in her satiric reading/photo-essay of the Shanghai Urban Planning Exhibition Hall (SUPEH), a huge six-story monument to city planning in Shanghai—its history and future development. Although all cities engage in real estate and urban development boosterism, SUPEH is

Figure 7. Shanghai Urban Planning Exhibition. Photo by Matt Tindell

particularly invested in managing the image of Shanghai in a celebratory mode, based largely on its centerpiece model of the city (seen in figure 7) and in three particular versions of the city: as a global city, eco-city, and city of imperialist nostalgia.[38]

Suburbanization in Shanghai reflects these trends—global city/eco-city/imperialist nostalgia—simultaneously. Shanghai's suburbanization markets the city's cosmopolitanism and livability *through* nature. Suburbanization communicates ideological messages and value hierarchies in the brave new world, about transportation and abstract nature over the chaos of hyperurbanization. SUPEH's monochromatic model shows all existing and approved buildings and is the center of a large room where you can walk along and above the model. The epic scale of Shanghai's model is meant to invite awe. Like most models, it is clean and orderly, nothing like the actual street life in the old historic core.

Campanella recounts the history of the development of Shanghai's signature Pudong skyline, how the city held an international architectural competition only to ultimately reject the international architects. The homegrown version emphasized the epic in all its full Chinese large-scale glory in a vision of China's urbanism as a city of "photogenic monumentality—a stage-set city intended to impress from a distance, from the Bund, from the air, from the pages of a glossy magazine," based around tall sky-scrapers and "central axes built around cars," producing a dead street life "more suited to a parade route than a place to walk."[39] Two decades after Pudong's development, Shanghai urbanization and suburbanization para-doxically recreated the monumentality of the skyline as mirrored by the stage-set miniaturization of nature, itself captured in the vortex of Shang-hai's real estate development model, which also has a dead street life and stage-set quality.

These sustainable developments are themselves captured by the flip side of Pudong's megaskyscrapers, two sides of the same coin. Krupar describes the eco-city romanticization of suburban lifestyles and its norms as "a pri-vate Eden of commodified residential real estate and lush greenery."[40] The lush greenery of the suburban small-scale models look like an inviting little dollhouse. I almost expected the miniature figures to jump out of this diorama. They are also the most accurate rendering of the actual experience of walking around in the suburban developments.

## NATURE SUCKS, DRIVE MORE CARS

Walking on the crowded streets near the historic Bund, I saw a T-shirt with the slogan "Nature Sucks, Drive More Cars" worn by a teenager. I did a dou-ble take, as this expression contrasted sharply with all of the sloganeering pro-environmental world expo ads that extolled low-carbon living. It also made me think of An Ting, developed in an area that is already one of the centers of China's automobile industry, both on the production side (a joint venture with the German firm Volkswagen), and as the site for China's first Formula 1 racetrack. An Ting is five square kilometers, built to accommodate eighty thousand people, and costs about ten billion yuan to build (1.2 billion U.S. dollars).[41]

The German architectural theorist Dieter Hassenpflüg offers a highly technical reading of An Ting's spatial attributes in relation to the typical

German cityscape.[42] Despite its flaws and failures, he contends that "An Ting New Town is a courageous project characterized by considerable motivation towards quality, in technical terms the Mercedes Benz, so to speak, among the thus far completed theme cities of the 'One City, Nine Towns-Plan.'"[43] Part of its "high quality" (quality discourse redux) is the exacting technical standards the architects embedded into the project. These are not just empty symbols or rhetoric; An Ting included better than usual standards in terms of energy efficiency, quality of materials, emission reduction, waste separation, a balanced supply of green and recreational spaces, and short walking distances. For example, the German Fichtner Company built an energy supply system using "natural energy" rather than air conditioners. Here, sustainability and technology are not just symbols, but based on highly exacting technical standards.

An Ting is, in contrast to Thames Town, the "Mercedes Benz" of the nine towns. What does it mean to extol the low-carbon lifestyle of the "original ecological German style apartments" so closely associated with the automobile production industry? In 2005, China surpassed Germany to become the third largest auto manufacturer in the world. The past two decades were truly an auto boom in China. Industry analysts estimate that by 2020 China will be the largest producer and consumer of cars, exceeding the United States. In Shanghai alone (from 1990 to 2003), the number of motor vehicles climbed from 212,000 to 1.2 million.[44] Like the industrial expansion of the past two decades, the scale and speed of highway expansion in China is dizzying. Americans have been a crucial part of China's twentieth-century auto history. They include men like Oliver Todd, a civil engineer who built the Hetch Hetchy Dam in the Sierra Nevada and spent eighteen years building a thousand miles of roads for the American Red Cross in the 1920s (John Muir protested the flooding of Hetch Hetchy, and thus kick-started the modern American preservation movement). They also include the city planner E. P. Goodrich, who built scenic roadways based on the Bronx River Parkway around the same time as Todd. In 1994, the Hong Kong developer and Stanford graduate Gordon Wu built the Guangzhou–Shenzhen expressway, based on the New Jersey Turnpike.[45]

As in the 1950s United States, the car is a cultural symbol of Chinese middle-class attainment, and highways the symbol of modernity. But, just as in the 1950s scourge of urban renewal, which the famed urbanist Jane Jacobs argued ripped apart central cities and tight-knit local communities in favor of the car, the psychological and human impact of the auto boom on the Shanghai landscape is immense. What differs now, in An Ting, is the idea that, through "German engineering," problems of climate change can be ameliorated by "superior" technology. Despite the attention to detail and high technology, fewer than 10 percent of the houses in An Ting were occupied, although most of them were sold.[46]

## NORTHERN EXPOSURE?

If cars in An Ting represent one end of the ecological spectrum, on the other end lies Luo Dian, one of the environmentally themed towns, described either as Scandinavian or Northern European. Golden Luodian Development, the investor behind Scandinavia Town, and SWECO, the builder, emphasize how environmentally friendly it is. According to one description of the town, "Luodian is a green, luxury getaway built on environmentally friendly principles imported from Sweden."[47] The surrounding area of Luo Dian is a mixture of wetlands and dusty roads lined with hardware stores and scrap metal businesses. The area set aside for the new community, however, has been reforested, complete with a residents-only lake, marina, and golf course complex. The town cost almost eight hundred million U.S. dollars to construct. Homes in Luo Dian cost five million yuan (U.S. $730,000) and apartments cost 580,000 yuan (U.S. $85,000).[48] Local media reported, as of 2009, that only eight of the forty-eight villas and 120 apartments had been sold.[49] At the same time, in 2009, Luo Dian was named a United Nations

Development Programme Pilot Town, and a National Development Reform Pilot Town by the United Nations Development and Reform Commission. According to its developers: "Luodian town is in the process of a rapid economic development. Many famous global companies have selected Luodian as an excellent strategic investment area including 50 foreign-invested enterprises from USA, Germany, France, Japan, Hong Kong and Taiwan" reaching U.S. $650 million and a 2009 industrial sales output of approximately 10.6 billion RMB.[50]

I traveled from Thames Town to Luo Dian. Traveling between two points on the outer edge in an urban megacity can take hours. The local bus that we took was crowded with rural migrants. On one side of the bus we saw fields and small manufacturing workshops. On the other side we saw the encroaching advance of Shanghai's urban development: malls, real estate developments, and car sales lots. My traveling companion, despite living not more than ten miles from the area we were passing through, was shocked by what she saw, which she likened to the rural poverty in the hinterlands. Her shock gave way to the familiar disappointment when we actually got to Luo Dian after two hours.

If there is any feeling that connects my experiences visiting the towns (except for Thames Town whose appearance matched the website version), it was a sense of uncertainty. Am I here? Is this it? I found that I began to imagine a stereotypical view of the so-called nation I was about to visit, and any deviation from that perception set me into a doubtful state of mind. In the case of Luo Dian, we didn't know we were actually there until I was reassured, not by a Scandinavian-style building, but by the statues. The first statue I spotted was a Viking helmet, with long braids attached. Next came the mini Viking ship with oars sticking out. The last was a tiny reindeer. These, apparently, are the markings of Northern Europe. The individual homes lacked cultural markers (but they did have individual garages, befitting the town's proximity to Shanghai's Volvo headquarters). The public squares were more spirited attempts to render a central town church and a common square. Campanella describes Luo Dian as a "Neo-Nordic" reinterpretation of Sweden's oldest town, Sigtuna, founded in 980 (Luo Dian's manmade lake is based on Sigtuna's Lake Mälare).[51] For good measure, the developers threw in monuments from Iceland and Denmark, replicas of the Althingi (Iceland's parliament), and a copy of the Little Mermaid statue.[52] I didn't see these replicas, but I did see statues of naked children playing and in free repose, with inscriptions at their bases reading "Hope" and "Expectation."

Hassenpflüg, who gave his grudging stamp of approval to An Ting, was far more scathing about Luo Dian, which he describes as "a travesty of the Chinese city. The satellite city is Chinese. Its centre is dressed in Scandinavian clothes. That's about it."[53] I would amend that Luo Dian is undressed in Scandinavian clothes. Here, nudity is the new element that makes the nature/nation dyad even kinkier. In other words, nature and freedom are the dyads here, in contrast to An Ting's heavy reliance on carbon-esque images and descriptions of highly technical advances.

But, despite the thrill of the promise of Scandinavian sexual promiscuity in the pastoral landscape, Luo Dian was pretty empty. Like Zhu Jia Jiao, the other environmental-themed development (near the region's famous ancient "water towns"), Luo Dian is a famous historical site. It was the location of an epic battle, the proverbial last stand before the Japanese invaded in 1937. The carnage and intensity of the battle earned Luo Dian the moniker "the grinding mill of flesh and blood."[54] Despite their three-to-one troop advantage, the Chinese were hampered by superior Japanese firepower. More than 50 percent of the Chinese troops were killed, and after Luo Dian was lost, the Japanese takeover of Shanghai was inevitable.

The stains of the past have been washed away by the supposed ecological freedoms of the Northern Europeans and the glorification of other invaders in faraway countries. It's not difficult to imagine why real estate developers ignore the bloody history of invasion in favor of the sanitized and surreal landscape of suburbia. But I suggest another cultural "invasion" is at play under the Nordic helmets.

## LOOKING FOR PU JIANG

If An Ting is the "Mercedes Benz" of the nine towns, and Luo Dian the Scandinavian sex-ski lodge, I suppose Pu Jiang aims to be the Versace (Fiat, Vespa?) of the bunch. Pu Jiang is the closest of the nine towns to downtown Shanghai and is supposed to hold eighty thousand residents and cost about five billion yuan to build.[55] Pu Jiang Town was developed by Shanghai High Power Investment OCT Corporation.[56] According to a luxury property sales brochure I collected (accompanied by gorgeous photographs for "Città de Pujiang"), the project "re-imagines the traditional positioning of the court-yard and villa structure, and the villa's light-filled sunken family room, ground floor living room and bedroom all enjoy fantastic views of the court-yard through elegant French windows."

We spent an hour looking at different real estate developments in the area without successfully finding Pu Jiang, until we found some elderly volunteers in orange vests, passing the time at a bus stop at nine on a Sunday morning, who finally pointed us in the right direction. We kept on expecting an Italian look, which my traveling companion imagined as something like Roman ruins. When we finally got to the Venice Bank and the advertisement contrasting two ancient doors, one medieval European, the other traditional Chinese, we finally found what we were looking for.

What buildings we did find looked more modern than classical, a result of the architect's more conceptual approach to the design. This approach to "Italian" design is expressed "in the interaction with the environmental conditions, intended as both natural elements and area conformation." The area, still dotted with agricultural land uses, is crisscrossed by water, invoking the Venetian urban waterscape. According to the designers, "The system of settlements is divided into . . . the 'top grade neighbourhood'; the 'standard neighbourhood'; the 'ecological neighbourhood'"; and a surrounding greenbelt.[57]

Pu Jiang is also the district where thousands of the eighteen thousand families displaced by the world expo were relocated, into a development known as Pu Jiang Expo Garden, the large-scale housing complex built as partial compensation for their homes. Project planners said that in order to stay in line with the theme of the 2010 Shanghai World Expo, Pu Jiang Expo Garden was designed as a new concept of urban life that provides "residents with not only regular services and facilities, but also something absent in many Chinese cities—a green environment, with streams and wooded areas." And "Green Pu Jiang" is not just in the aesthetics. According to Xing Tonghe, the chief architect of Pu Jiang Expo Garden, energy conservation technologies have been applied in building the houses, such as the use of outer wall heat preservation materials that could help save 50 percent of daily energy use.[58]

According to an explanatory panel at an off-site exhibit on the world expo that I visited before the official opening, "the relocation has been widely acclaimed by residents." Expo public relations material hammers this point relentlessly: "The relocation of households for the World Expo sticks to the people-first philosophy, and has lived up to its name of 'Sunshine Relocation,' as the relocation policy is transparent. The living conditions and qualities of the relocated families have been enhanced after the relocation. The World Expo relocation project was welcomed by the relocated families as it is in the interest of these households. . . . [M]ost of the relocated families were satisfied with the relocation work." Highly sensitive to critiques on human rights abuses, expo officials took every opportunity to point out how the relocation enacted the expo slogan of "Better City, Better Life" when extolling the "highly praised design" of the Pu Jiang Expo Garden. One of the centerpieces was a gigantic door, which "opens to new life," reminding us that the metaphor of the doorway is dual: both pathway to openness and means of closure.[59]

But, according to Human Rights in China and other activists, the Shanghai World Expo relocation has been a human rights disaster for local residents. For example, Hu Yan and her family faced a five-year ordeal when their home was demolished without their consent. They became the objects of official coercion, threats, and detention as they tried to petition the authorities, and Hu ultimately came to New York to (unsuccessfully) plead her family's case.[60]

## CONCLUSION

The eco-desire underpinning the idea of one planet/one world is a key part of the ideological rhetoric of the world expo, as I argue in the next chapter. At the same time, this idea of one planet/one world is part and parcel of the Disneyland "It's a Small World" ride, itself conceived at a world expo for an American corporate brand. Fifty years after the dolls put that chorus into the heads of millions of American and global consumers, the storyline is roaring back, but with new green twists in China and in global markets. From the postwar "American Century" and the globalization of American land-use patterns (suburbanization and auto-dependence), we now have suburbanization with Chinese characteristics. They are recognizably similar to each other in their green, antiurban form, even as they differ slightly on what elements of ecology they emphasize: clean air (Thames Town), low-carbon living (An Ting), water (Pu Jiang), or eco-friendly houses (Northern European Town). For real estate developers, the so-called green architecture trend did not die with the failures of the One City, Nine Towns initiative. Rather, the trend has accelerated throughout China, in developments called Eco Town, Garden Villa, Green World Garden, Greenery Villas, and Beautiful Garden. One recent chronicler of the phenomenon argues that this trend is less about actual green technologies or developments than about high-quality and luxury developments, quoting a developer that green "is a way to sell real estate in a competitive market."[61]

Green developments, thus, flourish despite their relative failure in the One City, Nine Towns context. The persistence of the nature/nation link is not surprising, given the larger cultural and social anxieties of the Chinese middle class over the conditions of their own environments. Thus, is it important to understand suburban nature not just as a pale imitation of its U.S. antecedents, since the real estate development, urban, and national contexts are radically different. The relationship between nature and nation carries particular ideological baggage in the context of the world expo, as we see in the next chapter.

# Imagining Ecological Urbanism
# at the World Expo

From the empty streets on Shanghai's periphery, I traveled to the city's glittering entrée to the global stage, the 2010 World Expo. Billed as the largest gathering of nations ever assembled, more than seventy million people visited the expo site on the Shanghai waterfront during a six-month span. In an old stereoscopic view of the 1893 Chicago Columbian Exposition that I own, a packed scene of thousands of men with moustaches wearing bowler hats and a few ladies in fashionable dresses faced the cameras with a line at the bottom describing the scene as "A Surging Sea of Humanity." Visiting the Shanghai World Expo is exactly how I imagined being in that surging sea of flesh. I waited a full three hours to merely get in through the gates (I faced an extra fifteen-minute delay, stopped by the gate checker fearful that my AIDS Walk T-shirt signaled that I was a possible protester rather than a clueless tourist who had grabbed the first clean shirt I could find). Once inside, I waited another three hours to go to the U.S. Pavilion. Another day, I waited three hours to get into the visually stunning U.K. Pavilion, and another two to get into Happy Street, a land of plastic sheep and stroopwaffel in the Dutch Pavilion. Two days after one of my visits, the single-day attendance total was more than one million people. This attendance represented the largest number ever to go to a world expo (and one of the larger single-day events in recent history). Even on relatively "low-attendance" days (in the 500,000 to 750,000 range), lines to get into the $164 million Saudi Arabian Pavilion (a.k.a. the Moon Boat, meant to evoke the desert) stretched to nine hours. Regular waits for the other popular national pavilions (Japan, Russia, Germany, and Spain) ranged from three to seven hours. Although I can't say why all those people waited in those long lines (Americans are well known, according to U.S. theme-park industry research, to resist lines that make us wait even one hour), I know why *I* did. I wanted to know what the Shanghai 2010 World Expo was all about, particularly its view of the ecological future it imagined and represented to its national and international audiences.

What shaped the twists and turns of the ecological plotline of the expo? First and foremost, the event was extolled as yet another sign of China's emerging ascendancy in global affairs, as the first expo organized in mainland Asia (previously, the only Asian host nation was Japan). Similar to how the United States used it various expos in the late nineteenth and early twentieth centuries, China used large-scale events like the Beijing Olympics and the Shanghai World Expo to project its power. Large international events both condensed and consolidated national and cultural identities, particularly as China is moving to global economic hegemon status and seeking the cultural power and influence to match.

Certainly, China's economic strength was a major factor in why it was awarded the event. The entire official expo budget was RMB 28.6 billion (4.2 billion U.S. dollars).[1] Following just two years after the global spectacle of the Beijing Olympics, the expo was Shanghai's turn to shine. The site was also the largest physical expo site in the history of these events, at 528 hectares (about one and a half times the size of New York City's Central Park) and split into two parts along the banks of the Huangpu River.[2] According to expo organizers, the Shanghai Expo is also host to the largest numbers of participating organizations and nations (almost two hundred) and the "first to take place in a developing country."[3]

The other major related storyline about the World Expo was about Shanghai, eager to paint itself as China's shining beacon to the world. Shanghai exemplified China's aspirations to leap out of its developing country status, from the first three decades of Communist rule until the 1980s. Shanghai is, and sees itself as, one of the leading cities in the world, equal to Hong Kong and Tokyo in Asia, and New York, Paris, and London in the West. One (non-official) expo guidebook suggests that the World Expo "is Shanghai amplified, distilled, and celebrated, in a festival of cosmopolitan exhibitionism. . . . Shanghai's global significance has nourished a self-absorption that would be insufferable, were it not that the city harbors the entire world within itself, its limitless self-regard entirely ameliorated by an equally unlimited openness. For Shanghai, hosting the world is a mission so natural it almost seems an *original destiny*."[4]

Since the inception of world expos, the relationship between city and nation has always been a complicated dance. This same account reads: "Cities accommodate Expos, significantly define them, participate in their glories, and absorb some . . . fraction of their impact. . . . [T]he Expo has been energized by creative tensions between the principal levels of large-scale social organization, provoking a prolonged public meditation upon relations between the individual, the city, the nation, and the world."[5] Since 1992, Shanghai has attracted some $120 billion in foreign direct investment. But, despite the red-hot economic climate in Shanghai, urban infrastructure and other living conditions have been relatively neglected. According to Daniel Vasella, the head of the International Business Leaders Advisory Council for the mayor of Shanghai and chairman of the global pharmaceutical firm Novartis, quality of life concerns matter to the large global workforce and expatriate community in Shanghai. He said, "The government is now more aware of quality-of-life issues. . . . They realize that if you can't deliver [a good standard of living], people won't want to live there."[6] Thus "quality of life," of which environment is a key (albeit vague) term, is an important component of Shanghai's urban and economic development strategy. Simply put, world expo preparation equals "urban development on steroids."[7]

Indeed, Shanghai took its mission seriously, spending far more than its "official direct cost" of $4.2 billion. The *China Economic Daily* reported that the "real cost" of the event was in the range of $45 billion to $58 billion (exceeding what was spent on the 2008 Beijing Olympics, themselves the most expensive Olympics ever).[8] Shanghai used the expo as a catalyst to build new infrastructure and improve transportation links (including a maglev train that attains speeds of up to 310 miles per hour); the city built new airport terminals, massively expanded its subway lines, constructed a $700 million riverfront promenade in a sprucing up of the historic Bund, resurfaced hundreds of roads, and repaved sidewalks. The growth of the subway system was particularly impressive. A system that began just fifteen years ago is now the largest in the world in terms of both the number of stations and the length of track (420 kilometers, outstripping both London at 408 kilometers and New York City at 368).[9]

Among these many storylines, the one that I am most interested in is how themes of ecology and urbanism were represented and communicated at the Shanghai World Expo, often to multiple and competing audiences. The official guide to the expo stated: "Expo 2010 is the first world exposition that focuses on the issues of [the] city." It explained that the event showcases "interesting examples of *sustainable development* and *harmonious society*."[10] China experimented with these themes in its pavilion at the expo in Aichi, Japan.[11] The official slogan in English in 2010 was "Better City, Better Life!" How did the expo represent "sustainable development" and "harmonious society"? What was at stake in these particular representations of "Better City, Better Life" at the expo?

To answer these questions, I looked at expo publicity documents and government press releases, and used my own wanderings on this so-called epic stage, especially in the theme pavilions. Compared to the more architecturally compelling national pavilions that reflected the worldview of the nations that hosted, designed, and built them, the theme pavilions are a more accurate worldview of the expo planners and the Chinese hosts (although only one of the five theme pavilions was designed by a Chinese company, they arguably still responded more directly to their Chinese clients). As in Dongtan and the One City, Nine Towns suburban developments, the image of ecology was everywhere, although the specific individuals and ecosystems are not. Again, eco-desire is about representation trumping polluted reality. The prominent narrative about ecology is not about valiant individuals fighting corporate polluters and enacting social, scientific, or legislative change (or signaled by heroic prophets in the U.S. historical and cultural context like Henry David Thoreau, John Muir, or Rachel Carson). Neither is the story about the quite significant economic investments in sustainability (which are indeed substantial) in China.

Rather, the major plotline of the story is the (old) techno-utopian fantasy that technology itself can solve multiple problems. These include environmental pollution and conflicts between rich and poor, urban and rural. Technology enables the imagined "harmonious" reconciliation of urban and rural development, and helps consolidate new middle-class consumption of ecological subjects in China. Eco-desire at the Shanghai World Expo was not just techno-utopianism unmasked, but its culmination. In that sense, the dominant story of Expo 2010 was actually a new Chinese version of a very old expo story, one that glorifies technology as savior, in this case, for a world facing environmental and social ruin.

Although technological utopianism at world expositions is not new (technologies that debuted at world's fairs include the telephone in 1876 in Philadelphia, and X-rays, the typewriter, and an early version of the fax machine in 1904 in St. Louis, in addition to the showcasing of electricity and the Ferris wheel in 1893 in Chicago), the "ecological branding" of world cities is relatively new.[12] The special theme pavilions are arguably the clearest manifestation of China's branding of sustainable urbanism. In this version of modernity, epic skyscrapers are not enough. Technology and sustainability take center stage to make the new growing world cities sources of wonder and order, rather than fear and chaos. Thus, Shanghai is contrasted with Lagos in the global imaginary or with Calcutta so famously described in all of its sensuous negativity in Paul Ehrlich's influential 1968 tract *The Population Bomb*. At the Shanghai World Expo, eco-desire is technology and sustainability conjoined, managed, and packaged by state and business to make urban growth desirable and not a diseased trend to be feared.

## WORLD'S FAIR DREAMING

Over the past 150-plus years, since the advent of world expositions in the mid-nineteenth century, they have always told a national story and explicitly aimed to leave their cultural, psychological, and architectural marks long after the actual fairgrounds have been dismantled.[13] The largest and most famous of the expositions are the so-called universal expositions, so named because they supposedly transcend time and place. They are, and have been, particularly effective repositories of memories, utopian fantasies, and primal fears. A recent French exhibit on the history of the world's fairs calls them "Dreamlands." The 1939 New York World's Fair highlighted a Salvador Dali-designed pavilion called "The Dream of Venus," where a melted façade contained inside it a choreographed water ballet and reproductions of Botticelli's *Birth of Venus* and Leonardo's *Mona Lisa*.

Historians have also noted the darker side of the fairs' dreams, which one writer describes as "the fascination with recreating the world in miniature, with controlling and shaping the world . . . the urge to gather the world together, to control and display it."[14] One place where this impulse to "control and display" was clearest was the Midway Plaisance in Chicago in 1893, where so-called authentic villages approximated those in the Philippines,

Alaska, and Hawaii. Colonialism, imperialism, and racism shaped these representations of the "world" at the same time that the inhabitants of these villages (often paid entertainers) created their own communities and resisted the racist and sexualized gaze of their predominantly white middle-class audiences.

Despite their supposed universalism and transcendence (a discourse that the world's fairs share with the modern Olympics, both of which emerged from Britain at the height of its imperial power), world's fairs reveal far more about the power and ambitions of their host nations and cities than about the "world" they purportedly represent. The very first of these in 1851, "The Great Exhibition of the Works of Industry of All Nations" (also known as the Crystal Palace), showed the glories of the Industrial Revolution at the height of Queen Victoria's reign and the global power of the British Empire. The Eiffel Tower is the most famous remnant of the 1889 World's Fair. Chicago's hosting of the 1893 Columbian Exposition paralleled America's increasingly imperial excursions in Cuba and the Philippines in that tumultuous decade. The 1915 Panama-Pacific International Exposition highlighted San Francisco's recovery from the devastations of the 1906 earthquake and fire; the 1939 New York World's Fair set up a technologically optimistic narrative through the GM Futurama Ride in the "World of Tomorrow," a testament to America's utopianism during the Great Depression on the brink of World War II; and the 1962 Seattle World's Fair left the Space Needle as an icon to the Space Age.

Examining the history of world expos reveals the particular historical contexts of the host countries and the cultural concerns of their time. To be sure, the old expo impulse to display and control are prominent in contemporary Chinese theme parks, most notably the Beijing World Park (the site of Jia Zhangke's melancholic film *The World*), Shenzen's Windows of the World (where you can ride a camel among the Egyptian pyramids, and a pony in the American West), and in the hundreds of "ethnic villages" that dot the

Chinese tourist landscape. Yet despite their particularity, expos also hold certain themes and approaches constant, chief among these the valorization and conflation of technology and spectacle.

## DEFINING BETTER CITY, BETTER LIFE

In earlier chapters, I discussed how the language of "betterment" and quality was applied to various land-use and development projects. The "natural capital" and ecological discourse that saturated Dongtan and Huangbaiyu represent the desire to add "value" to economically depressed rural spaces. This desire (value = rural + technology = ecology) was also a recurrent theme in the Shanghai World Expo. Shanghai's economic, urban, and environmental policy worked together to produce the improved city that promises a "Better City, Better Life," according to the official expo slogan. A vision of nature and environment is a key component to the city's recent history, what one U.S.-based planner working in Shanghai calls "the greatest transformation of a piece of earth in history."[15]

For local authors and politicians, the Shanghai World Expo was the primary agent of this urban transformation. Dreams of Shanghai hosting a world expo span more than a century. In 1905, the Shanghai-based novelist Wu Jianren rewrote the eighteenth-century novel *The Story of the Stone*, in which the hero, Jia Baoyu, visited a world expo staged in the city's Pudong area. In 1910, another Shanghai novelist, Lu Shi'e, predicted in his novel *New China* that the world expo would come to Shanghai one hundred years from then. According to one plot summary, the novel's protagonist, Lu Yunxiang, wakes up in an entirely new and unrecognizable Shanghai. In this new reimagined city, "extraterritoriality on foreign concessions is abolished, foreigners who used to be arrogant and dominating are now respectful to the Chinese, and innumerable changes have taken place in the street, those trams which used to have lots of accidents with pedestrians are now changed into underground trains . . ., the ground is hollowed to make way for tunnels, where rails are installed and electric lights are lit day and night, and trains flow to and fro like flying. . . . [A] huge bridge is built across Huang Pu River to link Pu Dong with Shanghai, . . . so as to facilitate the big Exposition to be held in Pu Dong, which is already as thriving as Shanghai."[16] At the time, responses to this novel were mixed, with the audience finding it too utopian and unrealistic. With the actualization of the "dream" of the Shanghai World Expo, these authors have been widely celebrated as prescient visionaries.

These dreams are immortalized in a bronze statue at the Shanghai Urban Planning Exhibition Center that commemorates the actual moment when the seven members of the BIE awarded the expo to Shanghai in 2002. For much of the next eight years after the initial announcement, ubiquitous slogans and images about the world expo blanketed the city, ranging from corporate advertising to state-sponsored exhortations. Banners proclaimed, "Thank people for their understanding and support for relocation," often on the sites where large-scale demolition of housing and businesses had occurred. Other banners proclaimed, "Hand in hand, eradicate messiness and untidiness."[17]

These notions of "messiness" and "untidiness" bring us back to James Scott in *Seeing Like a State*. He argues that governments and bureaucrats "see" the conditions that "need" improvement in vastly different ways than the actual inhabitants of these so-called defective places. Thus, where the state (in this case, the Shanghai municipality) seeks to consolidate and exercise its power using the guise (even if earnestly believed) of improvements as its raison d'être, local residents often argue that such improvements create new harms or are based on new logics that do not necessarily represent their own worldview.

Take, for instance, the case of the much-vaunted Shanghai subway system. Experiences and opinions vary greatly, depending on the particular circumstances and subject position of the person asked. Anecdotally, one family friend lost their business due to new station construction, but was able to receive partial compensation, which she used for college tuition for her daughter. Another of my mother's oldest friends complains bitterly about the cost of the metro system, preferring the bus instead. Of course, as a U.S.-based visitor to Shanghai, I love the trains, with the mobility they afford me, and the clear maps that make the city accessible to me as a tourist. In theory, I love the bus too, because bus systems are aimed at locals, particularly old people and people with kids, but the reality is that I only ever was on the bus with my mom and her friends. Once, on a bus ride with my mom and her friend, a rural migrant to the city was transporting extremely large packages and taking up several seats. One cranky Shanghainese lady complained loudly about the rural migrants who didn't know how to behave ("low-quality") and was shouted down by other locals who pointed out that the city relied on the labor of the migrants. That was a moment that could have happened only on a bus, as the migrant wouldn't have been allowed on the metro (the packages were too large to fit through the security screening machine), a moment where public space and political discourse about migrants in the city exploded into cacophonous view.

The rather obvious point I'm trying to make here, is that "better" means different things to different people, and people's ideas of whether something was indeed an improvement may change over time. The notion of "betterment" is not complete but contingent and highly contested. The variability of "better" is also quite literal in the expo case. Despite the prominence of "betterment" in the official expo slogan, the official meaning changes based on whether it is aimed at English- or Chinese-speaking audiences. There are often multiple layers of meaning at the expo, evident in the actual translation of official materials. In Chinese, the slogan is literally 城市,让生活更美好! Chengshi, rang shenghuo geng meihao! (roughly, "The city makes life better or more beautiful").

As one China scholar notes, the expo slogan and advertising simultaneously enact a discourse on modernity and "proper behavior," and a notion of behavior historically and culturally based on the concept of *wenming* (crudely translated as "civilized"). Leo Ou-Fen Lee identified the genealogy of the term from its Japanese roots at the turn of the century, through its propagandist uses by the nationalist movement in the 1930s and its relationship to hygiene discourse and injunctions on proper behavior. *Wenming* in the world expo context was used by the government to exhort the Shanghainese to move away from their local customs and poor behavior and toward a global cosmopolitan worldview.[18] Government action included the banning of wearing pajamas in public and explicit descriptions of how to ride an escalator and ride on the bus (another scholar gives these examples: "stand on the right, walk on the left, use the escalators in a wenming way." "Don't spit on buses, be more wenming").[19] For example, bringing gigantic packages on a bus would be an example of a non-wenming thing to do. One young Shanghainese journalist criticized the pajama ban (and explained its roots). He described the bans on inappropriate attire and exhortations of "Pajamas don't go out of the door; be a civilized resident for the Expo,'" and the volunteer "pajama policemen" who patrolled the neighborhoods and told pajama wearers to go home and change.[20]

In other instances, the slight differences between the English and Chinese versions of the expo publicity materials were equally discordant. According to the online English explanation of the expo theme, "Better City, Better Life" represented "the commonality of the whole humankind for a better living in future urban environments." In contrast, the Chinese description of the theme explained that the expo "is a festival of discussing human urban lives. It is a symphony of creativity and fusion (of different cultures and traditional culture). This will become a wonderful conversation about human civilization." Where the urban environment is dominant in the English version, the Chinese version also discusses cities, but more around the issues of culture and civilization. The symbolism of the emblem and the mascot also differ. The English version of the emblem described the image as three people (you, me, him/her holding hands symbolizing the big family of mankind). The Chinese description claimed that it derives its image from the Chinese character "shi (世)" ("world") which represents the concept of the world expo: "Understanding, communication, happy-together, and cooperation." Most obviously, the English version of the website highlighted the pavilions from other nations, whereas the Chinese version highlighted the pavilions from the outlying Chinese provinces. A close reading of the differences between the official expo-related materials (text descriptions, videos, and photographs) revealed important content shifts depending on the audience, with the Chinese content receiving considerably less "environmental" material· than the English-language version, while increasing the "cultural" content in discussing the expo themes.

Despite the lack of formal usage of the "betterment" discourse in Chinese, the closest linguistic equivalent circulates around city "health" and city "illness." Around 1998–2002, influential urban research introduced the discourse of *chengshi bing* (city illness). These early works define *chengshi bing* as the problems that occur during the process of a city's development, which include traffic, shortages of water and energy, polluted environments, and an "imbalance" of energy inputs. In addition, city illness is caused by over-population and the speed and scale of urbanization processes.[21] The core idea is that sick cities can be remedied with physical infrastructure that clears up the various "clogs" in the system, a representation of ideal city life that runs through the Pavilion of City Being, the only theme pavilion designed by Chinese companies, as I'll discuss below.

## HAIBAO HARMONY

If you traveled to Shanghai from 2002 to 2010, you probably saw lots of Haibao, the official mascot of the Shanghai World Expo. According to the English version of the expo website, the mascot was created from a Chinese character meaning people, and embodies "the character of Chinese culture." The Chinese version focused on the meaning of Haibao from the perspective of the characters themselves (*hai* = sea, and *bao* = treasure). Created by a Taiwanese designer and selected through competition, each of Haibao's elements is imbued with meaning—"the blue color: implying inclusivement [*sic*] and imagination, symbolizing China which is full of hope and potential of development. Hair: resembling the rolling waves. . . . Face: simplistic cartoonish expression, Eyes: round body, evoking beautiful feelings for harmonious life, cute and lovely, Fist: the thumb is raised to praise and welcome friends from the whole worlds, Big feet: standing firmly on the ground and giving strong support to the outspread arms, which implies that China has the capability and determination to hold a wonderful world exposition."[22] Most important (to the organizers), Haibao symbolized that "only by supporting each other and living in *harmony* between man and nature, people and society, and people among themselves can urban life be better."[23] For most people, Haibao was a souvenir, sold everywhere on Shanghai streets. Others note its resemblance to Gumby.[24] My own favorite picture of Haibao was one I took on a department store escalator, which told people to use *wenming* behavior, to "properly use the elevator because the World Expo concerns everyone."

Haibao's purported representation of the "harmony between man and nature, people and society, people among themselves" is tied to another important question about the world expo. Just how "green" was it? In the one hand, infrastructure investments, particularly the expansion of the subway, were a long-term strategy that may reduce air pollution associated with cars. A mostly positive in-depth 2009 assessment of the environmental dimensions of the world expo conducted by the United Nations Environment Program praised Shanghai for having improved its energy mix and reduced its reliance on coal to 51 percent of its energy needs in 2007 from 64 percent in 2001, and for improving its air quality (a major critique leveled at Beijing during the Olympics).[25]

On the other hand, one of the main defining features of the expo is that it was, by its central fact, unsustainable. A minicity of more than two hundred buildings was built on a space large enough to accommodate hundreds of thousands of people, and virtually none of the buildings remained six months later.[26] Yet, the park and recreational infrastructure left behind is "green." Some nations transported their buildings back home or donated them to provinces in China. Another journalist wrote of an "apparent, and glaring, contradiction," that is, that with "the promotion of sustainable urban development practices a key goal, the huge international event champions priorities that hardly seem to square with spending hundreds of millions of dollars on the construction of nearly 200 booths and buildings, nearly all of which are designed to last only for the six-month duration of the show."[27] The expo site was also home to the cradle of the industrial history of Shanghai, most emblematically the 130-year-old Jiangnan Shipyard. The shipyard was moved to Changxing Island, an island on the way to Chongming Island. Thus, in one sense, the transformation of the Shanghai waterfront as a place of leisure and "green" activities echoes a broader global transformation of working waterfronts in gentrifying cities. Polluting industry and manufacturing is moved out of the central city as land values rise, connected to the improving quality of life and the environment, what one U.S. urban and environmental scholar calls "the greenwave" of gentrification.[28]

## DREAMING THE GREEN FUTURE IN THE THEME PAVILIONS

Despite the glaring contradictions embedded in rapid construction and rapid deconstruction of the expo and the various transportation and environmental costs of getting the seventy-six million visitors to the site, the event highlighted its so-called green features. These green building features were clearest in the Expo Boulevard, built by the U.S.-based architects SBA

Figure 8. World Expo. Happy Valley with China National Pavilion in the background.
Photo by author, 2010

and engineered by the German firm Knippers Heibig. The Boulevard was lined with six large "Sunny Valleys" made of steel and plastic that operated as gigantic light and rain collectors. The water collected was channeled to the plants on the site.[29] Shanghai organizers made audience seats out of milk packages, handbags and tissues out of recycled paper, and used low-energy-consuming LED screens, acoustic devices, and electricity-powered vehicles in the Expo Park.

Three of the theme pavilions (Urbanian, City Being, and Urban Planet) were housed in a gigantic structure (one of the few buildings that remained in place after the expo). The west exhibition hall was the largest column-free interior space in the world. According to the official guide, the building was inspired by the concept of "paper folding" and the traditional Shanghai shi-kumen housing architectural style. The remaining pavilions (Footprint and Future) were held on the Puxi side, in repurposed industrial buildings. Four of the five pavilions were designed by non-Chinese companies, representing the same tensions and dynamics of nationalism/transnational cultures in the broader city and eco-city-building trends discussed in earlier chapters.

The large theme pavilion structure was also defined by "green building standards," which included green walls, solar paneled rooftops, and energy-saving design. The five-thousand-square-meter green walls were billed as the largest vertical eco-surfaces in the world, while the rooftop panels had an annual generating capacity of 2.8 million kilowatts.[30] Like the Shanghai Tower discussed in chapter 3, green-building structures in Shanghai have become a symbol of technological and ecological sophistication in excess. Large-scale (the "largest and best" solar panels, green walls, etc.) instruments received far more attention than individual behaviors, although argu-ably both are necessary to achieve environmental benefits.

The City Being, Urban Planet, and Future pavilions were the most sig-nificant centerpieces at the expo in terms of representing the dreams and aspirations of the "City" and the "Environment." Each one was unique in its presentation of technology and the experience of the visitors through space and time. For instance, the Pavilion of City Being presented a fascinating view of the city through the theme of "vigor" and metabolism, which most clearly illustrates the opposite of "city illness." This pavilion was designed and planned by President Xu Jiang and Vice President Song Jianming of the China Academy of Art. Xu Jiang said in an interview, "We really hope that our audiences come here not for a fad or just for fun. They come here to understand the city and to know what the city is. This is the original goal of the expo and this is also why our country invested so much money in this expo to make Chinese people make them realize their world citizenship."[31] The pavilion design changed eight times. According to Xu, the original idea and symbol of the pavilion was to represent the life of the city as a tree with the branches of the tree being streets. However, this idea proved unpopular. In the final design, the pavilion followed a person's experience in a city. According to the designers, the pavilion followed the spatial experience of someone who enters a city, arriving in a city in a train station, taking a subway to city streets, city garden, and the city square. These matched the sections of the pavilion, which illustrate city life from a "human-scale perspective: *entering* the city, *feeling* the city, *reading* the city, and *hoping* a better city."[32]

As visitors entered the dark space of the pavilion, placards read, "A City is an Organism throbbing with energy and metabolism." After the panels, I was then channeled into a huge room flanked by old trains. The back of the room switched between a giant screen with a train schedule and global stock prices, flanked by "vigor stations" associate with various global sites: New York, Vatican City, Oxford, and Houston. According to the official expo guidebook, "in a metaphorical way with *high scientific technologies,* a city is compared to a living being consisting of body and soul. Metabolism and circulation are important for it to function properly."[33] These metaphors were visually represented by a five-minute audio-visual show. The ceiling was covered in a large number of screens that start as a bright blue sky.

Suddenly a large airplane flew over the crowd, which elicited gasps from the surprised crowd (I watched this scene more than twenty times, and each time the reaction was the same). The image transformed to a series of bouncing dots, with an aural accompaniment of trains, then moved into a series of fantastic lights, and the hyper–*Blade Runner* city views; orange images of traffic ran through the skyscrapers as the city shrank in size, surrounded by a series of circling blue lights, exploding finally into lights that end up as a visual of circuits and computer bits as numbers (financial information and markets) distilled into a rainbow of lights, individual water blobs, each with organic self-contained cities.

The organic and self-contained cities visually resembled Arup's plans for Dongtan. The view of these unnamed networked cities dove down suddenly, à la Google Earth, zooming in on Shanghai and the expo site itself. That pavilion also situated Shanghai among the great cities of the world in a sur-round-sound film, in a teleological narrative of travel, progress, and tech-nology. The video, along with the entire City Being Pavilion itself, enacted a theory of the technological, networked global finance/world city.[34]

This concept of experiencing the city as a resident may at first glance represent the ideological opposite of *Seeing Like a State*. But that's not the case in the City Being Pavilion. In "Seeing Like an Eco-City," the political scien-tist Warren Magnusson argues that to "see like a city" means to "recognize that the static order we so often associate with the state is an illusion. Things are in flux." While seeing like a state involves a search for order and control, to see like a city is to be uncertain about "the politics of the moment" or its meaning. Rather, we can only "trace its patterns, note its instabilities, and keep watch for signs of change."[35] On the one hand, the pavilion mirrors the "experience" of entering the city, but its optic is still more like that of a state in its search of control and order. In the Pavilion of City Being's imaginings, you entered a globally networked city, one that prioritized the airplane, travel of people, and unfettered flow of financial information, and where the advanced network eco-city reigns supreme.

In another section of the same building, the Pavilion of Urban Planet dis-plays similar ideologies through its visualization of the core themes of "humanity in symbiosis with the city and planet."[36] Here, environmental images and themes were more explicit, beginning with a cowboy Haibao with a giant globe greeting people entering the line. This pavilion was designed by Triad Berlin, which won the commission over 150 other firms. According to its website, Triad is one of Germany's most successful communication agencies, specializing in creating "emotionally intelligent communication formats in spaces."[37] According to the expo website, the logic of the pavilion was split:

"The scenography combines traditions of Western narratives with motives taken from the Chinese Feng shui heritage. With a two-part structure, the exhibition focuses on the ambivalent character of cities: On the one hand, they destruct the environment, on the other, they are also places for creating value, prosperity and technological innovations."[38]

Nonetheless, this "ambivalence" was a source, not of tension, but of the essential "Taoist" philosophy. Here, according to Triad, "If the balance of the elements is preserved, this dynamic will progress in harmony. However, if the balance gets lost, it can also unleash destructive forces. Both aspects are reflected in the two-part structure of the exhibition as well as in the overall architecture of the pavilion."[39] Thus, in Triad's words, the architecture of the "experience" ascended through a "Road of Crisis," whereas the "Road of Solutions" suggested what will "solve" the crisis—technology. The problems sections—the Road of Crisis—was split into five sections that built on and adapted "natural elements" essential to Chinese philosophy: water—fire—metal—wood—earth. Thus, according to the designers, the "Road of Crisis" visualized "water shortage, water pollution, the massive burning of fossil fuels as well as the possible consequences in terms of climate change, depletion of our resources of oil, steel or copper, the extinction of species, and, last but not least, the production of non-perishable waste."[40] To visualize the crisis, five gigantic ticking metronomes represented that "time is running out." Although German-designed, the ecological information was presented in terms most understandable for Chinese audiences. For example, the "water crisis" display was a large water tank that is covered in the different national statistics on "per capita" consumption (in this case, per capita consumption in China is 89 liters per day versus 295 liters per day in the United States).

The other "chapters" provided little visual surprise. The section on energy juxtaposed pictures of crowded urban streets filled with cars alongside melting ice caps, recalling Arup's contrast between the crowded Shanghai streets and the ecological calm of Dongtan. The room on

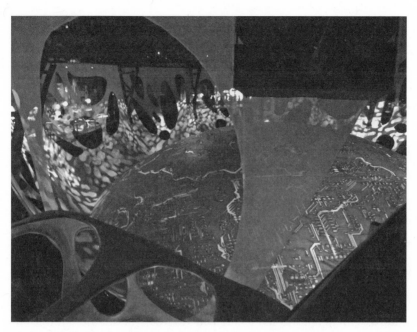

Figure 9. Triad. Photo by author, 2010

"industrialization" was filled with photos of scarred landscapes, similar to Burtynsky's China series. This section focused on apocalyptic environmental destruction, which was then followed by one titled "Nature, an Archive of Pictures." In it, robotic sounds and looping female voices emanated from brightly lit miniskyscrapers that showed images of bicycles and birds (Is it Chongming? I wondered). The last section in the "Road of Crisis" took the audience alongside a gigantic single mural of trash heaps with frightening texts about high lead rates in children.

From this depressing journey through environmental exploitation, the exhibit then switched gears to what Triad calls its "Eureka moment." Audience members walked into a completely separate room, the centerpiece of which is a giant globe, illuminated with a light and image show. Here, the visitors experienced "five spectacular metamorphoses of the hemisphere, which go along with a visible dynamic of change and adaptation. The Earth is now telling its own story."

The ideology in the "Road of Solutions" was embedded in the image of the Earth itself. The light display was clearly reminiscent of the ceiling of the City Being Pavilion, with its passage through time, space, and light. The ultimate image, the circuits that connect the "networked" globe, showed that the solutions to environmental crises are technological rather than moral or political.

Alongside the large globe, the audience walked down against minidisplays about "solutions." The sections on "ecotopia" were fascinating in this regard, as was the spotlighting of ecological design projects, ranging from the reconstruction of the New York City Highline Park to an entire eco-city panel. The eco-city section showed pictures of the San Francisco Treasure Island development and the Masdar eco-city being built in the United Arab Emirates. Dongtan was not mentioned anywhere in this section (the one mention of a Chinese ecological city on the wetlands is Liaoning). The section contained a number of pictures of spray robots, green cars, and panels extolling plans for "modern icebergs made entirely of garbage" (although why this plan would be an environmental good was never explained).

The content and structure of this exhibit argued that the solutions to environmental crises were ultimately technological. The story was about pollution's destructiveness and how new technologies restore "balance." The faith in new technologies was evident from the prominence that "bionic forms" such as space-age green cars are given. According to one description accompanying the fifteen-foot-high form, "bionics are said to be derived from the green bion and means life-like. It is the science of imitating the special abilities of plants and animals."

This faith in technology to solve the environmental crisis transcends nations and cultures. However, Triad's German origins shaped its representation of what the exhibit highlights as the "100 best practices in both the German and the international context," through global leaders in environmental technologies like Bosch and Daimler/smart. Many of the panels along the "Road of Solutions" borrowed ideas from the "Cradle to Cradle" design movement, as defined by the manifesto by the American architect William McDonough and the German environmental activist/chemist Michael Braungart. Their call is to look to nature to solve environmental problems. McDonough was, of course, the main force behind Huangbaiyu. They argue that many environmental problems can be solved by better design, and that designers should look to nature and natural systems to create healthy products, buildings, and societies. The exhibit highlighted this perspective through the repetition of bionic structures. According to Triad, these bionic forms formed the core "sceneography" (in their words) in this section: "Three-dimensional sculptures are the dominating design elements. . . . With their structures showing both a coolly technoid and a biomorphic structure, they symbolize the amalgamation of nature and technology: *Without technology there will be no eco-friendly change.* The forms of the three-dimensional sculptures are duplicated in the two-dimensional reliefs, which are used as displays for the content of the respective topics" (emphasis added).

## PAVILION OF THE FUTURE

The fetish for technology was echoed, albeit in slightly different form, in the Pavilion of the Future. Located on the older Puxi side of the river, the pavilion took place in a repurposed industrial building. A hybrid of the Chinese-designed City Being, and the German Pavilion of the Urban Planet, this pavilion was also designed by a European company but with a significant Chinese influence in the original films. Utopia and dystopia quite literally permeated the exhibit. According to the official guide, the pavilion tells how a city was "envisaged, planned and realized" in history. This view of planning draws heavily from science fiction in the opening "Dreams of Yesterday" sequence, which spotlighted dystopian views of the city through large and repeating clips from the German classic film *Metropolis*. These images were accompanied by large banners that set the scene, "a scenario composed of modern architecture and mythological buildings witness[ing] a world where Gods rule over humans." Moving from these black and white clips, the audience moved through a giant room of books on urban planning. These oversized piles of books included Fourier, Archigram, Thoreau's *Walden*, and David Harvey's *Spaces of Hope*. This odd collection of books was set against various utopian city planning schemes, including Frank Lloyd Wright's Broadacre City and Ebeneezer Howard's Garden City of Tomorrow.

The next room highlighted gigantic sculptures that represented the "9 themes of urban development." These included "Sustainability" envisioned as a scale balanced between building and trees, "Harmonious Growth" as a cluster of multicolored light rods, "Nature" as a big shiny rock (what it was—gold or uranium—was unclear), and "Urban Planning" as gigantic ants on a big rock. Narratively, the next section proclaimed that "the future is here," but to get there, the audience walked past two lonely male mannequins of so-called old-time Shanghai industrial laborers. After the exhausting walk through ideas, space, and time, a dimly lit room highlighted brilliant and strange cartoon images in a revolving loop depicting what the cities of the future—"eco city, space city, intelligence city and energy city"—will look like.

Here, the convergence of utopia and dystopia returned. In the text introduction to the "Intelligence City," the screen read: "Well, I'd like to live in a knowledge city. A Chip would let me learn without any effort at all and I'd spend my time trying to understand more complicated things. There would be big screens in the streets that would help us reflect and learn." The text for "Eco City" read: "I'd like to live in a city full of woods and animals, full of historic monuments. The factories and traffic would be under the ground and all of the space above ground would be for walking and entertaining."

The overall concept of this pavilion originated from the Spanish INGE-NIAqed Company. The Shanghai World Expo Affairs and Coordination Bureau also invited Mrs. Carmen Bueno from INGENIAqed to work as an independent consultant to help develop the concepts and themes of the Shanghai World Expo. Thus, INGENIAqed's influence was greater than the single pavilion.[41] According to an interview with Bueno, "Dream is the 'engine' that we made to 'run' this pavilion. It will lead the beautiful future-oriented trip for all thinkers, technocrats, scientists, and visitors." When asked what kind of urban experience inspired Bueno in selecting the content, she answered, "some surrealist films and literature including the utopian works which are beyond the reality gave us inspiration. This inspiration can provide various points of view. For example, we can use different ways of thinking to think about city. We can think about the question of how to build a more idealistic city."[42]

Hua Bu, a Beijing-born thirty-seven-year-old artist, designed the original animated films in this pavilion. The cartoons on the films were visually fantastic and the music contributed to the surreal atmosphere. In the "Eco City" film (see figure 10), the beginning images were of a space ship, followed in succession by a Roman bath, a magical unicorn, pipes and a factory, and a girl zapping a dragon out of a handheld machine. The factories produced a "delicious nanometer cake," and as the multiracial children jump on space age pods, a deer runs away, leading to the next city of "diverse possibilities." Here, we return in spirit to Dali's *Dream of Venus*, only this time the dream is of a surrealist and cyborgian hybrid of technology and nature.

COMPETING FUTURE NARRATIVES

How were tensions about the meaning of the city realized, expressed, and enacted at the world expo, and how did the event envision the Shanghai of the future? Before the expo, the site was home to the eighteen thousand residents discussed earlier, alongside the city's historic industrial sites, such as

Figure 10. Eco-City Film. Photo by author, 2010

*Chapter Five*

the massive Jiangnan Shipyard, the first manufacturer of rifles, cannons, and hydraulic presses, and several ten-thousand-ton ships for the United States. The ecological future in these pavilions denied and actually sublimated any place for manufacturing and industry in its vision. Industry and manufacturing were cast as vestiges of the archaic and polluted past that must be removed in the clean new technological future. Of course, this discourse, ideology, and urban development praxis are not unique to Shanghai but are ascendant in a number of "world" cities, including London and New York, that are adjusting to transitions from their historical economies and maritime pasts.[43]

One of the most striking counternarratives against the rhetoric of harmony and inevitable change could be found in listening to the stories of some of the eighteen thousand people relocated to make way for the expo site, which reveal a fundamentally different perspective. For instance, the housing rights activist Feng Zhenghu was under house arrest for his attempt to organize an "online expo" of judicial injustice for a six-month period to coincide with the world expo.[44]

Another counternarrative concerns the ideological centrality (or not) of the peasant or the industrial worker at the world expo, the implicit target for national improvement and betterment. At the same time as the expo, Cai Guoqiang, a Chinese artist, staged an art show at the Rockbund Art Museum titled "Peasant da Vincis." He conceived the show as an artistic counterpoint to the official expo narratives by celebrating the ingenuity of peasant-built inventions, including submarines, plywood airplanes, and robots. "These peasants' objects are different from the type of national, corporate power connected with the Expo," said Cai. "Until now, you only hear the collective voice of Chinese, but this is about individuals' voices."[45] Another of his slogans was "Peasants make a better city, better life," a play on the official expo slogan. He recounted that "this city's construction, its labor force, is all made up of peasants. These tall buildings, these roads, these subways, they

Figure 11. Huaming. Photo by author, 2010

were all built by peasants."[46] One of the peasants whose work is highlighted in the exhibit is named Wu Yulu. He built several talking robots, robot rats, a robot infant, artist robots that dripped paint on canvas, and a robot Damian Hirst, which created art out of colored dots. With just five years of official schooling, Wu Yulu has been mocked for years by other peasants for his robot obsession, but he expressed great pride at being included in the exhibit: "It's hugely significant. I'm representing peasants at this exhibition. I'm winning glory for peasants. It seems like peasants have been a bit neglected in the official Expo."[47] In highlighting the voices and perspectives of peasants, Cai's critique of the expo slogan foregrounded just how contested this idea of "betterment" and progress is on the ground, and showed that these terms and ideas are not objective facts to be measured. Rather, discourses saturated with "betterment" and "quality" have real-world impacts that are a source of both pride and sadness—sometimes at the same time—within a person, family, or community.

This insistent focus on the peasant contrasts to the miniaturized diorama that highlighted the "People's New Life in Huaming Model Town" (see figure 11). The little animated lifestyle figures showcase the new lives for local peasants in Tianjin eco-city in new apartments. This vision comes after an upbeat description of the model town as a "happy" example of "ecological, harmonious and habitable" living in the brave new future under the eco-city regime.

## CONCLUSION

The ultimate experience in the Pavilion of the Urban Planet was a film of tranquil nature images (trees) and sounds (birds chirping) on the domed ceiling of a small room. According to the designers, audiences reached the "exciting conclusion" after the "Road of Solutions" in the heart of the "Blue Planet" in a "fascinating panorama" show. The last message is: "We have only one world."

From the first image of the Earth from space taken by the Apollo 17 crew in 1972, the image and idea of "one world" has been central to Western environmental discourse. Its adoption within a Chinese environmental context is not itself surprising. But as the last image and idea in the special pavilions, the idea of one path has a particular cultural and ideological resonance, which dovetails with discourses of harmony and technological utopianism. The path is clear, and it's not about carbon reduction or personal choices and practices.

Rather, the one world, one path idea is grounded in technology, top-down solutions to environmental crises and a teleological narrative. Peasants have little to do with the vision but can be transformed by it into proper political and ecological subjects in the bold new future that China imagined for itself in the world expo. Although the call for "Better City, Better Life" imagines otherwise, the city/life metric is based on technology, control, and order. It is opposite to actually being in/seeing a city. The Shanghai World Expo mimics seeing like a state while it celebrates the urban. As Magnusson writes, "To see like a city is difficult, because a city is much more complicated than a state. We have to position ourselves as inhabitants, not governors, and come to terms with an order that often appears chaotic" (53).

# Conclusion

This book situates sustainability discourses in Shanghai as a particularly significant case study of ideological formations of the "environment" in a specific place at a particular moment. I have used a multimethodological analysis that takes different spatial and temporal scales into account in understanding what happened on Chongming Island, at Dongtan, in the suburbs, and at the world expo in Shanghai in the latter half of the first decade of what has been called the coming "Chinese Century." At the same time that I argue that my case study is unique and exceptional, I also suggest that the failures of imagination that animated Dongtan and the other cases are all too prominent outside of the Shanghai and Chinese context.

The methodological approach taken in this study contests those tendencies to see the "environment" as a thing fixed in time and space, but rather to see "environments" through multiple lenses—from above, below, and sideways and in the past, present, and future simultaneously. Rather that fixate on an "environmental good" or any single eco-city to rescue society from the specter of climate change—a fantasy island of ecological virtue, in other words—we need accounts of multiple environmentalisms. These multiple environmentalisms look different, situated in particular ecological and political systems. A properly situated sustainability is one that takes power and people seriously, rather than as an afterthought to the techno-fetishism that eco-desire inhabits, glorifies, and draws its breath from.

Scholars like Melissa Checker, Anne Rademacher, and Miriam Greenberg have focused squarely on reinserting the political dimensions of "sustainability" just as this language gains a foothold in multiple domains—from policy to activism to everyday life. The anthropologist Checker argues against the idea of environmental and land-use development as a mode of "postpolitical" governance in her articulation of environmental gentrification. She argues, drawing from social movements for environmental justice, that sustainability must be interlinked with justice concerns, and thus not be reduced to "green amenities." Greenberg focuses on "critical" urban sustainabilities in her work on Northern California. Rademacher focuses on what the actual ecological architectural practices look like in India, rather than as a traveling discourse from the global elites, which has been the focus of the examples in my case.

What I learned by "situating" sustainability in Shanghai is that environmentalism is a powerful and flexible discourse, one that can be used by politicians, developers, and transnational architects and engineers in completely different ways and for different ends. Ideologies about environmentalism, like pollution itself, travel in multiple directions and in complex ways. As the scale and scope of environmental problems continue unabated, scholars and the general public need more examples of sustainability that works in actually stemming the tide of environmental disaster, not sustainability schemes that merely abet it.

China is a good place to "see" the state of global transnational environmental sustainability schemes, because of the particular historical and national contexts that are amenable to its adoption as policy, if not practice. Although the aim of this book is not policy prescription, I do agree that critique without construction is not "useful." What is the alternative to a critique of techno-fetishism and techno-utopianism? I would argue that there is nothing inherently "wrong" with eco-desire, just the ways in which eco-desire is mobilized in the cases that I discussed in this book. What it more necessary and more complex is what is missing in these cases: a sense of humility, a "pause" on capitalist growth and development, and the ability to get past a staunch refusal to see how technological and engineering solutions create their own environmental and social burdens.

What characterizes the city optic (what Warren Magnusson calls seeing like a city) versus Scott's "seeing like a state" is a fundamental faith in change, fluidity, and humility. Scott explores these values suppressed by the state in the Greek concept of mêtis. Mêtis is practical and cunning intelligence, and it stands as an effective antidote to the natural and social failures of state power. The essence of mêtis—the characteristic that failed state projects disregard—is knowledge about when and how to apply rules of thumb to concrete situations. In his exhaustive study of contemporary Chinese environmentalism, the journalist Jonathan Watts interviewed hundreds of dedicated environmentalists working today. In just one tiny yet illustrative example of mêtis, he quotes an expert on alpine ecology working in Yunnan to show how village forest collection practices are demonstrably more sustainable than current government and business practice. This call to revalue traditional ecological and indigenous knowledge has strong scientific bases when analyzing the data, but it not merely a scientific imperative. It is also a rejection of the state-sanctioned impulse to "see like a state" and to seek mastery over nature.

We need more humility and self-reflexivity in the pressing nature of environmental problems in what has been called the Anthropocene, or the era in which human impacts have shaped geologic time. In the very decade in which overall carbon emissions from China have exceeded that of the United States, a sophisticated analysis of global environmental problems, such as climate change, that takes race, space, history, and global power seriously seems particularly necessary. The default position would be to fall back on racialized tropes that see the rise of China and India through the same interpretive lenses that framed Asian "population" growth in apocalyptic terms in the 1950s and 1960s. The larger political dimensions of Asian American, Pacific Islander, immigrant, and refugee environmentalism in the United States cannot be separated from global environmental discourses and how they shape international power relations.

Put simply, I ask that these questions be discussed and considered when framing environmental and sustainability projects: Does this project create environmental benefits—and what kind? But also, does it create more justice or less? Who (or, in the case of birds, what) benefits, how and why? We need more fiction, imagination, curiosity, humility, and wonder, not less of these forces—and not only of a techno-utopian, engineering variety. I asked these questions from the vantage point of someone curious about Dongtan, who wanted to understand what the broader calls for ecological Shanghai meant as an environmentalist, as a diasporic Shanghainese, and as an inhabitant of a world in which what China does means a lot to the planet. As my colleague Sheldon Lu writes, "In the heart and mind of a local Shanghainese or a diasporic Shanghainese, the city may well transcend the myopic scope of the nation-state and occupy a special place that is like no other in China or the world."[1] It is from my own fractured place of nostalgia, memory, and diaspora that I examined this focus on the technological and the ecological in the most hyperurban of cities.

In summation, although this book is about Shanghai, it's also about the United States. My perspective comes from a uniquely American vantage point, the prototypical immigrant offspring. Growing up in the 1970s and 1980s, I, along with millions of other Americans, did not yet know how much China was going to matter to American lives on the factory floor, in the stuff we use in our houses, in the clothes we wear on our bodies, and in the air we breathe. I wrote this book as a grandchild of Shanghai and

Chongming living across the Pacific Rim. I'm writing as an Asian American suspicious of China-bashing as much as a committed environmentalist rightfully afraid of what global climate change has already begun to do to the world that we know.

The goals of environmental justice movements, in the United States and globally, have focused significant attention on the disproportionate impacts of climate change on those who are the least culpable and the most affected. Businesses are preparing for climate change in terms of identifying new regions for agriculture and in developing carbon markets. Militaries and governments increasingly take into account climate change and the political upheavals it will bring as they do risk and strategic planning. My broad goal in this book has been to look at a few projects in a particular city, in order to interject some healthy skepticism into the eco-city trend. To do so is to necessarily warn against any simple design or technological fix that seeks to create ecological fantasy islands (that conveniently make money), while the rest of the world falls apart. I hope that I have succeeded in that task, that accompanying me on this tour of what I learned has been useful to you, and that these lessons learned can be applied in a critical yet constructive fashion. Borrowing from Gramsci, our shared (environmental) future depends on a nonnaive optimism of the spirit.

INTRODUCTION

1. The difference depends on whether one counts Taiwan. China claims Taiwan; Taiwan claims differently. Thus, descriptive features of the island—its size and relative ranking—run into immediate political complications.

2. Julie Sze and Yi Zhou, "Imagining a Chinese Eco-City: Environmental Criticism for the 21st Century," in *Environmental Criticism for the Twenty-first Century*, ed. Stephanie LeMenager, Teresa Shewry, and Ken Hiltner (New York: Routledge, 2011), 216–230.

3. The Shanghai government approved development plans announced for eastern Chongming Island in 2004 that allowed for a short-term population in Dongtan—as an extension of Chenjia Town—of only twenty-four thousand people, with long-term development serving up to fifty thousand. Shannon May, "Dongtan, China," in *Green Cities: An A-to-Z Guide,* ed. Nevin Cohen and Paul Robbins (Thousand Oaks, Calif.: SAGE Publications, 2011). Retrievable at http://www.sage-ereference.com/greencities/Article_n48.html.

4. Dialects develop in part because of divergent migration patterns. Historically, Chongming residents came from Jiangsu province to the north, in contrast to the Suzhou roots of Shanghainese.

5. The Italian cheese connection is facilitated by the Sino-Italian Coopera-tion Program sponsored by the Italian Trade Commission and the Italian Minis-try of the Environment. Yan Zhao and Herbert Girardet, *Shanghai Dongtan: An Eco-City* (Shanghai: SIIC Dongtan Investment & Development, 2006); also see "Overview of the Project," Sino-Italian Cooperation Program for Environmental Protection website, accessed October 1, 2012, http://www.sinoitaenvironment. org/indexe02.asp.

6. "Chongming County Introduction," Chongming County website (English version), accessed July 9, 2009, http://cmx.sh.gov.cn/cm_website/html/ DefaultSite/portal/index/index.htm.

7. The most recent wave of this migration is detailed in Leslie T. Chang's *Fac-tory Girls: From Village to City in a Changing China* (New York: Spiegel and Grau, 2008).

8. Baorong Huang, Zhiyun Ouyang, Hua Zheng, Huizhi Zhang, and Xiaoke Wang, "Construction of an Eco-Island: A Case Study of Chongming Island, China," *Ocean and Coastal Management* 51, nos. 8–9 (2008): 575–588. Also, see note 3 in this chapter.

9. Scale is first a *technical* measurement of the ratio between the size of objects in the world and their size on a map (for example, a cartographic scale of one to one million). Scale functions as a shorthand for an areal unit on a map, or for what geographers call an "analysis scale," as well as a "phenomenon scale," which is the size at which geographic structures exist and over which geographic processes exist in the world.

10. Nathan Sayre, "Ecological and Geographical Scale: Parallels and Poten-tial for Integration," *Progress in Human Geography* 29, no. 3 (2005): 276–290.

11. Nathan Sayre, "Climate Change, Scale, and Devaluation: The Challenge of Our Built Environment," *Washington and Lee Journal of Climate, Energy, and the Environment* 1, no. 1 (2010): 93–105.

12. Stephanie LeMenager, Teresa Shewry, and Ken Hiltner, "Introduction," in *Environmental Criticism for the Twenty-first Century*, ed. Stephanie LeMenager, Teresa Shewry, and Ken Hiltner (New York: Routledge, 2011), 10.

13. Sayre, "Climate Change, Scale, and Devaluation," 97.

14. Jeffrey N. Wasserstrom, *Global Shanghai, 1850–2010: A History in Frag-ments* (New York: Routledge, 2009).

15. Leo Ou-Fan Lee, *Shanghai Modern: The Flowering of a New Urban Culture in China, 1930-1945* (Cambridge, Mass.: Harvard University Press, 1999).

16. *China's Prophecy: Shanghai* was the third exhibition in a series called *Future City, 20/21,*, which started with *New York Modern*, chronicling New York City's place as the birthplace of the skyscraper at the turn of the century to the 1930s, followed by a second exhibition that explored Hong Kong from the 1960s onward. "China Prophecy: Shanghai," on the Skyscraper Museum's website, accessed October 1, 2012, http://www.skyscraper.org/EXHIBITIONS/CHINA_PROPHECY/china_prophecy.htm.

17. Ibid.

18. Wasserstrom, *Global Shanghai, 1850-2010.*

19. This passage, published in 1949 in *Jingji Zhoubao*, a Communist Party newspaper, is quoted in Peter G. Rowe and Seng Kuan, eds., *Shanghai: Architecture and Urbanism for Modern China* (Munich: Prestel, 2004), 44.

20. Gary Gang Tian, *Shanghai's Role in the Economic Development of China: Reform of Foreign Trade and Investment* (Westport, Conn.: Praeger, 1996). Tian provides a thorough account of Shanghai's shifting economy in the reform era, which began in 1978—as the metropolis moved from being a key supplier of manpower, technology, and money for Mao's literal centralist policies, which diverted power away from the coast into the heart of the mainland—and its subsequent floundering, reform, and eventual recovery. Market forces and political reforms transferred responsibilities to major cities, which resulted in increased international investment. Shanghai benefited greatly from these reforms and changes.

21. Xiangming Chen, ed., *Rising Shanghai: State Power and Local Transformations in a Global Megacity* (Minneapolis: University of Minnesota Press, 2009).

22. Much has been written about the discourse of harmony. A brief scan of three working papers from the Shanghai Academy of Social Sciences shows various elements of this discourse: Rongua Wang, "Harmony and Peace: The Global Implications of Chinese Development," Shanghai Academy of Social Sciences Working Paper 1, no. 1 (2008); Xuejin Zuo, "Reform of the Social Security System and the Building of Harmonious Society," Shanghai Academy of Social Sciences Working Paper 1, no. 2 (2008); Shijun Tong, "Pay Extra Attention to Harmonious Improvement of Spiritual Life and Material Life," Shanghai Academy of Social

Sciences Working Paper 1, no. 1 (2008). Christopher Connery, "Better City: Better Life," *Boundary 2* 38, no. 11 (2011): 207–227.

23. Wasserstrom, *Global Shanghai, 1850–2010*, 68.

24. Jeffrey N. Wasserstrom, "Is Global Shanghai 'Good to Think'? Thoughts on Comparative History and Post-Socialist Cities," *Journal of World History* 18, no. 2 (2007): 199–234.

25. Thomas J. Campanella, *The Concrete Dragon: China's Urban Revolution and What It Means for the World* (New York: Princeton Architectural Press, 2008), 24–25.

26. Miriam Greenberg, "The Sustainability Edge: Competition, Crisis, and the Rise of Eco-City Branding in New York and New Orleans," in *Sustainability in the Global City: Myth and Practice*, ed. Melissa Checker, Cindy Isenhour, and Gary McDonough (Cambridge: Cambridge University Press, 2014).

27. Julie Sze and Gerardo Gambirazzio, "Eco-Cities without Ecology: Constructing Ideologies, Valuing Nature," in *Resilience in Urban Ecology and Design: Linking Theory and Practice for Sustainable Cities*, ed. S. T. A. Pickett, M. L. Cadenasso, and Brian McGrath (Heidelberg: Springer, 2013), 289–297.

28. Arthur P. J. Mol and Gert Spaargaren, "Ecological Modernisation Theory in Debate: A Review," in *Ecological Modernisation around the World: Perspectives and Critical Debates*, ed. Arthur P. J. Mol and David Allan Sonnefeld (London: Frank Cass, 2000), 17–49.

29. Dana R. Fisher and William R. Freudenburg, "Ecological Modernization and Its Critics: Assessing the Past and Looking toward the Future," *Society and Natural Resources* 14, no. 8 (2001): 701–709; Richard York and Eugene A. Rosa, "Key Challenges to Ecological Modernization Theory: Institutional Efficacy, Case Study Evidence, Units of Analysis, and the Pace of Eco-Efficiency," *Organization and Environment* 16, no. 3 (2003): 273–288; Stephen C. Young, "Introduction: The Origins and Evolving Nature of Ecological Modernisation," in *The Emergence of Ecological Modernisation: Integrating the Environment and the Economy?*, ed. Stephen C. Young (New York: Routledge, 2009), 1–39; Joan Martinez-Alier, "The Distributional Effects of Environmental Policy," *Ecological Economics* 63 (2007): 246–247.

30. Lisa Rofel, *Desiring China: Experiments in Neoliberalism, Sexuality, and Public Culture* (Durham, N.C.: Duke University Press, 2007).

31. John R. Gillis, *Islands of the Mind: How the Human Imagination Created the Atlantic World* (New York: Palgrave Macmillan, 2009).

32. Ibid., 14.

33. Paul Boyer, *Urban Masses and Moral Order in America, 1820–1920* (Cambridge, Mass.: Harvard University Press, 1978).

34. Hwang examines this tension in a number of plays, most recently in *Yellow Face* and *Chinglish*.

35. Mel Y. Chen, "Racialized Toxins and Sovereign Fantasies," *Discourse* 29, nos. 2–3 (2007): 367–383.

36. Donovan Hohn, "Through the Open Door: Searching for Deadly Toys in China's Pearl River Delta," *Harpers*, September 2008, 58.

37. Mel Y. Chen, *Animacies: Biopolitics, Racial Mattering, and Queer Affect* (Durham, N.C.: Duke University Press, 2012).


1. FEAR, LOATHING, ECO-DESIRE

1. Sara Bongiorni, *A Year without "Made in China": One Family's True Life Adventure in the Global Economy* (Hoboken, N.J.: Wiley, 2007).

2. Thomas L. Friedman, *Hot, Flat and Crowded: Why We Need a Green Revolution—and How It Can Renew America* (New York: Farrar, Straus, and Giroux, 2008), 172.

3. Ibid., 372–373.

4. Ibid., 345.

5. Joseph Kahn and Jim Yardley, "As China Roars, Pollution Reaches Deadly Extremes," *New York Times*, August 26, 2007, accessed October 5, 2012, http://www.nytimes.com/2007/08/26/world/asia/26china.html?pagewanted=all.

6. Some recent studies estimate that ten billion pounds of airborne pollutants from Asia—ranging from dust and soot to mercury, heavy metals, pesticides, PCBs, mercury, ozone, carbon dioxide, nitrogen dioxide, and sulfur dioxide—reach the United States annually. See Les Blumenthal, "Scientists Track Asian Pollution," *News Tribune*, September 4, 2008, accessed October 5, 2012, http://www.thenewstribune.com/2008/09/04/471063/scientists-track-asian-pollution.html.

7. David Bunker, "Donner Summit Air Station Detects Chinese Pollution," *Sierra Sun*, July 21, 2006, accessed October 5, 2012, http://www.sierrasun.com/article/20060731/NEWS/60731006.

8. Andrew Szasz, *Shopping Our Way to Safety: How We Changed from Protecting the Environment to Protecting Ourselves* (Minneapolis: University of Minnesota Press, 2007).

9. Keith Bradsher and Matthew Wald, "A Measured Rebuttal to China over Solar Panels," *New York Times*, March 20, 2012, accessed October 5, 2012, http://www.nytimes.com/2012/03/21/business/energy-environment/us-to-place-tariffs-on-chinese-solar-panels.html?pagewanted = all.

10. Carin Hall, "The Future of Urban Development," Energy Digital Global Energy Portal, February 18, 2012, accessed October 3, 2012, http://www.energy-digital.com/green_technology/the-future-of-urban-development-tianjin-eco-city.

11. Diane Cardwell, "Solar Tariffs Upheld, but May Not Help in the U.S.," *New York Times*, November 7, 2012, accessed November 7, 2007, http://www.nytimes.com/2012/11/08/business/energy-environment/us-affirms-tariffs-against-chinese-solar-companies.html.

12. "Waste Management in China: Issues and Recommendations," Urban Development Working Papers, East Asia Infrastructure Department, World Bank, Working Paper no. 9, May 2005, accessed April 19, 2013, http://siteresources.worldbank.org/INTEAPREGTOPURBDEV/Resources/China-Waste-Management1.pdf.

13. This is distinct from Chinese anxieties about pollution and their cultural effects. See Sheldon Lu and Jiayan Mi, eds., *Chinese Ecocinema in the Age of Environmental Challenge* (Hong Kong: University of Hong Kong Press, 2009).

14. These plans include a massive water transfer from south to north, and a campaign to develop the restive west. See Judith Shapiro, *Mao's War against Nature: Politics and the Environment in Revolutionary China* (Cambridge: Cambridge University Press, 2001), 205.

15. James C. Scott, *Seeing Like a State: How Certain Schemes to Improve the Human Condition Have Failed* (New Haven, Conn.: Yale University Press, 1998).

16. Elizabeth Economy, *The River Runs Black: The Environmental Challenge to China's Future* (Ithaca, N.Y.: Cornell University Press, 2004).

17. Synthesizing many of these critiques, Michael Dorsey defines climate injustice as the idea that harm from the deleterious effects of climate change and the production and materialist processes associated with it is unevenly distributed, and deliberately falls disproportionately on the marginalized and the disadvantaged. See Dorsey's "Climate Knowledge and Power: Tales of Skeptic Tanks, Weather Gods, and Sagas for Climate (In)justice," *Capitalism Nature Socialism* 18, no. 2 (2007): 7–21.

18. Greg McCarthy. "The Climate Change Metanarrative, State of Exception and China's Modernisation," *Journal of Indian Ocean Region* 6, no. 2 (2010): 252–266.

19. Kahn and Yardley, "As China Roars, Pollution Reaches Deadly Extremes."

20. Edmund Russell, *War and Nature: Fighting Humans and Insects with Chemicals from World War I to Silent Spring* (Cambridge: Cambridge University Press, 2001).

21. Joseph Kahn and Mark Landler, "China Grabs West's Smoke-Spewing Factories," *New York Times*, December 21, 2007, accessed October 5, 2012, http://www.nytimes.com/2007/12/21/world/asia/21transfer.html?pagewanted = all.

22. Ibid.

23. Fiona Harvey, "Britain Merely 'Outsourcing' Carbon Emissions to China, Say MPs," *The Guardian*, April 18, 2012, accessed April 19, 2013, http://www.guardian.co.uk/environment/2012/apr/18/britain-outsourcing-carbon-emissions-china.

24. McKinsey Global Institute, "Preparing for China's Urban Billion," March 2009, accessed October 5, 2012, http://www.mckinsey.com/insights/mgi/research/urbanization/preparing_for_urban_billion_in_china.

25. Jasmin Sasin, "Shenzhen Ranks Fifth in the World in Terms of Population Density," *Shenzhen Standard*, May 30, 2012, accessed October 5, 2012, http://www.shenzhen-standard.com/2012/05/30/shenzhen-ranks-fifth-in-the-world-in-terms-of-population-density.

26. Campanella, *The Concrete Dragon*, chapter 5.

27. Sheldon Lu, "Tear Down the City: Reconstructing Urban Space in Cinema, Photography, Video," in *Chinese Modernity and Global Biopolitics* (Honolulu: University of Hawaii Press, 2007), 167.

28. Ibid., 167. Also see Michael Meyer's *Last Days of Old Beijing: Life in the Vanishing Backstreets of a City Transformed* (New York: Walker Books, 2008).

29. David Naguib Pellow, *Resisting Global Toxics: Transnational Movements for Environmental Justice* (Cambridge, Mass.: MIT Press, 2007).

30. CBS News, "Following the Trail of Toxic E-Waste," *60 Minutes*, January 8, 2010, accessed May 31, 2014, http://www.cbsnews.com/news/following-the-trail-of-toxic-e-waste/; Huo et al., "Elevated Blood Lead Levels of Children in Guiyu, an Electronic Waste Recycling Town in China," *Environmental Health Perspectives* 115, no. 7 (2007): 1113–1117.

31. Renwei Huang, "Comments on Debate Points Regarding Shanghai's Current Phase of Development," Shanghai Academy of Social Sciences Working Paper 1, no. 3 (2008).

32. McCarthy, "The Climate Change Metanarrative."

33. "Zenyang Renshi he Lijie 'Jianshe Shengtai Wenming'" [How to Understand "The Construction of Ecology"], *Xinhua Wang* [*Chinaview*], November 9, 2006, accessed June 16, 2009, http://news.xinhuanet.com/politics/2007-11/09/content_7038963.htm.

34. Jingtao Hu, "Report to the Seventeenth National Congress of the Communist Party of China" [A Special Topic on the Seventeenth National Congress of the Communist Party of China], *Xinhua Wang* [*Chinaview*], October 24, 2007, accessed 16 June, 2009, http://news.xinhuanet.com/newscenter/2007-10/24/content_6938568.htm.

35. Kahn and Yardley, "As China Roars, Pollution Reaches Deadly Extremes."

36. Kathy Le Mons Walker, "'Gangster Capitalism' and Peasant Protest in China: The Last Twenty Years," *Journal of Peasant Studies* 33, no. 1 (2006): 1–33.

37. "The government has gradually increased the proportion of GDP allocated to environmental protection from 0.72 percent in 1989 to 1.33 percent in 2003. Between 1998 and 2002, 580 billion yuan was invested in environmental protection and ecological construction across China, 1.8 times the total investment in this area for the 48 years between 1950 and 1997. In 2003, 136.34 billion yuan was invested in treatment of environmental pollution, 23.2 percent more than in 2002. Of the total investment, 78.53 billion yuan was used in construction of environmental infrastructure in urban areas, 18.84 billion yuan in treatment of sources of industrial pollution, and 38.97 billion yuan in environmental protection in new construction projects." "National Climate Change Program," China.org.cn, June 4, 2007, accessed July 17, 2009, http://www.china.org.cn/english/environment/213624.htm.

38. In 2002, the output value of China's environmental protection industry reached 220 billion yuan, compared to 4 billion yuan in 1992. See "Environmental Protection Funds and Environmental Protection Industry," Chinese Government's official web portal, accessed July 17, 2009, http://english.gov.cn/2006-02/08/content_182523.htm. In 2008, China invested the equivalent

of 156 million U.S. dollars in renewable energy. In 2009, 2.1 billion yuan was to be invested in eco-construction and energy-saving projects.

39. The "Report on the Outline of the Eleventh Five-Year Plan" clarified the goals for 2006 to 2010. They are to decrease energy consumption by 20 percent and decrease the release of polluted material by 10 percent. "National Climate Change Program."

40. "To prevent and control environmental pollution, protect nature and ecology, supervise nuclear safety, safeguard public health and environmental safety, and promote harmony between man and nature." "Zhuanjia Jiedu Huanbao bumen 30nian fazhan" [Experts Explain the Thirty-Year Development of the Department of Environmental Protection], Henan sheng zhengfu menhu wang [Henan Government official website, 2008], February 27, 2008, accessed July 20, 2009, http://www.henan.gov.cn/ztzl/system/2009/03/05/010122517.shtml.

41. Kahn and Yardley, "As China Roars, Pollution Reaches Deadly Extremes."

42. Ibid.

43. Center for Climate and Energy Solutions: Working Together for the Environment and the Economy, "Buildings and Emissions: Making the Connection," n.d., accessed October 5, 2012, http://www.c2es.org/technology/overview/buildings.

44. "Committing to the Development of an Ecological Civilization," *Ma Kai Qiushi Journal* 5, no. 4 (October 1, 2013). (*Quishi* is the organ of the Central Committee of the CCP.) Accessed May 31, 2014, http://www.chinadaily.com.cn/regional/2011-07/15/content_15573296.htm.

45. Ibid. These include Hainan, Jilin, Heilongjiang, Fujian, Zhejiang, Shandong, Anhui, Jiangsu, Hebei, Sishuan, Guangxi, Tianjin, Liaoning, and Shanxi.

46. "Zhongguo shouge 'shengtai wenming jianshe guihua dagang' bianzhi wancheng" [China's First "Plan of Construction of Ecological Civilization" Completed], *Sohu Xinwen* [*Sohu News*], September 19, 2008, accessed July 19, 2009, http://news.sohu.com/20080919/n259652480.shtml.

47. Eco-counties must complete a local construction plan based on the "Construction Plan of Eco-Counties and Eco-Cities" issued by the Ministry of Environmental Protection. The local plan should pass an examination by the local People's Congress and be reported to the Ministry of Environmental Protection. The county should have an independent organization for environmental

protection. There should be no serious environmental pollution accidents within the previous three years. In addition, the plan must save energy and include information such as the local peasants' annual income, forest coverage rate, air quality, and water quality. For the eco-county, 80 percent of its subordinated villages/townships must achieve the "National Standards of Environmental Beautiful Village/Township" [ huanjing youmei xiangzhen]. For the eco-city, 80 percent of its counties must be approved and named as national eco-counties. For the eco-province, 80 percent of its cities must be approved and named as national eco-cities. From Zhongguo Renming gongheguo huanjing baohubu [People's Republic of China Ministry of Environmental Protection], "Guanyu yinfa 'shengtai xian, shengtai shi, shengtai sheng jianshe zhibiao (xiudinggao)' de tongzhi" [Notice on the Issuance of "Eco-Counties, Eco-Cities, and Eco-Province Construction Index (Revised Draft)"], December 26, 2007, accessed July 22, 2009, http://www.mep.gov.cn/gkml/zj/wj/200910/t20091022_172492.htm.

48. Joseph Kahn, "In China, a Lake's Champion Imperils Himself," *New York Times*, October 14, 2007, accessed October 5, 2012, http://www.nytimes.com/2007/10/14/world/asia/14china.html.

49. Italics added.

50. "'Shengtai cheng' gainian fengmi bange zhongguo" [The Concept of "Eco-City' Overwhelms Half of China], Xianning chengshi guihua wang [Xianning City Planning Network], November 3, 2008, accessed July 23, 2009, http://xncg.gov.cn/xnsghj_web/website/20080326092514812/20080326092719421/info_20081103075248828.shtml.

51. Gaia Vince, "China's Eco-Cities: Sustainable Urban Living in Tianjin," BBC, May 3, 2012, accessed October 8, 2012, http://www.bbc.com/future/story/20120503-sustainable-cities-on-the-rise/2.

52. Jonathan Watts, *When a Billion Chinese Jump: How China Will Save Mankind—or Destroy It* (New York: Scribner, 2010). Also see Keith Bradsher, "Bolder Protests against Pollution Win Project's Defeat in China" *New York Times*, July 4, 2012, accessed October 5, 2012, http://www.nytimes.com/2012/07/05/world/asia/chinese-officials-cancel-plant-project-amid-protests.html.

53. These include Huzhou (Zhejiang province), Wuxi (Jiangsu province), Shenyang (Liaoning province), and Ji'nan (Shandong province), in addition to Shanghai Dongtan and Langfang in Heibei province.

54. Matt Tyrnauer, "Industrial Revolution, Take Two," *Vanity Fair,* May, 2008, accessed October 8, 2012, http://www.vanityfair.com/culture/features/2008/05/mcdonough200805. McDonough was also listed as one of the Vanity Fair 100 in 2010, a list of "influential" public figures.

55. Shannon May, "Ecological Citizenship and a Plan for Sustainable Development," *City* 12, no. 2 (2008): 237–244.

56. "Zhongguo shengtai chengshi: Zaochan de wutuobang" [Chinese Eco-City: Abortive Utopia], *Huaxia dili zazhi* [*National Geographic*], April 21, 2009, accessed July 23, 2009, http://www.huaxia-ng.com/web/?action-viewnews-itemid-61961.

57. Michael Ziser and Julie Sze, "Climate Change, Environmental Aesthetics and Global Environmental Justice Cultural Studies," *Discourse* 29, no. 2 (2007): 384–410.

58. Alex Pasternack and Clifford A. Pearson, "National Stadium: Herzog & De Muron Creates an Icon That Reaches beyond the Olympics," *Architectural Record* 196, no. 7 (2008): 92–99.

59. Ziser and Sze, "Climate Change, Environmental Aesthetics and Global Environmental Justice Cultural Studies."

60. Tom Dyckhoff, "We Can Help Change China Say Architects Herzog and De Meuron," *The Times* [London], March 12, 2008, accessed October 8, 2012, http://www.thetimes.co.uk/tto/arts/visualarts/architecture/article1887501.ece.

61. Ibid.

62. Campanella, *The Concrete Dragon*, 131–132.

63. Jasper Becker, "Transforming Beijing," *Travel and Leisure*, February 2004, accessed October 8, 2012, http://www.travelandleisure.com/articles/seeing-red/1.

64. Meyer, *Last Days of Old Beijing*; Campanella, *The Concrete Dragon*.

65. Jonathan Glancey, "Secrets of the Bird's Nest," *The Guardian*, February 11, 2008, accessed October 8, 2012, http://www.guardian.co.uk/artanddesign/2008/feb/11/architecture.chinaarts2008.

66. Xuefei Ren discusses the various controversies related to the Bird's Nest in "Olympic Spectacles, Critical Architecture, and New State Spaces," in *Building Globalization: Transnational Architecture Production in Urban China* (Chicago: University of Chicago Press, 2011), especially 152–158.

67. Michael Wines, "After Summer Olympics, Empty Shells in Beijing," *New York Times*, February 6, 2010, accessed October 8, 2012, http://www.nytimes.com/2010/02/07/weekinreview/07wines.html.

68. "Green Dream Park Promotes Low-Carbon Lifestyle," *China Daily*, July 16, 2010, accessed October 8, 2012, http://www.chinadaily.com.cn/imqq/china/2010-07/16/content_10118361.htm..

69. See these blog postings at http://www.thebeijinger.com/blog/2010/07/21/Confirmed-Beijing-has-World-s-Worst-Theme-Park and http://www.bullfax.com/?q = node-worst-theme-park-world-chinas-olympian-bid.

70. Kate Springer, "Soaring to Sinking: How Building Up Is Bringing Shanghai Down," *Time*, May 21, 2012, accessed October 8, 2012, http://science.time.com/2012/05/21/soaring-to-sinking-how-building-up-is-bringing-shanghai-down/.

71. Coco Liu, "Shanghai Struggles to Save Itself from the Sea," *New York Times*, September 27, 2011, accessed October 8, 2012, http://www.nytimes.com/cwire/2011/09/27/27climatewire-shanghai-struggles-to-save-itself-from-the-s-43368.html.

72. "Carbon Emission Rights Trading Scheme Launched," *China Daily*, August 17, 2012, accessed October 3, 2012, http://www.chinadaily.com.cn/china/2012-08/17/content_15682368.htm.

73. Michael Dorsey and Gerardo Gambirazzio, "A Critical Geography of the Global CDM," in *The CDM in Africa Cannot Deliver the Money*, ed. Patrick Bond et al. (Durban: University of KwaZulu-Natal Centre for Civil Society, 2012), 26–35. The main line of these critiques is that since existing structures of capitalism and development created the problems related to climate change, market mechanisms will reproduce and exacerbate existing social and global inequalities. See Larry Lohmann, "Carbon Trading, Climate Justice and the Production of Ignorance: Ten Examples," *Development* 51 (2008): 359–365.

74. Campanella, *The Concrete Dragon*.

75. Xiangming Wu, "City Case Study of Shanghai," in *Megacity Management in the Asian and Pacific Region*, vol. 2, *City and Country Case Studies*, ed. Jeffry Stubbs and Gilles Clarke (Manila: Asian Development Bank, 1996), 203–225.

76. Tingwei Zhang, "Striving to Be a Global City from Below: The Restructuring of Shanghai's Urban Districts," in *Shanghai Rising: State Power and Local*

*Transformations in a Global Megacity*, ed. Xiangming Chen (Minneapolis: University of Minnesota Press, 2009), 167-189.

77. See China Human Rights Defenders, "Thrown Out: Human Rights Abuses in China's Breakneck Real Estate Development," February 9, 2010, accessed October 8, 2012, http://chrdnet.com/2010/02/thrown-out-human-rights-abuses-in-chinas-breakneck-real-estate-development/.

78. Liza Weinstein and Xuefei Ren, "The Changing Right to the City: Urban Renewal and Housing Rights in Globalizing Shanghai and Mumbai," *City and Community* 8, no. 4 (2009): 407-432.

79. Ibid., 412.

80. Greg Girard, *Phantom Shanghai* (Toronto: Magenta Foundation, 2007), 26.

81. Ibid., 10.

82. Campanella, *The Concrete Dragon*, 171.

83. According to the website, those interviewed must be born between 1978 and 1985, and they are given ten to thirty minutes to share memories associated with a particular location. The goal is less audio tour than audio diary. See *Growing Up with Shanghai Project*, accessed October 8, 2012, http://www.growingup-withshanghai.com.

84. Terence Lloren, *Growing Up with Shanghai*, MP3 on Soundcloud, 12.21.01, January 2, 2010, http://www.growingupwithshanghai.com.

85. Ren, *Building Globalization*, 130.

86. Liu, "Shanghai Struggles to Save Itself from the Sea."

87. Springer, "Soaring to Sinking."

88. Guoyuan Wu and Chun Shi, "Shanghai's Water Environment," in *The Dragon's Head: Shanghai, China's Emerging Megacity*, ed. Harold D. Foster et al. (Victoria, B.C.: Western Geographical Press, 1998), 93-103. World Bank, Australian International Development Assistance Bureau, Kinhill-PPK Joint Venture and Shanghai Academy of Environmental Sciences and the Shanghai Municipal Government, *Draft Shanghai Masterplan* (Shanghai: Kinhill-PPK Joint Venture and Shanghai Academy of Environmental Sciences, 1994).

89. Kin-che Lam, and Shu Tao, "Environmental Quality and Pollution Control," in *Shanghai: Transformation and Modernisation under China's Open Door Policy*, ed. Yue-man Yeung and Yun-wing Sung (Hong Kong: Chinese University Press, 1996), 469-492.

90. "Yangtze River Chemical Leak Raises Concern in China," BBC News China, February 8, 2012, accessed October 3, 2012, http://www.bbc.co.uk /news/world-asia-china-16940407; "China Pig Deaths: Toll from Shanghai Rivers Near 14,000," BBC News China, March 20, 2013, accessed April 19, 2013, http://www.bbc.co.uk/news/world-asia-china-21861987.

91. Peter Abelson, "Economic and Environmental Sustainability in Shanghai," *Applied Economics*, accessed October 10, 2012, http://www.appliedeconomics.com.au/pubs/papers/pa99_shanghai.htm.

92. Liu, "Shanghai Struggles to Save Itself from the Sea."

93. Kelly Sims Gallagher, *China Shifts Gears: Automakers, Oil, Pollution, and Development* (Cambridge, Mass.: MIT Press, 2006).

94. Blood lead levels are far above the threshold associated with impaired intelligence, neurobehavioural development, and physical growth. More than two-thirds of children in Shanghai have blood lead levels greater than 10 µg per deciliter (the official U.S. maximum acceptable limit). In industrial and congested areas, the levels averaged between 21 and 67 µg per deciliter. Abelson, "Economic and Environmental Sustainability in Shanghai."

95. Hongchang Zhou, Daniel Sperling, Mark Delucci, and Deborah Salon, "Transportation in Developing Countries: Greenhouse Gas Scenarios for Shanghai, China," Pew Center on Global Climate Change, July 2001, accessed July 23, 2013, http://www.c2es.org/publications/transportation-developing-countries-greenhouse-gas-scenarios-shanghai-china.

96. Campanella, *The Concrete Dragon*, 16.

97. Liu, "Shanghai Struggles to Save Itself from the Sea."

98. Abelson, "Economic and Environmental Sustainability in Shanghai."

99. Ibid. Factories can take advantage of financial incentives to upgrade their technologies, and residents receive subsidized prices for energy-saving light bulbs and more efficient air conditioners. See Liu, "Shanghai Struggles to Save Itself from the Sea."

100. See "Waste Management in China: Issues and Recommendations," note 9.

101. According to Mee Kam Ng, "in Shanghai, where sustainable development has become national development strategy, sustainability efforts have been

resource management–related, top-down and state-centered, with minor inputs from the 'market' or civil society if any." Mee Kam Ng, "Governance for Sustainability in East Asian Global Cities: An Exploratory Study," *Journal of Comparative Policy Analysis: Research and Practice* 9, no. 4 (2007): 368.

102. Ibid. Ng compares the perceptions, rhetoric, and commitment of four East Asian cities with strong government orientations, in contrast with a market-based civil society context.

## 2. CHANGING CHONGMING

1. "Wo Jiaoao, Wo shi chongmingren" [I Am Proud, I Am a Chongming Person, 2006–2010], Chongming ba [Chongming Online Club], accessed June 10, 2009, http://tieba.baidu.com/f?z = 108779482&ct = 335544320&lm = 0&sc = 0&rn = 30&tn = baiduPostBrowser&word = %B3%E7%C3%F7&pn = 0.

2. Bingbing Yu, "An Increased Profit in Land: Chongming Eco-City Is Still Waiting for a Breakthrough," *Shanghai Stock Newspaper*, January 7, 2010; Yuqin Yuan, "Shengtai wenming linian xia de Chongming shengtaidao jianshe" [Chongming Eco-Island's Construction under the Concept of Ecological Civilization], Shanghai Chongming Government official website, accessed June 6, 2009, http://www.cmx.gov.cn/cmwebnew/node2/node2611/node2693/userobject7ai58450.html.

3. On January 19, 2008, Blair's successor, Prime Minister Gordon Brown, and the Shanghai mayor Han Zheng witnessed the signing of another landmark memorandum of understanding in Shanghai on Dongtan. The congruence of national and industrial interest is evidenced by the signatories to a 2008 memorandum of understanding between SIIC, the London-based banking and financial services company HSBC, Arup, and the Sustainable Development Capital Group to develop the funding model for eco-cities in China. The memorandum reaffirmed support for the implementation of Arup's master plan for Dongtan, and sought cooperation on matching U.K. technology and expertise with Chinese public works projects, and fostering a Sino-U.K. Institute for Sustainability; the signatory representing the government of the United Kingdom is Arup's director for global research. Helen Castle, "Dongtan: China's Flagship Eco-City: An Interview with Peter Head," *Architectural Design* 78, no. 5 (2008): 64–69.

4. Douglas McGray, "China's Great Leap Forward," *Wired*, April 24, 2007, accessed October 12, 2012, http://www.wired.com/wired/archive/15.05/feat_popup_sb.html.

5. Ibid.

6. Ibid.

7. "A Chinese Eco-City: City of Dreams," *The Economist*, March 19, 2009, accessed October 12, 2012, http://www.economist.com/node/13330904?story_id = 13330904.

8. Roger Wood, telephone interview by author, July 2009.

9. "Cities of the Future—Alejandro Gutierrez," July 28, 2010, http://www.youtube.com/watch?v = mb4GLhRRxS8.

10. Chongming Island was opened to foreign trade in the late nineteenth century. Jürgen Osterhammel, "Britain and China, 1842-1914," in *The Oxford History of the British Empire*, vol. 3, *The Nineteenth Century*, ed. Andrew Porter and William Roger Louis (Oxford: Oxford University Press, 1999), 146-169.

11. This is a source of considerable consternation among some Chongming residents, who feel that their development has gotten short shrift from Shanghai. In the Yuan Dynasty (founded A.D. 1277), Chongming was subordinated to the Yangzhou government (currently in Jiangsu province). Chongming Island was subordinated to the Jiangsu government in the Chinese Republican period (1927-1935). In 1936, it was incorporated into Shanghai municipality, but later, in 1945, it became a part of Jiangsu province again. This regionalism was kept from 1949 to 1958, after the new China was founded by the CCP. In December 1958, Chongming was reincorporated into Shanghai city. Zhang Jun and Fu Yong, "Shanghai and Yangtze River Delta: A Revolving Relationship," in *Regional Economic Development in China*, ed. Swee-Hock Saw and John Wong (Singapore: ISEAS, 2009), 123-154.

12. Ramsar is an intergovernmental treaty that provides the framework for national action and international cooperation for the conservation and wise use of wetlands and their resources. The Ramsar Convention is the only global environmental treaty that deals with a particular ecosystem, and the Convention's member countries cover all geographic regions of the planet. See "The Ramsar Convention on Wetlands," http://www.ramsar.org/. For Chongming's bird species and "important bird area" status, see http://www.birdlife.org/datazone/sitefactsheet.php?id=15643.

13. Timothy Brook, *Collaboration: Japanese Agents and Local Elites in Wartime China* (Cambridge, Mass.: Harvard University Press, 2005), 201–202.

14. Lan Yao, "Surviving War Crimes," *Shanghai Star*, April 4, 2002, accessed October 12, 2012, http://app1.chinadaily.com.cn/star/2002/0404/pr22-1.html.

15. Brook, *Collaboration*, 199.

16. "60-Year Sadness of Chinese Comfort Women," *People's Daily*, September 18, 2000, accessed October 12, 2012, http://english.peopledaily.com.cn/english/200009/18/eng20000918_50734.html.

17. The Chongming dialect differs from the Shanghai dialect because of the historical direction and migration source in the late nineteenth and twentieth centuries.

18. Dingfeng Lu, "Shenru yanjiu Chongming de lishi fangwei yu weilai fazhan" [Deep Analysis of Chongming's Historical Position and Future Development], Shanghai Chongming Government official website, accessed June 6, 2009, http://www.cmx.gov.cn/cmwebnew/node2/node2611/node2693/userobject7ai58444.html.

19. In 2003, 3,400 students left Chongming for undergraduate education but only 512 came back to Chongming in the same year. Zhiyuan Zhang, "Chongming jingjifazhan de kunhuo, yuanyin ji lujing tupo" [The Confusion, Reason, and Path Breakthrough of Chongming's Economic Development], Shanghai Chongming Government official website, accessed June 11, 2009, http://www.cmx.gov.cn/cmwebnew/node2/node2611/node2693/userobject7ai58483.html.

20. Ibid., accessed June 6, 2009.

21. Shuqing Zhao, Liangjun Da, Zhiyao Tang, Hejun Fang, Kun Song, and Jingyun Fang, "Ecological Consequences of Rapid Urban Expansion: Shanghai, China," *Frontiers in Ecology and the Environment* 4 (2009): 341–346.

22. Pudong was long an inhabited and active place of agriculture and, to a lesser extent, industry. According to Campanella, Pudong was "the blank slate on which the future of Shanghai would be written. It was not, of course, all that blank to begin with; there are more than a million people living in Pudong's several towns and rural villages" (Campanella, *The Concrete Dragon*, 71). The development process involved leading architects and urban designers from around the world, although that process was used primarily as a process to "glean good ideas" from the competition (79).

23. "China to Build Own Neverland as Michael Jackson Tribute," BBS China Forum, July 10, 2009, accessed October 12, 2012, http://bbs.chinadaily.com.cn /thread-641214-1-1.html.

24. Paul Hawkens, Amory Lovins, and L. Hunter Lovins, *Natural Capitalism: Creating the Next Industrial Revolution* (Boston: Little, Brown, 1999).

25. Lisa Heinzerling and Frank Ackerman, *Pricing the Priceless: Cost-Benefit Analysis of Environmental Protection* (Washington, D.C.: Georgetown Environmental Law and Policy Institute and Georgetown University Law Center, 2002); Stefano Pagiola, "How Useful Is Ecosystem Valuation?" (paper presented at the conference Economics and Conservation in the Tropics: A Strategic Dialogue, convened by the Conservation Strategy Fund, Gordon and Betty Moore Foundation, and Resources for the Future, San Francisco, January 31–February 1, 2008), accessed September 30, 2013, http://www.rff.org/Documents/08_Tropics_Conference/ Tropics_Conference_Papers/Tropics_Conference_Pagiola_Ecosystem_Valuation. pdf; Mark Sagoff, "Environmental Economics and the Conflation of Value and Benefit," *Environmental Science and Technology* 34, no. 8 (2000): 1426–1432; Kerry R. Turner et al., "Valuing Nature: Lessons Learned and Future Research Directions," *Ecological Economics* 46, no. 3 (2003): 493–510.

26. James Boyd and Spencer Banzhaf, "What Are Ecosystem Services? The Need for Standardized Environmental Accounting Units" (Resources for the Future, Discussion Paper no. RFF DP 06–02, 2006); Rudolf S. de Groot, Matthew A. Wilson, and Roelof M. J. Boumans, "A Typology for the Classification, Description and Valuation of Ecosystem Functions, Goods and Services," *Ecological Economics* 41, no. 3 (2002): 393–408; François Schneider, Giorgios Kallis, and Joan Martinez-Alier, "Crisis or Opportunity? Economic Degrowth for Social Equity and Ecological Sustainability: Introduction to This Special Issue," *Journal of Cleaner Production* 18, no. 6 (2010): 511–518.

27. Paul Robbins, *Lawn People: How Grasses, Weeds, and Chemicals Make Us Who We Are* (Philadelphia: Temple University Press, 2007); Maria Kaika, *City of Flows: Modernity, Nature, and the City* (New York: Routledge, 2005).

28. "Eco²Cities : Ecological Cities as Economic Cities," World Bank, accessed August 12, 2013, http://web.worldbank.org/WBSITE/EXTERNAL/TOPICS/EXTU RBANDEVELOPMENT/0,,contentMDK:22643153~pagePK:148956~piPK:216618~t heSitePK:337178,00.html.

29. Hiroaki Suzuki et al., *Eco²Cities: Ecological Cities as Economic Cities* (Washington, D.C.: World Bank, 2010).

30. Erik Gómez-Baggethun et al., "The History of Ecosystem Services in Economic Theory and Practice: From Early Notions to Markets and Payment Schemes," *Ecological Economics* 69, no. 6 (2010): 1209–1218.

31. Joachim H. Spangenberg and Josef Settele, "Precisely Incorrect? Monetising the Value of Ecosystem Services," *Ecological Complexity* 7, no. 3 (2010): 327–337.

32. The idea that islands are hothouses of nature has a long history, particularly in the Pacific, where women have long served as "muses" to a larger colonial project. See Adria L. Imada, *Aloha America: Hula Circuits through the U.S. Empire* (Durham, N.C.: Duke University Press, 2012).

33. Huang et al., "Construction of an Eco-Island."

34. Andrew Kipnis, "Suzhi: A Keyword Approach," *China Quarterly* 186 (2006): 295–313.

35. T. E. Woronov, "Governing China's Children: Governmentality and 'Education for Quality,'" *Positions* 17, no. 3 (2009): 567–589.

36. Andrew Kipnis, "Neoliberalism Reified: *Suzhi* Discourse and Tropes of Neoliberalism in the People's Republic of China," *Journal of the Royal Anthropological Institute* 13, no. 2 (2007): 383–400.

37. Peter Samuel, "Shanghai Opens Spectacular Toll Bridge and Tunnel to Yangste River Mouth Islands," *Tollroads News*, November 1, 2009, accessed October 12, 2012, http://www.tollroadsnews.com/node/4425.

38. Campanella, *The Concrete Dragon*, 225–229.

39. Burkhard Bilger, "The Long Dig," *New Yorker*, September 15, 2008, accessed May 11, 2014, http://www.newyorker.com/reporting/2008/09/15/080915fa_fact_bilger#ixzz0qrvb4dUl.

40. Non Arkaraprasertkul, "Power, Politics, and the Making of Shanghai," *Journal of Planning History* 9, no. 4 (2009): 232–259.

41. Ibid.

42. Gillis, *Islands of the Mind*, 3.

43. Although not without controversy and divided opinions. See Gillis, *Islands of the Mind*, 146.

44. Ibid., 155.

45. Articulated in David Harvey, *The Condition of Postmodernity: An Enquiry into the Conditions of Cultural Change* (Oxford: Blackwell, 1989).

46. Quoted in Gillis, *Islands of the Mind*, 147.

47. Campanella, *The Concrete Dragon*, 77.

48. "Limit Set for Tourists to Chongming Island," Information Office of Shanghai Municipality, November 19, 2009, accessed November 20, 2009, http://en.shio.gov.cn/news/2009/11/19/1150276.html.

49. Huang et al., "Construction of an Eco-Island."

50. Yan and Girardet, *Shanghai Dongtan*.

51. One study examined how different sectors of the population differed in ranking sustainability indicators on Chongming. While teachers, government workers, farmers, and students all ranked the environment high on their list, students prioritized employment, government workers and teachers ranked family higher, and farmers were most concerned with incomes. See Wen Yuan et al., "Development of Sustainability Indicators by Communities in China: A Case Study of Chongming County, Shanghai," *Journal of Environmental Management* 68, no. 3 (2003): 253–261.

52. "Wo Jiaoao, Wo shi chongmingren" [I Am Proud, I Am a Chongming Person, 2006–2010].

53. Ibid.

54. Malcolm Moore, "China's Dongtan Trial Eco-City Project Suspended," *Xingdao Global Newspaper*, October 20, 2008, accessed August 18, 2009, http://www.stnn.cc/ed_china/200810/t20081020_882305.html.

55. "Daqiao zaozai chenjiazhen heli ma?" [Is It Reasonable to Build the Bridge in Chenjia Town?], Chongming ba [Chongming Online Club], accessed March 22, 2009, http://tieba.baidu.com/f?kz = 722428077.

56. Zhuodan Gu, "Chongming xianwei shuji Peng Chenlei yu wangming jiaoliuhuodong huifu wangming tiwenhuizong" [Chongming Party Secretary Chenlei Peng Converses with Internet Users, Answering a Collection of Questions from the Internet Users], Eastday.com, May 18, 2009, accessed June 11, 2009, http://sh.eastday.com/qtmt/20090518/u1a575741.html.

57. "Wo Jiaoao, Wo shi chongmingren" [I Am Proud, I Am a Chongming Person, 2006-2010].

58. Ibid.

## 3. DREAMING GREEN

1. In the U.S. context, this association of nature and wilderness has been most thoroughly discussed by William Cronon, "The Trouble with Wilderness; or, Getting Back to the Wrong Nature," in *Uncommon Ground: Rethinking the Human Place in Nature*, ed. William Cronon (New York: W. W. Norton, 1995), 69–90.

2. Daniel Faber, *Capitalizing on Environmental Injustice: The Polluter-Industrial Complex in the Age of Globalization* (Lanham, Md.: Rowman & Littlefield, 2008).

3. Ren describes Beijing as a "concept-driven" city where images and representation dominate in the real estate development context. See chapter 3, "Architecture, Media, and Real Estate Speculation," in *Building Globalization*.

4. My interview requests to SIIC were repeatedly rebuffed, as were attempts to interview Shanghai Arup Dongtan staff. I interviewed the London-based project head, Roger Wood.

5. Duncan McCorquodale, ed., *Solutions for a Modern City: Arup in Beijing* (London: Black Dog Publishing, 2008).

6. David Owen, "The Anti-Gravity Men," *New Yorker*, June 25, 2007, accessed August 28, 2013, http://www.newyorker.com/reporting/2007/06/25/070625fa_fact_owen#ixzz0qrsh4h7z.

7. "Searching for More Heights to Conquer," *Sunday Times*, June 6, 2010, accessed October 15, 2012, http://www.sundaytimes.lk/100606/Plus/plus_01.html.

8. Arup became involved in 2004 after McKinsey & Co. was hired to consult on the development of Dongtan, and sought out Arup to analyze the impact of development on the Dongtan wetlands. May, "Dongtan, China."

9. Wayne Forster and Dean Hawkes, *Energy Efficient Buildings: Architecture, Engineering and Environment* (New York: W. W. Norton, 2002).

10. McCorquodale, *Solutions for a Modern City*, 52.

11. Arup Associates, *Unified Design*, ed. Paul Brislin (Chichester: Wiley, 2008).

12. Ibid., 54.

13. SIIC's first solicitation was for town and land-use planning of an expanded area of 174 square kilometers that included Chenjia town and Dongtan. Plans were submitted by Atkins Group (United Kingdom), Philip Johnson (United States), and the Architecture Studio (France) in 2001. Shanghai Urban Planning

Research Institute was hired to execute a comprehensive plan, which was approved in 2002. SIIC again sought international design collaboration in 2002 for an international leisure park from EDAW (United States), Kuiper Compagnons (Netherlands), and Groep Planning (Belgium), and for a wetlands park from Sasaki (United States), Groep Planning (Belgium), Alterra (Netherlands), Japan Comprehensive Planning, and Fleming (United States). May, "Dongtan, China."

14. Victoria Schlesinger, "Treasure Island Building Plans Draw Fire," *San Francisco Public Press*, November 29, 2010, accessed October 15, 2012, http://sfpublicpress.org/news/san-francisco/treasure-island.

15. Others, like the racial Bantustans, were not so prescient.

16. Marius de Gues, "Ecotopia, Sustainability, and Vision," *Organization and Environment* 15 (2002): 187–201.

17. David Pepper, "Utopianism and Environmentalism," *Environmental Politics* 14, no. 1 (2005): 3–22.

18. Paolo Soleri, *Arcology: The City in the Image of Man* (Scottsdale, Ariz.: Cosanti Press, 2006).

19. By the end of 2014, local officials and a consortium of private developers were to begin to finalize legal papers for Treasure Island's future as a high-density eco-city.

20. Journalists have closely documented the consolidation of power and corruption involved in the deal in a process driven by "power and influence," with lack of accountability, in which critics were harshly punished and "political friends got plum jobs and contracts. . . . City and state conflict-of-interest laws were waived. Independent inquiries and the will of voters were nakedly rebuffed." Alison Hawkes and Bernice Yeung, "Through Two Mayors, Connected Island Developers Cultivated Profitable Deal," *San Francisco Public Press*, July 1, 2010, accessed October 15, 2012, http://sfpublicpress.org/news/2010-06/through-two-mayors-connected-island-developers-cultivated-profitable-deal.

21. Roger Wood, telephone interview by author, July 24, 2009.

22. Bilger, "The Long Dig."

23. McCorquodale, *Solutions for a Modern City*.

24. Ibid.

25. "Shanghai Tower," *Gensler Design Update*, accessed May 16, 2013, http://www.gensler.com/uploads/documents/Shanghai_Tower_12_22_2010.pdf.

26. According to email correspondence with a senior press officer for Arup in May 2010, the book was written to "share learnings," although it was not intended for general sale. It was also produced in line with the convention in China of publishing books to commemorate big projects. The senior press officer for Arup was unable to confirm how many books were printed, and Arup did not give permission to use images from the book. In *Building Globalization*, Ren discusses the particular genres of magazines and books that transnational design firms use in China.

27. The yellow line signifies the eventual transportation infrastructure linking the three places—Shanghai, Chongming, and Jiangsu. The first part of the project, the Shanghai-Chongming bridge, opened in October 2010. The bridge connects, for the first time, a rural and predominantly poor island to the megaregion of China's richest city. After the bridge opened, weekend day-trippers from Shanghai reached one hundred thousand on an island with a total population of approximately seven hundred thousand.

28. Although the original plan called for fifty thousand residents, Arup increased that number to five hundred thousand because they believed that a denser population was needed from an energy perspective, in that the demonstration site could sell energy back to the grid.

29. Judith Williamson, *Decoding Advertisements: Ideology and Meaning in Advertising* (London: Boyars, 1994).

30. Wood, telephone interview by author, July 24, 2009.

31. Yan and Girardet, *Shanghai Dongtan*, 113.

32. Wood, telephone interview by author, July 24, 2009.

33. Yan and Girardet, *Shanghai Dongtan*, 28.

34. Ibid., 48.

35. The visual problematic of alienation is reminiscent of art and photography about China's modernization and its environmental impacts. On pages 80–81, the entire two-page spread is a photo of a single, large, completely anonymous apartment building. The windows are largely bereft of individual decorations. The photo is reminiscent of the work of the Canadian photographer Edward Burtynsky, who takes epic shots of China's transformation at a number of sites like the Three Gorges Dam, as well as photos of Shanghai's urban transformation (Ziser and Sze, "Climate Change, Environmental Aesthetics and Global Environmental Justice Cultural Studies").

36. Yan and Girardet, *Shanghai Dongtan*, 105.

37. Ibid., 171.

38. Louisa Schein, "The Consumption of Color and the Politics of White Skin in Post-Mao China," *Social Text* 41 (1994): 141–164.

39. Yan and Girardet, *Shanghai Dongtan*, 175.

40. All quotations in this paragraph are from ibid., 177.

41. Ying Shen, "Dongtan chenfu shimo" [The Vicissitudes of Dongtan], *GE huanqiu qiyejia* [*GE Global Entrepreneur Magazine*], March 20, 2009, accessed July 23, 2009, http://www.gemag.com.cn/14/11202_1.html.

42. Ibid.

43. One government official from the Ministry of National Land and Resources told the *GE Global Entrepreneur Magazine* that the quantities of China's farming lands shrank dramatically since many local governments implemented very loose policies to permit turning farmland to commercial use. Thus, the central government requires that all corporations' and local governments' development plans have to pass an examination by the State Council if the lands are more than seventy hectares. The Dongtan eco-city would use 12.5 square kilometers, far beyond the average level. Therefore, it is difficult for the project to gain permission even during the period of the Eleventh Five-Year Plan and the Twelfth Five-Year Plan.

44. However, SIIC took Dongtan out of the whole plan of Chenjia town development and wanted to implement an independent eco-city project in Dongtan. The result was that the Dongtan project cannot keep the same pace. Ying, "Dongtan chenfu shimo."

45. Wenming Song, "Dongtan shengtai cheng miwu" [The Secret of Dongtan Eco-City], *Zhongguo jingying bao* [*China's Business Newspaper*], November 2, 2008, accessed August 28, 2013, http://money.163.com/08/1102/21/4PP9USQF00251HJP.html.

46. Ibid.

47. Treasure Island, a manmade island constructed out of sea dredging spoils poured into rock walls and covered with soil, sits in the middle of the Bay Bridge between the East Bay and San Francisco. Treasure Island was built in 1939 for the Golden Gate International Exposition. The theme of this world's fair was "Pageant of the Pacific," symbolized by "The Tower of the Sun" and a giant eighty-

foot statue of Pacifica, goddess of the Pacific Ocean. During World War II, Treasure Island was turned into a naval base and remained as such until 1998, when it was decommissioned and left highly polluted as a Superfund site.

48. Shenjing He and Fulong Wu, "Property-Led Redevelopment in Post-Reform China: A Case Study of Xintiandi Redevelopment Project in Shanghai," *Journal of Urban Affairs* 27, no. 1 (2005): 1–23.

49. Not coincidentally, Enquist also did the master plan for Abu Dhabi. D'Arcy Doran, "Bridge Opens China's 'Last Virgin Island' for Development," November 1, 2009, accessed October 29, 2012, http://www.physorg.com/news176270468.html.

50. Jesse Fox, "China's Zero-Carbon City Dongtan Delayed, but Not Necessarily Dead, Says Planner," January 24, 2010, accessed on October 29, 2012, http://www.treehugger.com/files/2010/01/arup-peter-head-dongtan-interview.php.

51. Kahn and Yardley, "As China Roars, Pollution Reaches Deadly Extremes."

52. de Gues, "Ecotopia, Sustainability, and Vision."


4. IT'S A GREEN WORLD AFTER ALL?

1. Jonathan Glancey, "Pubs, Privet and Parody as China Builds Little Britain by the Yangtse," *The Guardian*, August 15, 2006, accessed October 29, 2012, http://www.theguardian.com/uk/2006/aug/16/world.china; Hannah Beech, "Ye Olde Shanghai," *Time*, February 7, 2005, accessed September 13, 2013, http://www.time.com/time/magazine/article/0,9171,1025219,00.html.

2. Dieter Hassenpflüg, "European Urban Fictions in China," EspacesTemps.net, Works, November 10, 2008, accessed September 13, 2013, http://www.espacestemps.net/en/articles/european-urban-fictions-in-china-en/.

3. Bianca Bosker, *Original Copies: Architectural Mimicry in Contemporary China* (Honolulu: University of Hawaii Press, 2013). Bosker suggests that the principal elements are individual structures, the master plan, and the nonmaterial signifiers (39).

4. Robbins, *Lawn People*.

5. Ellen Hanak and Matthew Davis, "Lawns and Water Demand in California," *California Economic Policy* 2, no. 2 (2006), accessed October 29, 2012, http://www.ppic.org/content/pubs/cep/ep_706ehep.pdf.

6. Bosker, *Original Copies*, 34.

7. Pow argues that the cultural politics of neoliberalism are a core value in the suburban aesthetic of middle-class landscapes. Choon-Piew Pow, "Neoliberalism and the Aestheticization of New Middle-Class Landscapes," *Antipode* 41, no. 2 (2009): 371–390.

8. Beech, "Ye Olde Shanghai."

9. "Pujiang New Town, Shanghai China," Designbuild-network.com, n.d., accessed October 29, 2012, http://www.designbuild-network.com/projects/ pujiang.

10. Ultimately the "Chinese team" won the competition, but the inclusion of international architects from the United States and France was central to the prestige politics of the project. Arkaraprasertkul, "Power, Politics, and the Making of Shanghai."

11. Hassenpflüg, "European Urban Fictions in China"; Gregory Bracken, "Thinking Shanghai: A Foucauldian Interrogation of the Postsocialist Metropolis" (Ph.D. diss., TU Delft, 2009).

12. Charlie Q. L. Xue and Minghao Zhou, "Importation and Adaptation: Building 'One City and Nine Towns' in Shanghai: A Case Study of Vittorio Gregotti's Plan of Pujiang Town," *Urban Design International* 12 (2007): 21–40.

13. The Tenth Five-Year Plan was the first five-year plan for the twenty-first century, scheduled from 2001 to 2005. Shanghaishi difang zhiban gongshi [Shanghai Chorography Office], "Shanghai nianjian 2005: Yicheng jiuzheng jianshe" [Shanghai 2005 Yearbook: The Construction of "One City, Nine Towns"], accessed June 18, 2009, http://www.shtong.gov.cn/node2/node19828/ node72707/node72895/node72897/userobject1ai83762.html.

14. The plan's goal was to "use industrialization to speed up urbanization, and use urbanization to develop industry." Furthermore, "industrial development is the basis for the development of towns, and 'one city, nine towns' should develop into industrial towns, commodity towns, port towns, tourist towns, satellite towns etc. according to the whole city plan of industry and [the towns' unique] functional positions." Ibid.

15. This model included one central city, eleven new cities, twenty-two central towns, and eighty-eight normal towns. The new (satellite) towns were the towns where the county/district governments were located. Later the "one city"

and "nine towns" were selected from among these chosen areas as trial sites. The goals were to shape the expansion of the central districts, to transform rural towns' status and decentralization vis-à-vis the central city, and to construct the new urban plan: "Central city—new city—central town—small town." Thus, the government hoped the new city and the nine central towns would stimulate other small towns' economies, shape industrial parks, attract residents from the central districts (and alleviate housing, environmental, and transportation pressures through an advanced service network), and create an urbanized group of towns. Ibid.

16. In other words, urban policy had many goals: spatial, social, and economic. "One City, Nine Towns" was superseded by the "'1966' City-Town-Village Plan" in 2005. This new construction plan is to develop one central city (six hundred square kilometers), nine new (satellite) cities, about sixty new towns, and about six hundred central villages. Some of these cities overlapped with the earlier One City, Nine Towns planning, including Qingpu, Song Jiang (where Thames Town is located), and Lingang New City. These cities are planned to attract 5.4 million people. "Jianshe nianjian: Cunzhen jianshe zongzu" [The Construction Yearbook: A Summary of the Construction of Counties and Towns], Shanghai shi Chenxiang jianshe he jiaotong weiyuanhui [The Shanghai Committee of Urban Construction and Communications], 2006, accessed June 17, 2009, http://www.shucm.sh.cn/gb/shucm/node18/node942/node943/node951/userobject1ai33948.html.

17. Since the 1980s, major new industrial/residential areas have been developed in the Baoshan-Wusong area on the southern bank of the Yangtzse River and in the Jinshanwei-Caojing area on the northern bank of Hangzhou Bay. Satellite towns, such as Minhang, Jiadang, Song Jiang, and An Ting, with separate industrial districts, were established thirty to forty kilometers away from the city center. For a brief overview, see Xiangming Chen, ed., *Shanghai Rising: State Power and Local Transformations in a Global Megacity* (Minneapolis: University of Minnesota Press, 2009).

18. Li Zhang, "Spatiality and Urban Citizenship in Late Socialist China," *Public Culture* 14, no. 2 (2002): 311-334.

19. Campanella, *The Concrete Dragon*, 210.

20. Helen Lansdowne, "Thamestown, China, Simulacra and the Realm of Make Believe" (presented at the Forty-second Annual Conference of Asian

Studies on the Pacific Coast, Crossing Boundaries in the Asia-Pacific, Victoria, Canada, June 13-15, 2008), accessed April 25, 2013, http://capiconf.uvic.ca/viewabstract.php?id = 187&cf = 3.

21. Encyclopedia of Shanghai Editorial Committee, "Songjiang District," in *The Encyclopedia of Shanghai* (Shanghai: Shanghai Science & Technology Publishing House, 2010), accessed April 25, 2013, http://zhuanti.shanghai.gov.cn/encyclopedia/en/Default2.aspx#358.

22. Xue and Zhou, "Importation and Adaptation."

23. "Sweco Designs Ecological City in China," *World Architecture News*, September 6, 2011, accessed April 25, 2013, http://www.worldarchitecturenews.com/index.php?fuseaction = wanappln.projectview&upload_id = 17490.

24. Ren discusses the Xintiandi project in the framework of nostalgia and development, in "History, Cosmopolitanism, and Preservation," chapter 4 of *Building Globalization*.

25. He and Wu, "Property-Led Redevelopment in Post-Reform China."

26. Frederik Balfour, "Shanghai Rising," *Bloomberg Business Magazine*, February 18, 2007, accessed May 13, 2013, http://www.businessweek.com/magazine/content/07_08/b4022055.htm.

27. Julie V. Iovine, "Our Man in Shanghai," *New York Times*, August 13, 2006, accessed September 13, 2013, http://www.nytimes.com/2006/08/13/arts/design/13iovi.html.

28. "Shanghai Suburbs: Hot Land for Investment," *Shanghai Agriculture and Suburb Development*, n.d., accessed April 27, 2013, http://en.shac.gov.cn/jdxw/200307/t20030707_74813.htm.

29. Shanghai shi Chengxiang jianshe he jiaotong weiyuanhui [Shanghai Committee of Urban Construction and Communications], "Shanghai renminzhengfu 'guanyu shanghaishi cujin chengzhen fazhan de shidian yijian'" [Shanghai Government: "A Proposal for Speeding Up Experimental Sites of Shanghai Towns' Development"], 2006, accessed May 11, 2014, http://law.eastday.com/epublish/gb/paper20/1/class002000001/hwz562963.htm.

30. Ibid.

31. Following the Second World Congress on Cities and Adaptation to Climate Change, mayors from more than sixty countries unanimously adopted the 2011 Bonn Declaration of Mayors committing to globally coordinated local climate

action. United Nations Office for Disaster Risk Reduction, "Mayors Unanimously Adopt Declaration to Build Urban Resilience and Fight Climate Change," June 14, 2011, accessed April 27, 2013, http://www.unisdr.org/archive/20319.

32. "Shanghai yixie weixingcheng biancheng 'youling cheng'" [Some of Shanghai's Satellite Cities Have Become "Ghost Cities"], Huanqiu wang, accessed August 10, 2009, http://china.huanqiu.com/eyes_on_china/2008-03/80661 .html.

33. Shiloh Krupar, "Shanghaiing the Future: A Detour of the Shanghai Urban Planning Exhibition," *Public Culture* 20, no. 2 (2008): 307-320.

34. "Shanghai Building Collapses, Nearly Intact," *Wall Street Journal—China*, June 29, 2009, accessed April 27, 2013, http://blogs.wsj.com/chinarealtime /2009/06/29/shanghai-building-collapses-nearly-intact/.

35. Alex Scobie, *Hitler's State Architecture: The Impact of Classical Antiquity* (University Park: Pennsylvania State University Press, 1990), 93-95.

36. Recently, Angela Schönberger has argued that this "theory of ruin value" was a euphemism that hid the real reason why this building technique was preferred: the economic necessity to minimize the use of iron, which was urgently needed for the armament program. Angela Schönberger, *Die neue Reichskanzlei von Albert Speer. Zum Zusammenhang von nationalsozialistischer Ideologie und Architektur* (Berlin: Gebrüder Mann Verlag, 1991), 168-169.

37. David Barboza, "Market Defies Fear of Real Estate Bubble in China," *New York Times*, March 4, 2010, accessed September 13, 2013, http://www.nytimes. com/2010/03/05/business/global/05yuan.html.

38. Krupar, "Shanghaiing the Future."

39. Campanella, *The Concrete Dragon*, 81.

40. Krupar, "Shanghaiing the Future."

41. According to a spokesman, the town design was completed after five months of shared effort by seven German planning and engineering companies and three Chinese design institutes. "Town Planning German-Style," *China Daily*, December 27, 2002, accessed September 13, 2013, http://spanish.china. org.cn/english/2002/Dec/52244.htm.

42. Hassenpflüg writes: "The streets are too broad and the buildings too modernist to provide the impression of visiting a historic city centre. Many buildings with pitched, hipped, and shed roofs are oriented with their eaves

facing the street. Also, the few unadorned gable ends, reduced to pure functionality, are hardly capable of staging public urban space in an effective way. The curves of the streets feel aesthetically rather weak considering their width. In the end, the first completed construction phase of An Ting New Town seems like a late Fordist residential development forced into the corset of a medieval basic structure." For one thing, the designers decided on an "organic plan" with a typified spatial structure of the medieval European city as its basis. This appeared to be possible since the German city in its traditional layout shares this spatial grammar. Also, the medieval urban morphology is still characteristic of the urban core (important for both image and identity) of most German cities. In addition, to this day the German landscape is still characterized by small and medium-size cities—a circumstance that becomes even more apparent when comparing the German cityscape with its Chinese counterpart, with its many megacities and their millions of inhabitants. Hassenpflüg, "European Urban Fictions in China."

43. Ibid.

44. Campanella, *The Concrete Dragon*, 218.

45. Ibid.

46. Bosker, *Original Copies*, 98.

47. Ulrika K. Engström, "Luodian—A Slice of Sweden in China," Sweden.se, February 10, 2006, accessed April 27, 2013, http://www.sweden.se/eng/Home/Business/Reading/Luodian—a-slice-of-Sweden-in-China-/.

48. The average per capita disposable income of Shanghai residents is the equivalent of three thousand U.S. dollars per year, the highest in China. Annalyn Censky, "China's Middle Class Boom," CNN Money, June 26, 2012, accessed April 27, 2013, http://money.cnn.com/2012/06/26/news/economy/china-middle-class/index.htm.

49. Rachel Kaufman, "Shanghai's European Suburbs," Smithsonian.com, June 10, 2010, accessed April 27, 2013, http://www.smithsonianmag.com/people-places/Shanghais-European-Suburbs.html.

50. "Brief Introduction to Lupdian [*sic*] Town," Luodian website, accessed April 27, 2013, http://en.luodian.com/Brief_Luodian.html.

51. Campanella, *The Concrete Dragon;* Kaufman, "Shanghai's European Suburbs."

52. Campanella, *The Concrete Dragon*, 88–89. Interestingly, the real "Little Mermaid" statue was the anchor of Denmark's World Exposition pavilion.

53. Hassenpflüg, "European Urban Fictions in China."

54. One description explains: "Luodian was only a small town, but it was the transportation center connecting Baoshan, downtown Shanghai, Jiading, Songjiang and several other towns with highways. Therefore, the successful defense of Luodian was strategically paramount to the security of Suzhou and Shanghai. As early as August 29, German adviser Alexander von Falkenhausen told Chiang Kai-shek that the town of Luodian had to be held at all costs. For the fight for Luodian, the Chinese concentrated some three hundred thousand soldiers, while the Japanese amassed more than one hundred thousand troops, supported with naval ships, tanks and airplanes." C. Peter Chen, "Second Battle of Shanghai, 13 Aug 1937–9 Nov 1937," World War II Database, accessed April 27, 2013, http://ww2db.com/battle_spec.php?battle_id = 85.

55. "Pujiang New Town, Shanghai."

56. Xue and Zhou, "Importation and Adaptation."

57. Gregotti Associati International, "2001/2002 Shanghai (People's Republic of China) Urban Planning & Landscape Design Town of Pujiang, First Prize in the Closed International Design Competition," accessed April 27, 2013, http://www.webalice.it/s.zirilli/Eventi/Pujiangnewtown.htm.

58. XiaoQiao Pan, "Moving On Up?" *Beijing Review*, n.d., accessed April 27, 2013, http://www.bjreview.cn/EN/06-26-e/bus-1.htm.

59. Dai Qian, "Impression on Xinsong Park," *World Expo Magazine*, September 1, 2006, accessed April 27, 2013, http://www.expo2010.cn/expo/expoenglish/wem/node1245/userobject1ai36760.html.

60. "Home Demolished for World Expo, Shanghai Petitioners Seek Just Compensation," *Human Rights in China*, April 4, 2010, accessed April 27, 2013, http://www.hrichina.org/content/385.

61. Bosker, *Original Copies*, 124–125.

5. IMAGINING ECOLOGICAL URBANISM AT THE WORLD EXPO

1. Keith B. Richburg, "Shanghai Prepares World's Fair while Wondering about Costs," *Washington Post*, April 19, 2010, accessed May 13, 2013, http://www

.washingtonpost.com/wp-dyn/content/article/2010/04/18/AR2010041803376.
html.

2. Carol Huang, "China's Shanghai Expo 2010—by the Numbers," *Christian Science Monitor*, April 29, 2010, accessed May 13, 2013, http://www.csmonitor.com/World/Global-News/2010/0429/
China-s-Shanghai-Expo-2010-by-the-numbers.

3. Ibid.

4. Nick Land, ed., *Urbanatomy Shanghai: 2009* (Shanghai: Nan Kai University Press, 2008), 47. Emphasis added.

5. Ibid, 158.

6. Balfour, "Shanghai Rising."

7. Land, *Urbanatomy Shanghai*, 48.

8. The higher cost includes the infrastructure investments related to the expo. See Huang, "China's Shanghai Expo 2010—by the Numbers."

9. Yonah Freemark, "Shanghai's Metro, Now World's Longest, Continutes to Grow Quickly as China Invests in Rapid Transit," *The Transport Politic*, April 15, 2010, accessed May 13, 2013, http://www.thetransportpolitic.com/2010/04/15/
shanghais-metro-now-worlds-longest-continues-to-grow-quickly-as-china-invests-in-rapid-transit/.

10. *Expo 2010 Shanghai China Official Guidebook* (Shanghai: China Publishing Group, 2010), 4. Emphasis added.

11. The Shanghai Expo is not the first to deal with environmental themes, which have been a "metatheme" of world expositions since the 1960s: in Montreal in 1960; Seville, Spain, in 1992; Lisbon in 1998; Hanover, Germany, in 2000; and Aichi, Japan, in 2005, where China's pavilion theme was nature, city, harmony, art of life, and the idea of the city as a piece of nature.

12. Greenberg, "The Sustainability Edge."

13. There are three kinds of exhibitions: those historically known as universal (now known as registered), international, and horticultural. They are sanctioned by the Paris-based Bureau International des Expositions (BIE; English: International Exhibitions Bureau) and last anywhere from three weeks to six months.

14. Caroline Rossiter, "To Shanghai, Perchance to Dream," *The Faster Times*, n.d., accessed May 13, 2013, http://thefastertimes.com/visualarts/2010/06/03/
to-shanghai-perchance-to-dream/.

15. Balfour, "Shanghai Rising."

16. Tiangang Li, "A Long Love Affair," *Beijing Review*, May 9, 2009, accessed May 13, 2013, http://www.bjreview.com.cn/nation/txt/2009-05/09/content_194750.htm.

17. Translations of banners in 2010, from Will Thompson of New York University.

18. Gina Anne Russo, "Better City, Better Life," *The China Beat*, May 20, 2009, accessed May 13, 2013, http://www.thechinabeat.org/?tag = haibao.

19. Ibid.

20. Yu Bing Gao, "The Pajama Game Closes in Shanghai," *New York Times*, May 16, 2010, accessed May 13, 2013, http://www.nytimes.com/2010/05/17/opinion/17gao.html.

21. This article was from an academic paper, and UPLA uploaded it to its own website in 2007. The original article was published in *Urban Planning International* [*Guowai chengshi guihua*] in 2005. *Urban Planning International* is an academic journal that is organized, edited, and published by the Bureau of China's Urban Planning and Design (located in Beijing). The official website is: http://web.archive.org/web/20080428215606/www.upo-planning.org/index.asp. The website (UPLA.cn) was established in March 2006 by Bendao-Chongqing Company, which is a high-tech (Internet-based technology) company. This company /website aims to provide information, knowledge, business policy, and technology consultation for architects and landscape designers. This website also provides an online forum for users to discuss issues of urban planning ("About Us," UPLA.cn, accessed November 29, 2010, http://www.upla.cn/about/about .shtml).

22. *Expo 2010 Shanghai China Official Guidebook*, 4.

23. Ibid. Emphasis added.

24. Louisa Lim, "Tyranny of High Expectations," National Public Radio, April 23, 2010, accessed May 15, 2013, http://www.npr.org/templates/story/story.php?storyId = 126223052.

25. Both reports are available at http://www.unep.org.

26. Zhihao Tang, "Will They Stay or Will They Go?" *China Daily*, April 19, 2010, accessed May 13, 2013, http://www.chinadaily.com.cn/china/2010-04/19/content_9745597.htm.

27. Ted Plafker, "Shanghai Puts on a Green Face," *New York Times*, April 29, 2010, accessed May 13, 2013, http://www.nytimes.com/2010/04/30/world/asia/30iht-rshanover.html..

28. Melissa Checker, "Wiped Out by the 'Greenwave': Environmental Gentrification and the Paradoxical Politics of Urban Sustainability," *City and Society* 23, no. 2 (2011): 210–229.

29. *Expo 2010 Shanghai China Official Guidebook*, 233.

30. Ibid.

31. "Chengshi Shengming Guan: Quan 'Guochan' shibozhutiguan'" [City Being Pavilion: The Totally China-Made Pavilion], Xinhua-Shanghai News Net, April 28, 2010, accessed May 15, 2013, http://www.sh.xinhuanet.com/2010-04/28/content_19650050.htm.

32. Italics added.

33. *Expo 2010 Shanghai China Official Guidebook*, 18. Italics added.

34. The movie *Soul Square* was directed by Xia Su, the chair of the media department of China Academy of Art, who said that each story demonstrated the spirit of people who live in that city. Su said that after the devastating Sichuan earthquake, they included that site as well. "Shibo 'chengshishengmingguan' sheji bayiqigao" [The Design Plan of the Expo City Being Pavilion Was Changed Eight Times], *Sohu Culture News* [original source: *Oriental Morning Newspaper*], April 27, 2010, accessed May 15, 2013, http://cul.sohu.com/20100427/n271773817.shtml.

35. Warren Magnusson, "Seeing Like an Eco-City: How to Urbanize Political Science," in *Critical Urban Studies: New Directions*, ed. Jonathan Davies and David Imbroscio (Albany: State University of New York Press, 2010), 41–54.

36. *Expo 2010 Shanghai China Official Guidebook*, 19

37. "Triad Berlin Stands for Communication in Spaces," TRIAD, accessed May 15, 2013, http://www.triad.de/en/company.

38. "Urban Planet," TRIAD, accessed May 15, 2013, http://www.triad.de/en/expo2010-germany/topic.

39. Ibid.

40. Ibid.

41. "Shanghai shibo huishiwuxietiaoju" [Bureau of Shanghai World Expo Affairs and Coordination], Shanghai World Expo official website, accessed

November 11, 2010, http://www.expo2010.cn/expo/sh_expo/qt/zzjg/userob-ject1ai44546.html.

42. "Chengshiweilaiguan: Mengxiang yinling renlei chengshi de weilai [zhutu]" [Urban Future Hall: Dreams Lead Mankind's Future], Shanghai World Expo official website, June 12, 2009, accessed May 15, 2013, http://www.expo2010.cn/a/20090612/000025.htm.

43. Susannah Bunce and Gene Desfor, "Introduction to 'Political Ecologies of Urban Waterfront Transformations,'" *Cities* 24, no. 4 (2007): 251–258.

44. Louisa Lim, "In Shanghai, Alternatives to the World Expo," National Public Radio, May 4, 2010, accessed May 15, 2013, http://www.npr.org/templates/story/story.php?storyId = 126425172.

45. Ibid.

46. Ibid.

47. Ibid.

CONCLUSION

1. Lu, *Chinese Modernity and Global Biopolitics*, 125.

# ACKNOWLEDGMENTS

This book has been a long time coming. How long is not quite clear to me. Let's just use a more contained measure of time, say 2006 when I first read about Dongtan. Since then, I've had a second child—Leo, to join Sofia. My husband, Sasha Abramsky, has published a number of remarkable books. My main thanks, of course, go to my family, who keep me (somewhat) balanced as I fall down the rabbit hole of research. My first book was dedicated to Sofia in the hope of a world with more justice for all. This book is dedicated to Sofia and Leo with the same hope: it is sorely needed in a world that seems to have more injustice and environmental inequality with each passing year, despite our ever-growing technical knowledge. My dad always warned me against being book-smart and life-stupid. The older I get, the more I am convinced that book smarts and life smarts are needed, alongside a concern for social justice. These values include humility, wisdom, and the ability to ask better questions, not the arrogance of thinking that your answer (whether defined on the individual, cultural, or political level) is the right or only answer. Here's hoping that the next decades are better than the past few.

I traveled to Shanghai and the United Kingdom for book research. Thanks to the scholars at NYU, Brown, Stanford, the University of Montreal, and Columbia for inviting me to present on various chapters in progress and for providing invaluable feedback. Closer to home, research clusters at UC Santa Cruz, UC Berkeley, and UC Davis also invited me to present on the work. The collective research strengths in the University of California system are assets to be protected and preserved in the public university, not stripped away in times of economic crisis. Along that line, a number of China scholars at UC Irvine, including Jeff Wasserstrom and Ken Pomeranz (now at the University of Chicago), provided early help and encouragement. Other prominent China scholars such as Linda Cooke Johnson did the same.

A number of talented graduate students helped me along the way: Mayee Wong, Troy Crowder, Yi Zhou, and Terrence Tan. I learned something from all of you, and wish you the best of luck. I also had significant undergraduate assistance, from Amber Ma, Chelsea Jones, and Caylen Garrie as well as important staff assistance from Naomi Ambriz, Kathy Hayden, and others. I've been fortunate to have friends and colleagues stretching back from graduate school at New York University. There are too many to mention, but the continued and active support of my advisors, including Troy Duster and Harvey Molotch, is most appreciated. I give special shout outs to Andrew Ross and Arlene Davila. Mentorship from environmental justice scholars like Joni Adamson, David Pellow, and Noël Sturgeon has been critical throughout my career. I have wonderful colleagues, both in American Studies (Carolyn De La Pena, Grace Wang, Eric Smoodin, Caren Kaplan, Charlotte Biltekoff) and at my university. I want to thank my dean, Jessie Ann Owens, for her support, as well as the rich community of environmental humanists and social scientists (Ari Kelman, Tom Beamish, Louis Warren, Mike Ziser, Hsuan Hsu, Diana Davis, Jonathan London); the race and social justice scholars that overflow in Hart Hall (Kimberly Nettles, Richard Kim, Bettina Ngweno, Beth Rose Middleton, Sunaina Maira, Susette Min, Ines Hernandez Avila, Miroslava Chavez-Garcia), and throughout my campus, in the social sciences, engineering, and environmental sciences (Christina Cogdell, Bruce Haynes, Deb Niemeier, Mary Cadenasso, Fraser Shilling), and others I have accidentally forgotten to mention here. I want to thank my colleague Simon Sadler for his architectural musings at Thamestown, and for our numerous conversations about design and ideology, at the UC Humanities Research Institute SECT seminar in 2009 and since. Thank you to my good friends who have nothing to do with my work life whom I can call to talk about all kinds of things.

Audra Wolfe provided critical assistance at an important time in the research and writing of this book. I can honestly say that her assistance made all the difference in bringing this project to completion. At UC Press, my editor Niels Hooper has provided a steady and calming presence. Kim Hogeland has been eternally patient and incredibly efficient at the same time. Thanks also to all the very professional staff who are working on the technical and book production side, especially Madeleine Adams. I am particularly grateful to the external readers for providing extremely detailed and important advice that I incorporated in my final edits.

I have three last thoughts and thanks. To Sasha: for more than eighteen years, we have traveled and moved together, grown older, started a family, and continued to support each other both professionally and personally. That is a gift that I treasure every day, although I may not always express it. Thanks to my parents (Tony and Lily Sze), siblings (Betty and Lena), and their families (Brad, Liliana, Nakeeb, and Idris). Last, while I was writing this book my maternal grandmother died. Her life saw tremendous change and pain. As I write this, my other step-grandmother, from Chongming, is still alive, and I hope that when this book comes out she will still be here. Several of my mother's friends took me in and walked me around in Shanghai. As they enter the last stages of their lives, having experienced personal and political traumas far beyond my own experience, my hope is that their stories will not be buried in the surging sea of ecological modernization that is overtaking Shanghai.

Although change and death are inevitable parts of life, what is not inevitable are the forms of change that take place over time and in particular places. These are political and cultural choices that get made by individuals, businesses, and governments. Understanding the differences between multiple pathways, between the short and the long term, between responsibility and risk, is how we, in this warming world, might try to gain balance—environmental and otherwise—in an increasingly precarious world.

"A Chinese Eco-City: City of Dreams." *The Economist*, March 19, 2009. Accessed October 12, 2012. http://www.economist.com/node/13330904?story_id = 13330904.

Abelson, Peter. "Economic and Environmental Sustainability in Shanghai." *Applied Economics*. Accessed October 10, 2012. http://www.appliedeconomics.com.au/pubs/papers/pa99_shanghai.htm.

Arkaraprasertkul, Non. "Power, Politics, and the Making of Shanghai." *Journal of Planning History* 9, no. 4 (2009): 232–259.

Arup Associates. *Unified Design*. Edited by Paul Brislin. Chichester: Wiley, 2008.

Balfour, Frederik. "Shanghai Rising." *Bloomberg Businessweek Magazine*, February 18, 2007. Accessed May 13, 2013. http://www.businessweek.com/magazine/content/07_08/b4022055.htm.

Becker, Jasper. "Transforming Beijing." *Travel and Leisure*, February 2004. Accessed October 8, 2012. http://www.travelandleisure.com/articles/seeing-red/1.

Beech, Hannah. "Ye Olde Shanghai." *Time*, February 7, 2005. Accessed September 13, 2013. http://www.time.com/time/magazine/article/0,9171,1025219,00.html.

Bilger, Burkhard. "The Long Dig." *New Yorker*, September 15, 2008. Accessed May 11, 2014. http://www.newyorker.com/reporting/2008/09/15/080915fa_fact_bilger#ixzzoqrvb4dUl.

Bongiorni, Sara. *A Year without "Made in China": One Family's True Life Adventure in the Global Economy*. Hoboken, N.J.: Wiley, 2007.

Bosker, Bianca. *Original Copies: Architectural Mimicry in Contemporary China*. Honolulu: University of Hawai'i Press, 2013.

Boyd, James, and Spencer Banzhaf. "What Are Ecosystem Services? The Need for Standarized Environmental Accounting Units." Resources for the Future, Discussion Paper no. RFF DP 06-02, 2006.

Boyer, Paul. *Urban Masses and Moral Order in America, 1820-1920*. Cambridge, Mass.: Harvard University Press, 1978.

Bracken, Gregory. "Thinking Shanghai: A Foucauldian Interrogation of the Postsocialist Metropolis." Ph.D. diss., TU Delft, 2009.

"Brief Introduction to Luodian Town." Luodian website. Accessed April 27, 2013. http://en.luodian.com/Brief_Luodian.html.

Brook, Timothy. *Collaboration: Japanese Agents and Local Elites in Wartime China*. Cambridge, Mass.: Harvard University Press, 2005.

Bunce, Susannah, and Gene Desfor. "Introduction of 'Political Ecologies of Urban Waterfront Transformations.'" *Cities* 24, no. 4 (2007): 251-258.

Campanella, Thomas J. *The Concrete Dragon: China's Urban Revolution and What It Means for the World*. New York: Princeton Architectural Press, 2008.

Castle, Helen. "Dongtan: China's Flagship Eco-City: An Interview with Peter Head." *Architectural Design* 78, no. 5 (2008): 64-69.

Center for Climate and Energy Solutions: Working Together for the Environment and the Economy. "Buildings and Emissions: Making the Connection." N.d. Accessed October 5, 2012. http://www.c2es.org/technology/overview/buildings.

Chang, Leslie T. *Factory Girls: From Village to City in a Changing China*. New York: Spiegel and Grau, 2008.

Checker, Melissa. "Wiped Out by the 'Greenwave': Environmental Gentrification and the Paradoxical Politics of Urban Sustainability." *City and Society* 23, no. 2 (2011): 210-229.

Chen, C. Peter. "Second Battle of Shanghai, 13 Aug 1937–9 Nov 1937." World War II Database. Accessed April 27, 2013. http://ww2db.com/battle_spec.php?battle_id = 85.

Chen, Mel Y. *Animacies: Biopolitics, Racial Mattering, and Queer Affect.* Durham, N.C.: Duke University Press, 2012.

———. "Racialized Toxins and Sovereign Fantasies." *Discourse* 29, nos. 2–3 (2007): 367–383.

Chen, Xiangming, ed. *Shanghai Rising: State Power and Local Transformations in a Global Megacity.* Minneapolis: University of Minnesota Press, 2009.

"Chengshiweilaiguan: Mengxiang yinling renlei chengshi de weilai [zhutu]" [Urban Future Hall: Dreams Lead Mankind's Future]. Shanghai World Expo official website. June 12, 2009. Accessed May 15, 2013. http://www.expo2010.cn/a/20090612/000025.htm.

China Human Rights Defenders. "Thrown Out: Human Rights Abuses in China's Breakneck Real Estate Development." February 9, 2010. Accessed October 8, 2012. http://chrdnet.com/2010/02/08/thrown-out-human-rights-abuses-in-chinas-breakneck-real-estate-development/.

*China Prophecy: Shanghai.* The Skyscraper Museum. Accessed October 1, 2012. http://www.skyscraper.org/EXHIBITIONS/CHINA_PROPHECY/china_prophecy.htm.

"Chongming County Introduction." Chongming County website (English version). Accessed July 9, 2009. http://cmx.sh.gov.cn/cm_website/html/DefaultSite/portal/index/index.htm.

"Cities of the Future—Alejandro Gutierrez." July 28, 2010. http://www.youtube.com/watch?v = mb4GLhRRxS8.

"Committing to the Development of an Ecological Civilization." *Ma Kai Qiushi Journal* 5, no. 4 (October 1, 2013). Accessed May 31, 2014, http://www.chinadaily.com.cn/regional/2011-07/15/content_15573296.htm.

Connery, Christopher. "Better City, Better Life." *Boundary 2* 38, no. 2 (2011): 207–227.

Cronon, William. "The Trouble with Wilderness; or, Getting Back to the Wrong Nature." In *Uncommon Ground: Rethinking the Human Place in Nature*, edited by William Cronon, 69–90. New York: W. W. Norton, 1995.

"Daqiao zaozai chenjiazhen heli ma?" [Is It Reasonable to Build the Bridge in Chenjia Town?]. Chongming ba [Chongming Online Club]. Accessed March 22, 2009. http://tieba.baidu.com/f?kz = 722428077.

de Gues, Marius. "Ecotopia, Sustainability, and Vision." *Organization and Environment* 15 (2002): 187–201.

de Groot, Rudolf S., Matthew A. Wilson, and Roelof M. J. Boumans. "A Typology for the Classification, Description and Valuation of Ecosystem Functions, Goods and Services." *Ecological Economics* 41, no. 3 (2002): 393–408.

Dorsey, Michael. "Climate Knowledge and Power: Tales of Skeptic Tanks, Weather Gods, and Sagas for Climate (In)justice." *Capitalism Nature Socialism* 18, no. 2 (2007): 7–21.

Dorsey, Michael, and Gerardo Gambirazzio. "A Critical Geography of the Global CDM." In *The CDM in Africa Cannot Deliver the Money*, edited by Patrick Bond, Joan Martinez-Alier, Khadija Shariffe, Leah Temper, and Ruth Castel-Branco, 26–35. Durban: University of KwaZulu-Natal Centre for Civil Society, 2012.

"Eco²Cities : Ecological Cities as Economic Cities." World Bank website. Accessed August 12, 2013. http://web.worldbank.org/WBSITE/EXTERNAL/TOPICS/EXTURBANDEVELOPMENT/0,,contentMDK:22643153~pagePK:148956~piPK:216618~theSitePK:337178,00.html.

Economy, Elizabeth. *The River Runs Black: The Environmental Challenge to China's Future*. Ithaca, N.Y.: Cornell University Press, 2004.

Encyclopedia of Shanghai Editorial Committee. "Songjiang District." In *The Encyclopedia of Shanghai*. Shanghai: Shanghai Science & Technology Publishing House, 2010. Accessed April 25, 2013. http://zhuanti.shanghai.gov.cn/encyclopedia/en/Default2.aspx#358.

*Expo 2010 Shanghai China Official Guidebook*. Shanghai: China Publishing Group, 2010.

Faber, Daniel. *Capitalizing on Environmental Injustice: The Polluter-Industrial Complex in the Age of Globalization*. Lanham, Md.: Rowman & Littlefield, 2008.

Fisher, Dana R., and William R. Freudenburg. "Ecological Modernization and Its Critics: Assessing the Past and Looking toward the Future." *Society and Natural Resources* 14, no. 8 (2001): 701–709.

Forster, Wayne, and Dean Hawkes. *Energy Efficient Buildings: Architecture, Engineering and Environment*. New York: W. W. Norton, 2002.

Friedman, Thomas L. *Hot, Flat and Crowded: Why We Need a Green Revolution—and How It Can Renew America*. New York: Farrar, Straus, and Giroux, 2008.

Gallagher, Kelly Sims. *China Shifts Gears: Automakers, Oil, Pollution, and Development*. Cambridge, Mass.: MIT Press, 2006.

Gillis, John R. *Islands of the Mind: How the Human Imagination Created the Atlantic World*. New York: Palgrave Macmillan, 2009.

Girard, Greg. *Phantom Shanghai*. Toronto: Magenta Foundation, 2007.

Glaeser, Edward. *Triumph of the City: How Our Greatest Invention Makes Us Richer, Smarter, Greener, Healthier, and Happier*. New York: Penguin, 2011.

Gómez-Baggethun, Erik, Rudolf de Groot, Pedro L. Lomas, and Carlos Montes. "The History of Ecosystem Services in Economic Theory and Practice: From Early Notions to Markets and Payment Schemes." *Ecological Economics* 69, no. 6 (2010): 1209–1218.

Gregotti Associati International. "2001/2002 Shanghai (People's Republic of China) Urban Planning & Landscape Design Town of Pujiang, First Prize in the Closed International Design Competition." Accessed April 27, 2013. http://www.webalice.it/s.zirilli/Eventi/Pujiangnewtown.htm.

Greenberg, Miriam. *Branding New York: How a City in Crisis Was Sold to the World*. New York: Routledge, 2008.

———."The Sustainability Edge: Competition, Crisis, and the Rise of Eco-City Branding in New York and New Orleans." In *Sustainability in the Global City: Myth and Practice*, edited by Melissa Checker, Cindy Isenhour, and Gary McDonough. Cambridge: Cambridge University Press, 2014.

Hanak, Ellen, and Matthew Davis. "Lawns and Water Demand in California." *California Economic Policy* 2, no. 2 (2006). Accessed October 29, 2012. http://www.ppic.org/content/pubs/cep/ep_706ehep.pdf.

Harvey, David. *The Condition of Postmodernity: An Enquiry into the Conditions of Cultural Change*. Oxford: Blackwell, 1989.

Hassenpflüg, Dieter. "European Urban Fictions in China." EspacesTemps.net. Works. November 10, 2008. Accessed September 13, 2013. http://www.espacestemps.net/en/articles/european-urban-fictions-in-china-en/.

Hawkens, Paul, Amory Lovins, and L. Hunter Lovins. *Natural Capitalism: Creating the Next Industrial Revolution*. Boston: Little, Brown, 1999.

He, Shenjing, and Fulong Wu. "Property-Led Redevelopment in Post-Reform China: A Case Study of Xintiandi Redevelopment Project in Shanghai." *Journal of Urban Affairs* 27, no. 1 (2005): 1–23.

Heinzerling, Lisa, and Frank Ackerman. *Pricing the Priceless: Cost-Benefit Analysis of Environmental Protection*. Washington, D.C.: Georgetown Environmental Law and Policy Institute and Georgetown University Law Center, 2002.

Hohn, Donovan. "Through the Open Door: Searching for Deadly Toys in China's Pearl River Delta." *Harpers*, September 2008, 47–58.

Hu, Jingtao. "Report to the Seventeenth National Congress of the Communist Party of China." (A Special Topic on the Seventeenth National Congress of the Communist Party of China). *Xinhua Wang* [*Chinaview*], October 24, 2007. Accessed 16 June 2009. http://news.xinhuanet.com/newscenter/2007-10/24/content_6938568.htm.

Huang, Baorong, Zhiyun Ouyang, Hua Zheng, Huizhi Zhang, and Xiaoke Wang. "Construction of an Eco-Island: A Case Study of Chongming Island, China." *Ocean and Coastal Management* 51, nos. 8–9 (2008): 575–588.

Huang, Carol. "China's Shanghai Expo 2010—by the Numbers." *Christian Science Monitor*, April 29, 2010. Accessed May 13, 2013. http://www.csmonitor.com/World/Global-News/2010/0429/China-s-Shanghai-Expo-2010-by-the-numbers.

Huo, Xia, Lin Peng, Xijin Xu, Liangkai Zheng, Bo Qiu, Zongli Qi, Bao Zhang, Dai Han, and Zhongxian Piao. "Elevated Blood Lead Levels of Children in Guiyu, an Electronic Waste Recycling Town in China." *Environmental Health Perspectives* 115, no. 7 (2007): 1113–1117.

Imada, Adria L. *Aloha America: Hula Circuits through the U.S. Empire*. Durham, N.C.: Duke University Press, 2012.

Jun, Zhang, and Fu Yong. "Shanghai and Yangtze River Delta: A Revolving Relationship." In *Regional Economic Development in China*, edited by Swee-Hock Saw and John Wong, 123–154. Singapore: ISEAS, 2009.

Kahn, Joseph, and Jim Yardley. "As China Roars, Pollution Reaches Deadly Extremes." *New York Times*, August 26, 2007, accessed October 5, 2012, http://www.nytimes.com/2007/08/26/world/asia/26china.html?pagewanted = all.

Kaika, Maria. *City of Flows: Modernity, Nature, and the City*. New York: Routledge, 2005.

Kaufman, Rachel. "Shanghai's European Suburbs." Smithsonian.com, June 10, 2010. Accessed April 27, 2013. http://www.smithsonianmag.com/people-places/Shanghais-European-Suburbs.html.

Kipnis, Andrew. "Neoliberalism Reified: *Suzhi* Discourse and Tropes of Neoliberalism in the People's Republic of China." *Journal of the Royal Anthropological Institute* 13, no. 2 (2007): 383–400.

———. "Suzhi: A Keyword Approach." *China Quarterly* 186 (2006): 295–313.

Krupar, Shiloh. "Shanghaiing the Future: A Detour of the Shanghai Urban Planning Exhibition." *Public Culture* 20, no. 2 (2008): 307–320.

Lam, Kin-che, and Shu Tao. "Environmental Quality and Pollution Control." In *Shanghai: Transformation and Modernisation under China's Open Door Policy*, edited by Yue-man Yeung and Yun-wing Sung, 469–492. Hong Kong: Chinese University Press, 1996.

Land, Nick, ed. *Urbanatomy Shanghai: 2009*. Shanghai: Nan Kai University Press, 2008.

Lansdowne, Helen. "Thamestown, China, Simulacra and the Realm of Make Believe." Presented at the 42nd Annual Conference of Asian Studies on the Pacific Coast, Crossing Boundaries in the Asia-Pacific, Victoria, Canada, June 13–15, 2008. Accessed April 25, 2013. http://capiconf.uvic.ca/viewabstract.php?id = 187&cf = 3.

Lee, Leo Ou-Fan. *Shanghai Modern: The Flowering of a New Urban Culture in China, 1930–1945*. Cambridge, Mass.: Harvard University Press, 1999.

LeMenager, Stephanie, Teresa Shewry, and Ken Hiltner. "Introduction." In *Environmental Criticism for the Twenty-first Century*, edited by Stephanie LeMenager, Teresa Shewry, and Ken Hiltner, 1–15. New York: Routledge, 2011.

Li, Tiangang. "A Long Love Affair." *Beijing Review*, May 9, 2009. Accessed May 13, 2013. http://www.bjreview.com.cn/nation/txt/2009-05/09/content_194750.htm.

Lim, Louisa. "In Shanghai, Alternatives to the World Expo." National Public Radio, May 4, 2010. Accessed May 15, 2013. http://www.npr.org/templates/story/story.php?storyId = 126425172.

———. "Tyranny of High Expectations." National Public Radio, April 23, 2010. Accessed May 15, 2013. http://www.npr.org/templates/story/story.php?storyId = 126223052.

Lloren, Terrence. *Growing Up with Shanghai*. MP3 on Soundcloud, 12.21.01. Accessed January 2, 2010. http://www.growingupwithshanghai.com.

Lohmann, Larry. "Carbon Trading, Climate Justice and the Production of Ignorance: Ten Examples." *Development* 51 (2008): 359–365.

Lu, Dingfeng. "Shenru yanjiu Chongming de lishi fangwei yu weilai fazhan" [Deep Analysis of Chongming's Historical Position and Future Development]. Shanghai Chongming Government official website. Accessed June 6, 2009. http://www.cmx.gov.cn/cmwebnew/node2/node2611/node2693/userobject7ai58444.html.

Lu, Sheldon H. *Chinese Modernity and Global Biopolitics*. Honolulu: University of Hawaii Press, 2007.

Lu, Sheldon H., and Jiayan Mi, eds. *Chinese Ecocinema in the Age of Environmental Challenge*. Hong Kong: University of Hong Kong Press, 2009.

Magnusson, Warren. "Seeing Like an Eco-City: How to Urbanize Political Science." In *Critical Urban Studies: New Directions*, ed. Jonathan Davies and David Imbroscio, 41–54. Albany: State University of New York Press, 2010.

Martinez-Alier, Joan. "The Distributional Effects of Environmental Policy." *Ecological Economics* 63 (2007): 246–247.

May, Shannon. "Dongtan, China." In *Green Cities: An A-to-Z Guide*, edited by Nevin Cohen and Paul Robbins. Thousand Oaks, Calif.: SAGE Publications, 2011. Accessed May 11, 2014. http://www.sage-ereference.com/view/green-cities/n48.xml.

———. "Ecological Citizenship and a Plan for Sustainable Development." *City: Analysis of Urban Trends, Culture, Theory, Policy, Action* 12, no. 2 (2008): 237–244.

McCarthy, Greg. "The Climate Change Metanarrative, State of Exception and China's Modernisation." *Journal of the Indian Ocean Region* 6, no. 2 (2010): 252–266.

McCorquodale, Duncan, ed. *Solutions for a Modern City: Arup in Beijing*. London: Black Dog, 2008.

McGray, Douglas. "China's Great Leap Forward." *Wired*, April 24, 2007. Accessed October 12, 2012. http://www.wired.com/wired/archive/15.05/feat_popup_sb.html.

McKinsey Global Institute. "Preparing for China's Urban Billion." March 2009. Accessed October 5, 2012. http://www.mckinsey.com/insights/mgi/research/urbanization/preparing_for_urban_billion_in_china.

Meyer, Michael. *The Last Days of Old Beijing: Life in the Vanishing Backstreets of a City Transformed*. New York: Walker Books, 2008.

Mol, Arthur P. J., and Gert Spaargaren. "Ecological Modernisation Theory in Debate: A Review." In *Ecological Modernisation around the World: Perspectives and Critical Debates*, edited by Arthur P. J. Mol and David Allan Sonnefeld, 17-49. London: Frank Cass, 2000.

"National Climate Change Program." China.org.cn, June 4, 2007. Accessed July 17, 2009. http://www.china.org.cn/english/environment/213624.htm.

Ng, Mee Kam. "Governance for Sustainability in East Asian Global Cities: An Exploratory Study." *Journal of Comparative Policy Analysis: Research and Practice* 9, no. 4 (2007): 351-381.

Osterhammel, Jürgen. "Britain and China, 1842-1914." In *The Oxford History of the British Empire*, vol. 3, *The Nineteenth Century*, edited by Andrew Porter and William Roger Louis, 146-169. Oxford: Oxford University Press, 1999.

"Overview of the Project," *Sino-Italian Cooperation Program for Environmental Protection*. Accessed October 1, 2012. http://www.sinoitaenvironment.org/indexe02.asp.

Owen, David. "The Anti-Gravity Men." *New Yorker*, June 25, 2007. Accessed August 28, 2013. http://www.newyorker.com/reporting/2007/06/25/070625fa_fact_owen—ixzzoqrsh4h7z.

Pagiola, Stefano. "How Useful Is Ecosystem Valuation?" Presented at the conference Economics and Conservation in the Tropics: A Strategic Dialogue, convened by the Conservation Strategy Fund, Gordon and Betty Moore Foundation, and Resources for the Future, January 31-February 1, 2008. Accessed September 30, 2013. http://www.rff.org/Documents/08_Tropics_Conference/Tropics_Conference_Papers/Tropics_Conference_Pagiola_Ecosystem_Valuation.pdf.

Pan, XiaoQiao. "Moving On Up?" *Beijing Review*, n.d. Accessed April 27, 2013. http://www.bjreview.cn/EN/06-26-e/bus-1.htm.

Pasternack, Alex, and Clifford A. Pearson. "National Stadium: Herzog & De Meuron Creates an Icon That Reaches beyond the Olympics." *Architectural Record* 196, no. 7 (2008): 92-99.

Pellow, David Naguib. *Resisting Global Toxics: Transnational Movements for Environmental Justice*. Cambridge, Mass.: MIT Press, 2007.

Pepper, David. "Utopianism and Environmentalism." *Environmental Politics* 14, no. 1 (2005): 3–22.

Pow, Choon-Piew. "Neoliberalism and the Aestheticization of New Middle-Class Landscapes." *Antipode* 41, no. 2 (2009): 371–390.

"Pujiang New Town, Shanghai China." Designbuild-network.com., n.d. Accessed October 29, 2012. http://www.designbuild-network.com/projects/pujiang.

Qian, Dai. "Impression on Xinsong Park." *World Expo Magazine*, September 1, 2006. Accessed April 27, 2013. http://www.expo2010.cn/expo/expoenglish/wem/node1245/userobject1ai36760.html.

Ren, Xuefei. *Building Globalization: Transnational Architecture Production in Urban China*. Chicago: University of Chicago Press, 2011.

Robbins, Paul. *Lawn People: How Grasses, Weeds, and Chemicals Make Us Who We Are*. Philadelphia: Temple University Press, 2007.

Rofel, Lisa. *Desiring China: Experiments in Neoliberalism, Sexuality, and Public Culture*. Durham, N.C.: Duke University Press, 2007.

Rowe, Peter. G, and Seng Kuan, eds. *Shanghai: Architecture and Urbanism for Modern China*. Munich: Prestel, 2004.

Russell, Edmund. *War and Nature: Fighting Humans and Insects with Chemicals from World War I to Silent Spring*. Cambridge: Cambridge University Press, 2001.

Sagoff, Mark. "Environmental Economics and the Conflation of Value and Benefit." *Environmental Science and Technology* 34, no. 8 (2000): 1426–1432.

Sayre, Nathan. "Climate Change, Scale, and Devaluation: The Challenge of Our Built Environment." *Washington and Lee Journal of Climate, Energy, and the Environment* 1, no. 1 (2010): 93–105.

———. "Ecological and Geographical Scale: Parallels and Potential for Integration." *Progress in Human Geography* 29, no. 3 (2005): 276–290.

Schein, Louisa. "The Consumption of Color and the Politics of White Skin in Post-Mao China." *Social Text* 41 (1994): 141–164.

Schneider, François, Giorgos Kallis, and Joan Martinez-Alier. "Crisis or Opportunity? Economic Degrowth for Social Equity and Ecological Sustainability: Introduction to This Special Issue." *Journal of Cleaner Production* 18, no. 6 (2010): 511–518.

Schönberger, Angela. *Die neue Reichskanzlei von Albert Speer. Zum Zusammenhang von nationalsozialistischer Ideologie und Architektur.* Berlin: Gebrüder Mann Verlag, 1991.

Scobie, Alex. *Hitler's State Architecture: The Impact of Classical Antiquity.* University Park: Pennsylvania State University Press, 1990.

Scott, James C. *Seeing Like a State: How Certain Schemes to Improve the Human Condition Have Failed.* New Haven, Conn.: Yale University Press, 1998.

Shanghai shi Chengxiang jianshe he jiaotong weiyuanhui [Shanghai Committee of Urban Construction and Communications]. "Shanghai renminzhengfu 'guanyu shanghaishi cujin chengzhen fazhan de shidian yijian'" [Shanghai Government: "A Proposal for Speeding Up Experimental Sites of Shanghai Towns' Development"]. 2006. Accessed May 11, 2014. http://law.eastday.com/epublish/gb/paper20/1/class002000001/hwz562963.htm.

"Shanghai shibo huishiwuxietiaoju" [Bureau of Shanghai World Expo Affairs and Coordination]. Shanghai World Expo official website. Accessed November 11, 2010. http://www.expo2010.cn/expo/sh_expo/qt/zzjg/userobject1ai44546.html.

"Shanghai Suburbs: Hot Land for Investment." *Shanghai Agriculture and Suburb Development*, n.d. Accessed April 27, 2013. http://en.shac.gov.cn/jdxw/200307/t20030707_74813.htm.

"Shanghai Tower." *Gensler Design Update.* Accessed May 16, 2013. http://www.gensler.com/uploads/documents/Shanghai_Tower_12_22_2010.pdf.

Shanghaishi difang zhiban gongshi [Shanghai Chorography Office]. "Shanghai nianjian 2005: Yicheng jiuzheng jianshe" [Shanghai 2005 Yearbook: The Construction of "One City, Nine Towns"]. Accessed June 18, 2009. http://www.shtong.gov.cn/node2/node19828/node72707/node72895/node72897/userobject1ai83762.html.

Shapiro, Judith. *Mao's War against Nature: Politics and the Environment in Revolutionary China.* Cambridge: Cambridge University Press, 2001.

Shen, Ying. "Dongtan chenfu shimo" [The Vicissitudes of Dongtan]. *GE huanqiu qiyejia* [*GE Global Entrepreneur Magazine*], March 20, 2009. Accessed July 23, 2009. http://www.gemag.com.cn/14/11202_1.html.

Soleri, Paolo. *Arcology: The City in the Image of Man.* Scottsdale, Ariz.: Cosanti Press, 2006.

Spangenberg, Joachim H., and Josef Settele. "Precisely Incorrect? Monetising the Value of Ecosystem Services." *Ecological Complexity* 7, no. 3 (2010): 327–337.

Springer, Kate. "Soaring to Sinking: How Building Up Is Bringing Shanghai Down." *Time*, May 21, 2012. Accessed October 8, 2012. http://science.time.com/2012/05/21/soaring-to-sinking-how-building-up-is-bringing-shanghai-down/.

Suzuki, Hiroaki, Arish Dastur, Sabastian Moffatt, Nanae Yabuki, and Hinako Maruyama. *Eco²Cities: Ecological Cities as Economic Cities*. Washington, D.C.: World Bank, 2010.

Szasz, Andrew. *Shopping Our Way to Safety: How We Changed from Protecting the Environment to Protecting Ourselves*. Minneapolis: University of Minnesota Press, 2007.

Sze, Julie, and Gerardo Gambirazzio. "Eco-Cities without Ecology: Constructing Ideologies, Valuing Nature." In *Resilience in Urban Ecology and Design: Linking Theory and Practice for Sustainable Cities*, edited by S. T. A. Pickette, M. L. Cadenasso, and Brian McGrath, 289–297. Heidelberg: Springer, 2013.

Sze, Julie, and Yi Zhou. "Imagining a Chinese Eco-City: Environmental Criticism for the 21st Century." In *Environmental Criticism for the Twenty-first Century*, edited by Stephanie LeMenager, Teresa Shewry, and Ken Hiltner, 216–230. New York: Routledge. 2011.

Tian, Gary Gang. *Shanghai's Role in the Economic Development of China: Reform of Foreign Trade and Investment*. Westport, Conn.: Praeger, 1996.

Turner, Kerry R., Jouni Paavola, Philip Cooper, Stephen Farber, Valma Jessamy, and Stavros Georgiou. "Valuing Nature: Lessons Learned and Future Research Directions." *Ecological Economics* 46, no. 3 (2003): 493–510.

Tyrnauer, Matt. "Industrial Revolution, Take Two." *Vanity Fair*, May 2008. Accessed October 8, 2012. http://www.vanityfair.com/culture/features/2008/05/mcdonough200805.

United Nations Office for Disaster Risk Reduction. "Mayors Unanimously Adopt Declaration to Build Urban Resilience and Fight Climate Change." June 14, 2011. Accessed April 27, 2013. http://www.unisdr.org/archive/20319.

Walker, Kathy Le Mons, "'Gangster Capitalism' and Peasant Protest in China: The Last Twenty Years." *Journal of Peasant Studies* 33, no. 1 (2006): 1–33.

Wasserstrom, Jeffrey N. *Global Shanghai, 1850–2010: A History in Fragments*. New York: Routledge, 2009.

———. "Is Global Shanghai 'Good to Think'? Thoughts on Comparative History and Post-Socialist Cities." *Journal of World History* 18, no. 2 (2007): 199–234.

"Waste Management in China: Issues and Recommendations." Urban Development Working Papers, East Asia Infrastructure Department, World Bank, Working Paper no. 9, May 2005. Accessed April 19, 2013. http://siteresources. worldbank.org/INTEAPREGTOPURBDEV/Resources/China-Waste-Management1.pdf.

Watts, Jonathan. *When a Billion Chinese Jump: How China Will Save Mankind—or Destroy It*. New York: Scribner, 2010.

Weinstein, Liza, and Xuefei Ren. "The Changing Right to the City: Urban Renewal and Housing Rights in Globalizing Shanghai and Mumbai." *City and Community* 8, no. 4 (2009): 407–432.

Williamson, Judith. *Decoding Advertisements: Ideology and Meaning in Advertising*. London: Boyars, 1994.

"Wo Jiaoao, Wo shi chongmingren" [I Am Proud, I Am a Chongming Person, 2006–2010]. Chongming ba [Chongming Online Club]. Accessed June 10, 2009. http://tieba.baidu.com/f?z = 108779482&ct = 335544320&lm = 0&sc = 0&rn = 30&tn = baiduPostBrowser&word = %B3%E7%C3%F7&pn = 0.

World Bank, Australian International Development Assistance Bureau, Kinhill-PPK Joint Venture and Shanghai Academy of Environmental Sciences and the Shanghai Municipal Government. *Draft Shanghai Masterplan*. Shanghai: Kinhill-PPK Joint Venture and the Shanghai Academy of Environmental Sciences, 1994.

Woronov, T. E. "Governing China's Children: Governmentality and 'Education for Quality.'" *Positions* 17, no. 3 (2009): 567–589.

Wu, Guoyuan, and Chun Shi. "Shanghai's Water Environment." In *The Dragon's Head: Shanghai, China's Emerging Megacity*, edited by Harold D. Foster, David Chuenyan Lai, and Naisheng Zhou, 93–103. Victoria, B.C.: Western Geographical Press, 1998.

Xiangming, Wu. "City Case Study of Shanghai." In *Megacity Management in the Asian and Pacific Region*, vol. 2, *City and Country Case Studies*, edited by Jeffry Stubbs and Gilles Clarke, 203–225. Manila: Asian Development Bank, 1996.

Xue, Charlie Q. L., and Minghao Zhou. "Importation and Adaptation: Building 'One City and Nine Towns' in Shanghai: A Case Study of Vittorio Gregotti's Plan of Pujiang Town." *Urban Design International* 12 (2007): 21–40.

Yan, Zhao, and Herbert Girardet. *Shanghai Dongtan: An Eco-City*. Shanghai: SIIC Dongtan Investment & Development, 2006.

York, Richard, and Eugene A. Rosa. "Key Challenges to Ecological Modernization Theory: Institutional Efficacy, Case Study Evidence, Units of Analysis, and the Pace of Eco-Efficiency." *Organization and Environment* 16, no. 3 (2003): 273–288.

Young, Stephen C. "Introduction: The Origins and Evolving Nature of Ecological Modernisation." In *The Emergence of Ecological Modernisation: Integrating the Environment and the Economy?* edited by Stephen C. Young, 1–39. New York: Routledge, 2009.

Yuan, Wen, James Philip, Ken Hodgson, S. M Hutchinson, and C. Shi. "Development of Sustainability Indicators by Communities in China: A Case Study of Chongming County, Shanghai." *Journal of Environmental Management* 68, no. 3 (2003): 253–261.

Yuan, Yuqin. "Shengtai wenming linian xia de Chongming shengtaidao jianshe" [Chongming Eco-Island's Construction under the Concept of Ecological Civilization]. Shanghai Chongming Government official website. Accessed June 6, 2009. http://www.cmx.gov.cn/cmwebnew/node2/node2611/node2693/userobject7ai58450.html.

Zhang, Li. "Spatiality and Urban Citizenship in Late Socialist China." *Public Culture* 14, no. 2 (2002): 311–334.

Zhang, Tingwei. "Striving to Be a Global City from Below: The Restructuring of Shanghai's Urban Districts." In *Shanghai Rising: State Power and Local Transformations in a Global Megacity*, edited by Xiangming Chen, 167–189. Minneapolis: University of Minnesota Press, 2009.

Zhang, Zhiyuan. "Chongming jingjifazhan de kunhuo, yuanyin ji lujing tupo" [The Confusion, Reason, and Path Breakthrough of Chongming's Economic Development]. Shanghai Chongming Government official website. Accessed June 11, 2009. http://www.cmx.gov.cn/cmwebnew/node2/node2611/node2693/userobject7ai58483.html.

Zhao, Shuqing, Liangjun Da, Zhiyao Tang, Hejun Fang, Kun Song, and Jingyun Fang. "Ecological Consequences of Rapid Urban Expansion: Shanghai, China." *Frontiers in Ecology and the Environment* 4 (2009): 341–346.

Zhongguo Renming gongheguo huanjing baohubu [People's Republic of China Ministry of Environmental Protection]. "Guanyu yinfa 'shengtai xian, shengtai shi, shengtai sheng jianshe zhibiao (xiudinggao)' de tongzhi" [Notice on the Issuance of "Eco-Counties, Eco-Cities, and Eco-Province Construction Index (Revised Draft)"]. December 26, 2007. Accessed July 22, 2009. http://www.mep.gov.cn/gkml/zj/wj/200910/t20091022_172492.htm.

Zhou, Hongchang, Daniel Sperling, Mark Delucci, and Deborah Salon. "Transportation in Developing Countries: Greenhouse Gas Scenarios for Shanghai, China." Pew Center on Global Climate Change, July 2001. Accessed July 23, 2013.http://www.c2es.org/publications/transportation-developing-countries-greenhouse-gas-scenarios-shanghai-china.

"Zhuanjia Jiedu Huanbao bumen 30nian fazhan" [Experts Explain the Thirty-Year Development of the Department of Environmental Protection]. Henan sheng zhengfu menhu wang [Henan Government official website], February 27, 2008. Accessed July 20, 2009. http://www.henan.gov.cn/ztzl/system/2009/03/05/010122517.shtml.

Ziser, Michael, and Julie Sze. "Climate Change, Environmental Aesthetics and Global Environmental Justice Cultural Studies." *Discourse* 29, no. 2 (2007): 384–410.

*Note: Page numbers in italics indicate figures.*

eco-dreams and, 4–6, 89, 166n5; eco-future and, 5, 56, 75; ecological fantasy islands and, 14, 76–77; eco-Potemkin and, 58; eco-romantic notions and, 4, 166n5; eco-Shanghai and, 9–10, 12–15, 101; ecotopianism and, 101; ectopia in context of, 88–89; failed projects and, 9, 83, 96–98, 100–102, 188nn43–44; geographical discourse and, 58; "green" approach and, 3, 83; greenwashing and, 83, 108–9; harmony and, 17, 27, 100; ideology in context of ecology and, 28–29, 75, 82–83, 100; imagined future/new world and, 89, 90–96; international architects and engineers in context of, 70, 82–84, 87, 100, 185n13; land-use policy and, 97, 185n13; master plan and, 3, 91, 187nn27–28; monumental or iconic projects and, 90; moral discourse in context of, 67–68; nature in context of eco-development and, 66–67, 91, 118, 187n28; nature tourism and, 78, 95–96; politics and, 4, 28–29, 82, 96–98, 165n3, 188nn43–44; press coverage of, 57–58; publications and, 91–94, 187n26; "quest" in context of, 3, 42; real estate development and, 18, 83, 94, 101, 118; residents and, 94–95; rural population and, 4–5; rural spaces and, 4; scale and, 9, 95; SIIC and, 3–4; solid waste production and, 2; status of residents and, 78; sustainability and, 5, 82, 89, 98, 100; technological solutions and, 27, 70, 80, 89, 93–94, 98, 100; top down environmentalism, 76, 101–2; urbanism and, 5; wetlands and, 1, 3–4, 9, 81, 185n8; whites/whiteness

and, 94. *See also* Arup, and Dongtan; Chongming Island; Shanghai
dreams: built dream and, 189n3; green dream and, 41, 45, 83–84, 104–5. *See also* eco-dreams
Dutch/European town (Harbor New Town), *106*, 106–7, 113

eco-cities: overview of, 14–17, 38–39, 163, 174n47; betterment and, 57–58, 87; Chinese pollution and, 29, 54; ecological economics and, 65; ecotopianism and, 101–2; energy efficiency, 65; as failed projects, 9, 101; green capitalism and, 54; harmony and, 38–39; international architects and engineers and, 40, 56–57, 89, 98, 174n53, 179n3; real estate development and, 87; satellite, 109–11, 190nn13–15, 191n16; scale and, 9, 15, 66–67, 82–83, 183n32; technological solutions and, 65–66; as term of use, 88; Tianjin and, 39, 157; U.S. and, 15; utopianism and, 88–89. *See also specific eco-cities*
eco-desire: overview and definition of, 15–19, 161; Bird's Nest and, 42–46, *43*; China and, 17, 28; Dongtan, 18; Dongtan and, 18, 83, 86, 134; eco-authoritarianism and, 25–26, 28, 84; eco-development and, 16, 18; ecological fantasy islands, 17–18; economics and, 86; Shanghai and, 17–18; suburbanization and, 14, 18, 104–5, 107–8, 134; U.S. and, 26, 28; World Expo and, 14, 18, 134–35; World Exposition in 2010, 18
eco-development (environmental development): authoritarian political structures and, 27–28; CCP and, 31, 33, 39; on Chongming Island, 1, 12,

eco-development *(continued)*
58, 63–64, 63–67, 64, 75–77, 91,
187n28; Dongtan and, 5, 12, 66–67,
82, 91, 101, 118, 187n28; eco-desire
and, 16, 18; eco-modernization and,
16; economic costs and, 172nn37–38;
ecotopiainism and, 88; local context
and, 6–7, 40–41, 83, 86, 101; nature
in context of, 63–67, 91, 187n28; real
estate development and, 40, 108;
Shanghai and, 11, 29, 53–54, 98, 101;
space/spatial scale of, 15, 66–67,
82–83, 101, 183n32; U.S. in context of
Chinese, 20–21, 23–24, 162–63

eco-dreams: overview of, 8–10; Chongming Island and, 1, 75–76, 80;
downsides in context of, 40; green
dream and, 41, 45, 83–84, 104–5

eco-future: overview of, 163; of Chongming Island, 5, 56, 75; green future
and, 4, 91, 151–57; imagined future/
new world and, 89, 90–96

"ecologically harmonious socialist
society" *(shengtai wenming)*, 36–38

ecology: definitions of, 75–76; eco-
authoritarianism and, 25–26, 28, 84;
eco-counties and, 38, 173n47;
ecological fantasy islands and, 14–15,
17–18, 55–56, 66–67, 76–77, 82;
ecological fears/dystopianism and,
20, 26, 148–49, 151–52; eco-modernization and, 16; economics and, 65;
scale and, 7; urban ecology and,
12–14, 109. *See also* eco-cities;
eco-development (environmental
development); eco-dreams;
eco-future; ideology, in context of
ecology

economic development: building projects
and, 30–31, 33, 35–36, 38, 44, 48–50,
177n83; Chinese pollution in context

of, 24; on Chongming Island, 1;
climate change in context of, 21–22;
environmental impacts/disaster in
context of, 30–31, 33; equity in
context of sustainability and, 39;
frontier status and, 35–36; gendered
dimension of, 66–67, 183n32;
grassroots protests against, 39–40;
harmony and, 39; nature in context
of, 63–66; politics and, 21; property
destruction and, 33; public-private
entities and, 37; purchasing power of
China and, 21; relocation of populations due to building projects and,
30–31, 33, 44, 48–50, 177n83; scale
and, 33–34, 82; technological
solutions and, 54; urbanization in
context of, 32–33; U.S. and, 20–21,
23–24

eco-Potemkin, 17, 58, 116–17

eco-romantic notions, 4, 121, 166n5

eco-Shanghai, 9–10, 12–15, 17, 90–91,
101. *See also* Shanghai

ecotopiainism, 87–89, 99, 150, 186nn19–
20, 188n47

eco-villages, 40–41, 86, 137, 151

energy consumption, 38, 173n39

energy efficiency, 15, 38, 65, 101, 120

engineers, 70, 85. *See also* international
architects and engineers (transnational builders and engineers)

Enquist, Philip, 100, 189n49

environmental development (eco-
development). *See* eco-development
(environmental development)

environmental impacts/disaster: air
pollution in context of, 34; alienation
and, 93, 187n35; authoritarian
political structures and, 27–28;
building projects and, 38; Chinese
pollution in context of, 33–34; cost

Lake Tai, 30, 38
land-use policy, 37, 46–47, 53, 82, 97, 109, 111, 160, 185n13
late capitalism, 71
lawns, and suburbanization, 104–5, 190n7
Liujiazui district, 107, 190n10
local context, and eco-development, 6–7, 40–41, 83, 86, 101
Luo Dian (Northern European/Scandinavian/Swedish town), 106, 108, 113, 123–26, 194n48, 195n54

Mao Zedong, 30–31, 33, 167n20
maritime economy, 34, 143, 153, 155
Masdar eco-city, 15, 150
McDonough, William, 40–41, 151, 175n54
megaskyscrapers, 13, 64, 90–91, 99, 120–21. See also monumental (iconic) projects
methodology, 7, 9, 14–16, 19–20, 159–60
mêtis, 161
miniaturization, 121, 135–36, 156, 157
Ministry of Environmental Protection, 37–38, 173n40
modernization, and alientation, 93, 187n35
monumental (iconic) projects: overview of, 31; Arup, 57, 89–90; Beijing and, 44; Beijing Olympics in 2008, 44, 89; Dongtan and, 90; epic-scale projects and, 13, 19, 27, 31, 68, 187n35; Germany and, 44, 118–19; megaskyscrapers and, 13, 64, 90–91, 99, 120–21; Pudong district and, 64, 120–21; Shanghai and, 99; spectacles and, 12, 82, 131, 137; U.S. and, 72
moral discourse, 18, 67–68, 109, 150. See also environmental justice/injustice
Moses, Robert, 33, 52

multimethodological (interdisciplinary) analysis, 7, 14, 19–20, 159
multiple environmentalisms, 159–60
multiscalar analysis, 9, 19

nationalism: China and, 13, 20–21; climate change in context of, 21–22; nature/nation and, 105, 108, 114–16, 124–25, 129; real estate development in context of, 112; shi or "world" and, 140–41, 144–45, 157; U.S. and, 20, 24–25
nature: economic development in context of, 63–66; nature/nation and, 105, 108, 114–16, 124–25, 129; nature tourism and, 18, 67, 72–73, 78, 79, 80, 95–96, 99; One City, Nine Towns and, 104–5, 107, 115–16, 118; Pudong district in context of, 118, 121. See also harmony
neoliberalism, 8, 17, 32, 37, 190n7
Northern European/Scandinavian/Swedish town (Luo Dian), 106, 108, 113, 123–26, 194n48, 195n54

One City, Nine Towns: overview of, 105–7, 106, 128–29; An Ting or German town and, 106, 108, 113–14, 115, 117–18, 121–23, 125, 128, 191n17, 193nn41–42; betterment and, 104, 115; built dream in context of, 104, 189n3; carbon emissions/low carbon and, 108, 114, 122; Cheng Qiao or traditional southern Chinese town and, 106; clean air and, 108, 128; construction quality and, 104, 118; eco-desire and, 14, 18, 104–5, 107–8, 134; economic costs and, 114, 121, 123–24, 126, 194n48; energy efficiency and, 120; environmentalism and, 107; Feng Cheng or Spanish

18, 83, 94, 101, 118; eco-cities and, 87; eco-development and, 40, 108; greenwashing in context of, 108-9; nationalism in context of, 112; One City, Nine Towns and, 116-18; Shanghai and, 13, 72-73, 119-21, *120*; SIIC and, 57; suburbanization and, 18, 107-8

Register, Richard, 88

relocation of populations, and building projects: Beijing Olympics in 2008 and, 33, 44; building projects in context of, 33, 44; economic development in China and, 30-31, 33, 44, 48-50, 177n83; Shanghai and, 48-50, 113, 177n83; U.S. and, 30, 33; World Expo and, 127-28. *See also* environmental justice/injustice

ruin value theory, 118-19, 193n36

scale: climate change in context of, 6-7, 166n9; eco-cities and, 9; ecology and, 7; ecology in context of, 7; economic development in China and, 33-34, 82; environmental impacts/disaster in China and, 93; epic-scale projects, 13, 19, 27, 31, 68, 187n35; globalization, 8; global warming in context of, 8; multiscalar analysis, 9, 19; time/temporal, 7-9, 18, 71, 95, 145, 150, 152. *See also* space/spatial scale

Schumacher, E. F., 9

Schumpeter, Joseph, 33

"seeing like a city" (city-optic), 147, 158, 161

"seeing like a state," 27-28, 138, 147, 158, 170n17

self-reflexivity, 161-62

Shanghai: overview and history of, 11-12, 55-56, 61-62, 125, 195n54; air quality

and, 51-52, 178n94; anti-Shanghai spaces and, 17, 20, 90-91, 120; automobile industry and, 114, 122-23; betterment and, 53; bridges and infrastructure in, 72; Bund and, 49, 120-21, 133; carbon emissions and, 52, 178n94; carbon trading market and, 47, 176n73; city/nation relationship and, 132-33; construction quality and, 101, 118; eco-desire and, 17-18; eco-development and, 11, 29, 53-54, 98, 101; eco-Potemkin and, 17; eco-Shanghai and, 9-10, 12-15, 17, 90-91, 101; energy efficiency and, 101; environmental problems in, 29, 46-53; gentrification and, 143; global power and, 11-12, 132, 147; greenhouse gas emissions, 52; greenwashing and, 15, 145; harmony and, 12; housing and, 47; Japan and, 11; Jiangnan Shipyard and, 143, 153, 155; land-use policy and, 46-47, 53, 111; maritime economy and, 143, 153, 155; megaskyscrapers and, 13, 90-91, 120, 145; model for development and, 11-12, 116, 119-20, *120*, 167n20; modernization and, 12, 13, 16, 49, 60; monumental or iconic projects and, 99; politics and, 11-12, 167n20; real estate development and, 13, 72-73, 119-21, *120*; relocation of populations due to building projects in, 48-50, 113, 177n83; satellite eco-cities development and, 109-11, 190nn13-15, 191n16; sea level rise and, 46; solid waste production and, 53, 178n99; sustainability and, 17, 53, 178n101; top down environmentalism and, 178n101; transformations and, 5-6, 12-13, 137, 143, 153, 155, 187n35; urban development and, 47-51,

suzhi discourse, 67–68
SWECO, 113, 123

technological solutions: overview of, 27,
54; authoritarian political structure
in China and, 70; Dongtan and, 27,
70, 80, 89, 93–94, 98, 100; eco-cities
and, 65–66; eco-modernization and,
16; economic development and, 54;
environmentalism, 54; geographical
discourse and, 58, 71; green dream
and, 83–84; infrastructure construction and, 69–70; One City, Nine
Towns and, 122–23; politics and, 71;
suburbanization and, 27; World Expo
and, 27, 134–35, 148, 150–51; world
expositions and, 137. *See also* green
technology
Tenth Five-Year Plan, The, 110, 118, 190
Thames Town, 103–8, *108, 112*, 112–14,
117–19, 122, 124, 128, 191n16. *See also*
Song Jiang district
theme parks, 103, 107, 136–37
"Think Global—Act Local," 6–7
Thoreau, Henry David, 134, 152
Three Gorges Dam, 27, 31, 34, 60,
187n35
Tianjin eco-city, 39, *156*, 157
time/temporal scale, 7–9, 18, 71, 95, 145,
150, 152. *See also* scale
top down environmentalism, 16, 19, 25,
40, 76, 101–2, 157, 178n101
tourism: nature, 18, 67, 72–73, 78, 79, *80*,
95–96, 99; in U.K., 111; in U.S., 73, 111
transnational builders and engineers
(international architects and
engineers). *See* international
architects and engineers (transnational builders and engineers)
Treasure Island Sustainability Plan, 88,
99, 150, 186nn19–20, 188n47

Triad, 147–51, *149*

United Arab Emirates, 15–16, 150
United Kingdom, 32, 105, 111, 116, 155
United Nations Development Programme
Pilot Town, 123–24
United Nations National Development
Reform Pilot Town, 123–24
United States: authoritarian political
structure and, 54; automobiles and
automobile industry in, 116–17,
122–23; bridges and infrastructure in,
72; carbon emissions and, 21, 26–27,
38; consumerism in, 23–24, 26, 54;
eco-cities and, 15; eco-desire and,
26, 28; eco-development in China
and, 20–21, 23–24, 162–63; electronic
waste from, 34–35; environmental
impacts/disaster and, 30, 72–73;
environmental justice movement in,
163; equity in context of sustainability and, 39; green technology and,
26–27; international architects and
engineers and, 185n13, 190n10;
land-use patterns and, 128; lawns in
context of suburbanization and,
104–5, 190n7; magic lands in context
of western expansion in, 14;
maritime economy and, 155;
monumental or iconic projects and,
72; nationalism and, 20, 24–25;
nature tourism in, 73; relocation of
populations due to building projects
and, 30, 33; solid waste production
and, 27; suburbanization and, 104–5,
111, 116, 190n7; sustainability and,
39; tourism and, 73, 111; Treasure
Island plan and, 88, 99, 150,
186nn19–20, 188n47; utopianism
and, 136; water consumption in,
26, 148

solutions and, 137; urban development and, 133. *See also specific world expositions and world's fairs*

World Financial Tower, 90

World's Fair in New York in 1939, 107, 135, 136, 153

World's Fair in New York in 1964, 103, 107, 128

World's Fair in Paris in 1889, 136

World's Fair in Seattle in 1962, 136

Wright, Frank Lloyd, 152

Wu, Gordon, 69, 123

Xintiandi, 99, 113

Zemin, Jiang, 67

Zhu Jia Jiao (Chinese traditional town), 106, 113–14, 125